Psychology
Aweigh!

Psychology Aweigh!

A History of
Clinical Psychology
in the
United States Navy,
1900-1988

Frederick L. McGuire
Captain, MSC, USNR, Retired

AMERICAN PSYCHOLOGICAL ASSOCIATION
WASHINGTON, DC

Library of Congress Cataloging-in-Publication Data

McGuire, Frederick L., 1926–
    Psychology aweigh: A history of clinical psychology in the United States Navy,
1900–1988 / Frederick L. McGuire.
        250 pages.
    Includes bibliographical references.
    ISBN 1-55798-086-1
    1. Clinical psychology—United States—History—20th century.   2. Medicine,
Naval—United States—History—20th Century.   I. Title.
    [DNLM: 1. United States. Navy.   2. Naval Medicine—history—United
States.   3. Psychology, Clinical—history—United States.   WM 11 AA1 M4p]
RC466.83.U6M34   1990   616.89′008′8359-dc—20
DNLM/DLC for Library of Congress   90-279
                                                                                                            CIP

First Edition

Published by
American Psychological Association
1200 Seventeenth Street, NW
Washington, DC 20036

Copies may be ordered from:
Order Department
P.O. Box 2710
Hyattsville, MD 20784
Order Number 450-0100

Typesetting: Harper Graphics, Waldorf, MD
Printing: United Book Press, Inc., Baltimore, MD
Cover Design: Richard Steele, Washington, DC
Editor & Production Coordinator: Carlotta Ribar

Printed in the United States of America.

CONTENTS

Foreword ix
Preface xi
Acknowledgments xv

Prologue

1. The Beginnings of Clinical Psychology 3

The Evolution of Clinical Psychology in the U.S. Navy

2. Before World War I 11
3. World War I 17
4. Between the Wars 31
5. World War II 35
6. Enter the Medical Service Corps 49
7. The Korean War 55
8. The Vietnam Era 61
9. The Training Program at Bethesda 63
10. Women in Clinical Psychology and the Armed Forces 65
11. The Chief Clinical Psychologists, 1944–1988 71
12. The Civilian Consultants 73

Recruit Screening and Evaluation

13. Early Standards for Recruits 77
14. The Introduction of Binet-Type Testing 83
15. Recruit Screening in World War I 87
16. Recruit Screening in World War II 97
17. The Search for an Actuarial (Statistical) Approach to Screening 105
18. The Marginal Recruit 115

The Practice of Clinical Psychology
in the U.S. Navy—Then and Now

19. Introduction 121
20. Administration and Management 123
21. Direct Mental Health Services 125
    Hospitals and Clinics 125
    The Issue of Sexuality 132
    Health Psychology 135
    Alcohol and Drug Abuse 137
    Crisis and Postdisaster Intervention 141
22. Duty with the Operating Forces—Not Just *in* the Navy,
    But *of* the Navy 147
    The U.S. Naval Academy 147
    The Fleet Marine Forces 156
    The Submarine Service 165
    The Naval Air Service 171
    The SERE (Survival, Evasion, Resistance, and
        Escape) Program 179
    The SEALs (Sea–Air–Land Teams) 182
    Forensic Psychology 184
    The Marine Security Battalion 186
23. Research 189

Epilogue

24. The Personal World of a Navy Clinical Psychologist 201
25. The Future of Clinical Psychology in the U.S. Navy 207

References 221

Appendixes and Indexes

Appendix 1. Ranks in the U.S. Navy 235
Appendix 2. Uniformed Navy Clinical Psychologists on Extended
            Active Duty, Medical Service Corps, 1948–1988 237
Appendix 3. Suggestions for the Management of Psychological Services
            in the U.S. Navy 241
Name and Author Index 243
Subject Index 247

List of Tables

Table 1. Marine Corps Recruit Screening Tests, Binet-Type, 1915 85

Table 2. Comparison of Recruits' Test Scores With Performance Record, Marine Corps, 1915 85

Table 3. Service Records of Follow-Up Group of Marine Corps Recruits, 1915 86

Table 4. Comparison of Service Records of Suspect Group and Normal Control Group, Navy Recruit Screening Program, 1941–1944 100

Table 5. Comparison of Psychiatric Discharge Rates of Recruits at Three Naval Training Stations, 1943 101

Table 6. Comparison of Intelligence Test Scores With Year-End Academic Standing, Freshmen, U.S. Naval Academy, 1922–1923 150

List of Figures

Figure 1. Navy Recruit Screening Card, Brief History, 1919 89

Figure 2. Navy Recruit Screening Form, Reverse Side of Preliminary Psychiatric Test Sheet, List of "Character Descriptives," 1919 90

Figure 3. Navy Recruit Screening Form, Neurological Examination, 1919 91

Figure 4. Navy Recruit Screening Card, Life History, 1917–1918 93

FOREWORD

Excursions into little known chapters of the history of psychology have afforded me great enjoyment during the 31 years that I have been teaching a graduate seminar on this subject. Thus, it was with more than a little pleasure that I read Fred McGuire's chronicle of those developments in our history that relate to the evolution of clinical psychology in the U.S. Navy.

It is most appropriate that the American Psychological Association is publishing this book about a subset of American psychologists just as the association is preparing to celebrate the centennial of its founding, in 1992. For, as is clear from McGuire's lively account, which quotes liberally from documents of the period, the history of clinical psychology in the U.S. Navy during the twentieth century, in all its seemingly disparate facets, reflects the history of our country's clinical psychology more generally. Just as in recent years our universities, industries, schools, clinical facilities, and other agencies recruited graduates of our psychology departments whose advanced education included such subsets of our discipline as human factors, statistics, and clinical, experimental, physiological, social, and related areas of psychology, so also did the U.S. Navy recruit their classmates who also had just completed such advanced training in the same classrooms, laboratories, and practicum settings.

In regard to the major focus of this book, that subset referred to as clinical psychology, McGuire's book illustrates changing attitudes toward clinical psychology that prevailed not only in the Navy but also in civilian life. Specifically, he chronicles the evolution of Navy clinical psychology from its roots in Titchener's turn-of-the-century brand of experimental psychology, to the introduction of the Binet-Simon Scale in the Navy's earliest efforts to improve mental and psychological assessment, to the present high-level professional roles (in treatment, assessment, intervention, research, and administration) being exercised by today's generation of Navy clinical psychologists, all of which roles are similar to those engaged in by their civilian counterparts.

I particularly enjoyed reading McGuire's book because I served in the Navy from 1943 to 1947 and thereafter in the U.S. Naval Ready Reserve until 1987. Additionally, my PhD mentor (from 1948 to 1952) and lifelong friend was William A. Hunt, an academician-clinical psychologist who served from 1940 to 1945 as the Navy's first Chief of Clinical Psychology; he maintained his love for that service until his death in 1986. I had thought that both of these experiences provided me with fairly good firsthand knowledge of the history of clinical psychology in the U.S. Navy from 1940 to the present. In addition, I have served as the National Consultant in Clinical Psychology to the Surgeon General of the U.S. Navy continuously since 1981, and I have taught our department's History of Psychology seminar for three decades. However, McGuire's book was a pleasure to read because it introduced me to much that I did not know about the history of clinical psychology in the U.S. Navy.

Because it explores little-known territory, I believe that McGuire's book will be much appreciated by historians from several disciplines. Furthermore, I especially hope that the authors of our current books on the history of psychology will take time to read it. If books comparable to this one on the Navy were written on still other little-known chapters of our history (for example, psychologists working in industry, public schools, prisons, other government services, medical schools, and so forth), the content of our history of psychology textbooks, most of which has changed little during the past half century, would contain considerably more exciting material.

In a 1987 article in the *American Psychologist*, I argued that there is only a single core of knowledge that differentiates the discipline of psychology from the disciplines of mathematics, sociology, physics, English literature, and so on, and that what differentiates one psychologist from another (for example, a clinical versus an experimental versus a social psychologist) is the forum in which that common, identical core of psychological knowledge is applied. I believe that McGuire's book provides good support for my thesis; namely, that those clinical psychologists who served in the U.S. Navy during the past century were applying in the naval setting the same pool of knowledge, called psychology, that their civilian counterparts concurrently were applying in hospitals, clinics, industry, and university settings.

Joseph D. Matarazzo
Professor and Chairman
Department of Medical Psychology
Oregon Health Sciences University
Past President, American Psychological Association

PREFACE

Prior to the August 1986 annual meeting of the American Psychological Association in Washington, DC, a Navy Psychology Day was held at Bethesda Naval Hospital in Bethesda, Maryland. Attendees included a number of active-duty psychologists, members of the Naval Reserve, representatives of the other services, and the current clinical psychology internship class stationed at Bethesda. The program was chaired by Captain Frank A. Mullins, MSC, USN, Specialty Advisor for Clinical Psychology to the Naval Medical Command, and Dr. Melvin A. Gravitz, civilian Director of Psychology Training and Research at Bethesda.

In addition to a program of distinguished speakers, a number of informal discussions took place among the participants. As is common at such meetings, one of the main topics of conversation was recalling the "good old days," and it became evident there existed a huge gap in our so-called corporate memory. The collective experience of the senior clinical psychologists then on active duty extended back less than 20 years, and the "memory bank" of many of the important years of clinical psychology in the Navy now resides only with retired or reserve personnel. Furthermore, the January 1986 death of William Hunt, one of the first uniformed Navy clinical psychologists on active duty in World War II and an ardent supporter of Navy psychology during his successful career in civilian life, reminded us that these resources will not be available to us much longer.

Because of poor documentation and the fact that much of their work was buried in government publications, many of the unique contributions of clinical psychologists in the Navy have gone relatively unnoticed. This state of affairs has not been limited to the Navy. In 1953, the late Robert Watson, himself a Navy clinical psychologist during World War II and a distinguished professor of the history of psychology, noted that "clinical psychologists have been surprisingly ahistorical. Very little thought has been given to, and less written about, the origin and development of clinical psychology" (Watson, 1953). In

1956 Hunt wrote, "Because of the relative tardiness of recognizing and defining clinical psychology as a professional entity, much of its history is hidden elsewhere in psychology" (Hunt, 1956). A search of the literature showed the situation in 1987 to be relatively unchanged. Several books have been written about clinical psychology, but with the exception of an excellent book by Reisman (1976), the history has been relegated to an occasional chapter limited to a simple listing of sequential events rather than an in-depth analysis. A history should be written with a purpose in mind. In addition to simple documentation, it should become a useful tool for management and training.

The original conception of this book was that one could not write of the history of clinical psychology without also describing the history of its parent discipline: experimental, or scientific, psychology. The author believes that clinical psychology has never left its symbiotic relation with scientific psychology or its adherence to the scientific method of inquiry as its primary tool. Furthermore, it was deemed important that the younger psychologists and the nonpsychologists who read this book understand and appreciate the historical base of clinical psychology, including the contributions of such philosophers as Socrates (469–399 B.C.), Plato (428–348 B.C.); Aristotle (384–322 B.C.), St. Augustine (354–430), Leonardo da Vinci (1452–1519), and Rene Descartes (1596–1650), as well as the works of the early psychologists such as Gustave Fechner (1801–1887), Hermann von Helmholtz (1821–1894), Wilhelm Wundt (1832–1920), and Sir Francis Galton (1822–1911). It is disturbing to read recent publications in which the writer has "reinvented the wheel" or cloaked ancient ideas in fancy labels and offered them as being new or original.

However, to cover such a broad area proved to be an overly ambitious goal. Not only is this historical base so vast as to require a separate volume, but it was thought that this would distract from the primary focus of the book: the accomplishments of clinical psychology within the U.S. Navy. As one reviewer observed, "Those are two books, and you meant to write only one." For readers wishing to pursue this historical base without engaging in the tedious task of searching for original sources, many of which are not written in English, there are a number of secondary sources (Boring, 1929; 1950; Garfield, 1965; Korchin, 1976; Mora, 1967; Wolman, 1965, Zilboorg & Henry, 1941).

The usefulness of a history of clinical psychology in the U.S. Navy is no different from that in any field of human endeavor. First, an individual cannot be said to be well rounded in his or her field without a historical perspective. To quote Boring (1929), "The gift of professional maturity comes only to the psychologist who knows the history of the science. . . . A psychological sophistication that contains no component of historical orientation seems to me to be no sophistication at all" (pp. x, vii). In addition, and perhaps just as important, Navy psychologists have historically engaged in a wide variety of fascinating activities that are sure to be of more than passing interest to all students of clinical psychology, and their contribution to the field should be memorialized. Finally, clinical psychology in the U.S. Navy is on the verge of many significant changes that will cause it to occupy an increasingly important role in the future. Planning and implementing this future cannot be done with maximum efficiency without appreciation of what has gone before.

This author has chosen to limit this book to the relation of clinical psychology to the Navy and to focus further, although not exclusively, on the men and women in uniform—the so-called "deployables." However, the reader should know that a great deal of work relevant to the Navy took place among civilian psychologists in the federal civil service attached to Navy installations. In fact, some of the latter group have been some of our best "sailors." Work conducted by the Army, especially during World War I, is also included in this book because it not only relates to psychology in the Navy but also established a model for military psychology later followed by both services. Unfortunately, the Navy's participation in this model has been poorly documented, and the work done by Army personnel is presented herein as part of the historical base held in common by both services.

This history is based in part on accounts in the professional and official literature. Of particular note are the volumes of the *Naval Medical Bulletin*, the official in-house publication of the Navy Medical Department from 1907 through 1949, and its successor, the *Armed Forces Medical Journal*, and the usual array of psychological journals and books. A variety of Navy documents also provided a great deal of information; most of these now reside in government depositories and installations.

Large amounts of written material exist concerning all aspects of the history of the U.S. Navy but have not been catalogued or used. On numerous occasions the author has heard naval historians observe that all too often the general attitude of the Navy toward documentation of its own history has been to merely gather and store voluminous amounts of material without processing it, apparently with the attitude that should anyone care to write a history, the material is there. In addition, and especially when compared with the U.S. Army, the Navy has been slow in allotting financial resources to the documentation of its own history. Given this combination of inadequate cataloging, poor retrieval capability, and the lack of financial support, the result has been predictable. One naval historian remarked, "This situation is an absolute scandal."

The history of clinical psychology in the Navy during World War II is reasonably well documented due to the fact that so many of the nearly 500 psychologists of all types in Navy uniform were in a climate favorable to writing about their military experiences while on active duty and following their return to civilian life. However, since that time, what little has been written is scattered and has never been organized to serve a historical purpose.

Retrieving this information meant obtaining "oral histories" by recording interviews with the participants, as well as exchanging written and verbal communication. This part of the volume provides several open-ended and often freewheeling reminiscences of present and former clinical psychologists. Obviously, such input is vulnerable to the vagaries of memory and the recording technique, but, as the reader will find, it is not dull. The sources of data and opinions obtained by personal interview are not always identified; to do so might have inhibited the openness of their contributions. Whenever information depended solely on individual recall, it was always supported by the testimony of at least two persons. I have included my own opinions and personal interpretations in this book, but I have made an effort to make it obvious to the reader that the opinions and interpretations are mine.

Finally, keep in mind that this book was compiled over a 3-year period and that by the time it was published, certain facts and names may have changed, such as title and rank of some individuals and the structure and administration of some programs. It is hoped that none of these discrepancies, if any, will alter the substance of the text.

This volume targets all psychologists with an interest in history. For those younger psychologists entering the Navy, it may help give them an appreciation of the fact that they are part of an organization with its own history and tradition. Clinical psychology in the U.S. Navy is unique, but at the same time it is part of the field at large. It is hoped this book will make a contribution to both.

FREDERICK L. MCGUIRE
Captain, MSC, USNR, Retired
Professor Emeritus of Medical Psychology
University of California, Irvine

ACKNOWLEDGMENTS

This work was supported in part by a contract with the Naval Historical Center, Washington, DC.

A number of people donated time and material to this book, several of whom took the time to review a final draft in addition to their other contributions. Thanks are given to each of them, including Bruce Becker, Captain, MSC, USNR-R; Patricia W. Crigler, Captain, MSC, USN; William G. Cumming, Jr., Captain, MSC, USN, Retired; Robert S. Herrmann, Captain, MSC, USN, Retired; John F. House, Commander, MSC, USN, Retired; Robert D. McCullah, Captain, MSC, USN; Dr. Joan S. Guilford, Executive Director, Sheridan Psychological Services, Inc.; Allen E. McMichael, Captain, MSC, USN, Retired; Ivan N. Mensh, Captain, MSC, USNR, Retired, and Professor Emeritus, UCLA; H. Barry Molish, Commander, MSC, USNR, Retired, and Associate Professor, Baylor College of Medicine; Frank A. Mullins, Captain, MSC, USN; Dr. John A. Plag, Project Director, Naval Health Research Center, Retired; John E. Rasmussen, Captain, MSC, USN, Retired; Edwin S. Shneidman, Professor Emeritus, UCLA; and Walter L. Wilkins, Captain, MSC, USNR, Retired, and Scientific Director, Retired, Naval Health Research Center, San Diego, CA.

In addition, thanks are also given to those individuals who contributed interviews in which they described their current and past experiences, with special appreciation going to Drs. Alan S. Halpern, Randall R. Jones, and Ted D. Kilpatrick for their description of their experiences in Vietnam.

Invaluable cooperation and assistance was given by Mary Aldous, librarian at the Naval Health Research Center, and special appreciation is given to the efficient and courteous staff of the library at the University of California, Irvine Medical Center.

Thanks go to Carlsbad Publications, Carlsbad, California, and Mrs. Sue Bosio for her assistance in the preparation of the final draft of this book. Special recognition is due for the superior job done by my editor at APA, Carlotta Ribar.

Finally, an award goes to Mrs. Terry J. Stripling as my Indispensable Right

Hand. Kudos are especially due for her enthusiastic and effective secretarial support and the cheerful completion of the myriad of other tasks associated with the preparation of this book.

The following publishers were kind enough to grant permission for the use of copyrighted material:

From "Psychiatric Re-examination of Unsuitable Naval Recruits: A Two-Year Follow-Up" by J. A. Plag and R. J. Arthur, 1965, *American Journal of Psychiatry*, *122*(5), pp. 534–541. Copyright 1965 by the American Journal of Psychiatry. Reprinted by permission.

From *The Blue and Gold: The Annapolis Story* (p. 4) by Graydon DeCamp, 1974. New York: Arco Publishing Company, Inc. Copyright 1974 by Arco Publishing Company, Inc. Reprinted by permission of the publisher.

From "Aviation Clinical Psychology" by J. B. Parker, 1987, *Military Medicine*, *152*, pp. 349–350. Copyright 1987 by the Association of Military Surgeons in the U.S. Reprinted by permission.

From "An Investigation of Naval Neuropsychiatric Screening Procedures" by W. A. Hunt, in *Groups, Leadership and Men* (p. 250), edited by H. Guetzkow, 1951. Pittsburgh, PA: Carnegie Press. Copyright 1951 by Carnegie Press. Reissued 1963 by Russell and Russell, Inc., New York. Adapted by permission.

From *Eagle Against the Sun* (p. 18, pp. 393–394) by Ronald H. Spector, 1983. New York: The Free Press. Copyright 1983 by Ronald H. Spector. Reprinted by permission of The Free Press, a division of Macmillan, Inc.

From *Collected Papers*, Vol. I, Chapter VIII, 6th edition, by Sigmund Freud, "Heredity and the Aetiology of the Neuroses," p. 146. Published Authorized Translation under the supervision of Joan Riviere. Published by Basic Books, Inc., by arrangement with Hogarth Press Ltd. and The Institute of Psycho-Analysis, London. Reprinted by permission of Basic Books, Inc., publishers, New York.

From "Clinical Psychology in 1944–1945" by W. A. Hunt, 1975, *Journal of Clinical Psychology*, *31*, pp. 173–178. Copyright 1975 by Journal of Clinical Psychology. Reprinted by permission.

From *The Shame of the States* (pp. 50–51) by Albert Deutsch, New York: Harcourt, Brace and Company. Copyright 1948 by Albert Deutsch. Reprinted by permission of Lucy Kroll, The Lucy Kroll Agency, New York.

From *Architects of Adjustment* (pp. 99–102) by Donald S. Napoli. Published 1981 by Kennikat Press, Port Washington, NY. Reprinted by permission of Stonehill Publishing Co., Inc., New York, NY.

From W. A. Hunt, *The Clinical Psychologist* (p. 58), 1956. Courtesy of Charles C Thomas, Publisher, Springfield, Illinois.

From *Clinical vs. Statistical Prediction* (p. 4) by Paul E. Meehl, 1954. Minneapolis, MN: University of Minnesota Press. Copyright 1954 by the University of Minnesota. Reprinted by permission of the University of Minnesota Press.

Prologue

The Beginnings of Clinical Psychology

T he field of psychology is both a science and a profession. It shares its beginnings with philosophy, physiology, and, to a lesser degree, physics. Scientific psychology began to assume its own identity in the first half of the 19th century. By 1900, it had organized itself as a separate discipline, complete with a national association, academic titles and laboratories, separate university departments that granted doctoral degrees, and the publication of its own journals.

The Emergence of Clinical Psychology

Within the evolution of this "new science," as it was called, it is also possible to trace the elements of the emerging subspecialty of clinical psychology. By 1910 a small number of psychologists with the PhD degree could be identified as clinical psychologists (Wallin, 1961), the term *clinical psychology* had been formally coined, a university-based training program had been outlined and implemented (Witmer, 1907), the Binet-Simon test had been introduced, and professional journals dealing with clinical research and practice were being published.

The American Psychological Association (APA) was founded in 1892. Under the leadership of G. Stanley Hall, a meeting was held by 7 psychologists at Clark University on July 8 of that year. These men formed an organizational committee and held the first meeting at the University of Pennsylvania on December 27. In addition to these 7, 16 others were elected, including 2 physicians (Fernberger, 1932). In 1906, 22 new members were elected. This apparently so alarmed the members that steps were taken to tighten the membership requirements in order to prevent undesirable speed of growth. By 1938 the membership had grown to only 667. However, in the next 50 years, the numbers increased so much that in 1988 the APA had more than 65,000 members and more than 24,000 affiliates.

The growth of clinical psychology has followed a pattern similar to that of its parent organization. In 1890 James McKeen Cattell coined the term *mental tests* and urged the need for standardization of procedures and the use of norms. He also advocated the use of statistical analysis in the study of individual differences, a new idea at the time (Cattell, 1890). As a result, in 1896 Cattell chaired the APA Committee on Physical and Mental Tests, which marked the beginning of psychology's attempting to standardize and exercise quality control over testing. In 1915 this work culminated in the following resolution by the APA, a document that not only expressed a concern for the exercise of professional standards but also lent substance to the formal recognition of clinical psychology as a specialty within the general field of psychology:

> Whereas: Psychological diagnosis requires thorough technical training in all phases of mental testing through acquaintance with the facts of mental development and with various phases of mental retardation. And, Whereas: There is evidence of a tendency to appoint for this work persons whose training in clinical psychology is inadequate; Be it resolved: That this Association discourages the use of mental tests for practical psychological diagnosis by individuals psychologically unqualified for this work. (Fernberger, 1932, p. 46)

It is not clear whether the term *psychologically unqualified* referred to their training or their state of mental health.

Given the history of psychology, it is obvious that the first clinical psychologists came from the ranks of the experimental psychologists. A small number of those with the doctoral degree were identified as clinical psychologists between 1896 and 1910: 16 in all (Wallin, 1961). Most of them worked in hospitals for the insane or mentally retarded or in clinics. In December 1896, in an address before the APA, Lightner Witmer of the University of Pennsylvania coined the term *clinical psychology* and outlined a formal program of training and study. In fact, he designed a model for the field that has remained essentially unchanged (Witmer, 1907). In addition to offering formal courses, Witmer also founded, in 1907, a journal entitled *The Psychological Clinic*, which continued as a major outlet for his work and that of others until 1935.

The Growth of Professional Organizations

Because of its short history, small numbers, and lower status in the academic community, the profession of clinical psychology suffered from ambiguity and conflict surrounding its proper role and responsibilities. In spite of this, the group of 16 identified by Wallin continued to grow, and finally in 1917 a group of 45 psychologists with the doctoral degree held an organizational meeting in Pittsburgh and established the American Association of Clinical Psychology (AACP) (Symonds, 1937). In 1919, the APA accepted this group as a separate section within the national organization, and the AACP disbanded. In 1932, the Association of Consulting Psychologists (ACP) was formed, and in 1937 they founded the *Journal of Consulting Psychology*. The ACP served as a parent organization for the formation in 1937 of the American Association for Applied Psychology (AAAP), with four sections: Clinical, Education, Business and Industrial, and Consulting (Bernreuter et al., 1937). The AAAP remained the primary organization for clinical psychology until after World War II.

By 1988, however, the Division of Clinical Psychology of the APA had about 5,600 members, and about 2,000 individuals were certified in clinical psychology by the American Board of Professional Psychology (ABPP). Furthermore, each of the 50 states now licenses or legally certifies psychologists, most of them in some version of clinical psychology, and several thousand of them are not accounted for on the rolls of the APA membership. The APA central office now has an annual budget of more than $40 million and 370 full-time staff members (*The Monitor*, June 1987, p. 4).

Definitions of Clinical Psychology

In view of this tremendous growth, one might assume that today the field of clinical psychology is well defined; however, this is not the case. In spite of the legal incorporation of its many local, national, international, and affiliated organizations, the content of the field is not well identified, and there is no single definition of clinical psychology. Even Lightner Witmer, the founder of clinical psychology, believed that clinical psychology is not the exclusive province of the psychologist (Witmer, 1907). In his original position paper, Witmer (1907) noted that

> the methods of clinical psychology are necessarily invoked whenever the status of an individual mind is determined by observation and experiments, and . . . treatment applied to effect a change, i.e., the development of such [an] individual mind. (p. 9)

This rather succinct statement seems to have embodied the essence of the many varied and often lengthy attempts to define clinical psychology that have continued unabated to this day.

In 1939, Louttit attempted to find some consensus in the literature and, without exhausting the list, he compiled a total of 40 definitions (Louttit, 1939). In addition to efforts by individuals to create a definition, there have been numerous attempts by several groups. In 1937, the clinical section of the AAAP made such an attempt, and under the auspices of the APA, miniconventions have been held with a similar objective at Boulder, Colorado, in 1949 (Raimy, 1950); Stanford University, in 1955 (Strother, 1956); Miami Beach, Florida, in 1958 (Roe et al., 1959); Princeton, New Jersey, in 1961; Chicago, Illinois, in 1966 (Hoch et al., 1966); and Vail, Colorado, in 1973 (Korman, 1976). As of February 1987, additional meetings of various groups had this item on their agenda. Even though little progress has been made toward a satisfactory definition beyond that described by Witmer in 1907, the serious student of training in clinical psychology would do well to study these references.

A companion topic of these meetings was the issue of what should be the content of a clinical training program. In 1947, a committee of the APA recommended a program of graduate training that was generally adopted by all parties involved. It consisted of six primary areas of study: (a) general–experimental psychology, (b) psychodynamics of behavior, (c) diagnostic methods, (d) research methods, (e) related disciplines, and (f) psychotherapy. At least a 1-year internship in a clinical setting was also included, preferably before the awarding of the PhD.

In general, these six broad areas of training content have not changed, and attempts to become more specific have not been very successful. The assumption, of course, was that only by knowing what tasks the clinical psychologist is called on to do can one prescribe a course of training. However, the kinds of work done by clinical psychologists seem to be limited only by one's imagination and ability to recognize opportunities. In 1939, Louttit concluded that "there is little or no actual agreement as to what clinical psychology is, except that it deals with individuals" (Louttit, 1939). Witmer (1907) was not entirely happy with the word *clinical* but, as he wrote:

> I have borrowed the word "clinical" from medicine because it is the best term I can find to indicate the character of the *method* I deem necessary for this work. Words seldom retain their original significance and clinical medicine is not what the word implies—the work of a practicing physician at the bedside of a patient. The term "clinical" implies a method and not a locality. (p. 8)

As a method, clinical psychology has found applications in nearly every field of human endeavor. Basically, the work of the clinical psychologist involves diagnosis—including interviewing and testing—research, and therapy. To this might be added, a la Witmer, "and the application of the clinical method." To describe where these activities occur would only result in a long list of locations such as institutions, schools, industry, business, the military, and so forth. Many clinical psychologists have used their background in statistics, computer science, experimental psychology, and social psychology to produce a wide mixture of skills and knowledge, thus expanding the application of their clinical talents even further. In addition, even though clinical psychologists are usually identified as working with the individual client or patient, they frequently work with both small and large groups. For example, they may work with the entire environment of a hospital, business, or factory in order to enhance the collective mental health and well-being. They also have the additional task of interpolating and applying to individual cases research findings based on group studies.

This problem of definition is not peculiar to clinical psychology. James McKeen Cattell, president of the APA in 1895, once wittily defined general psychology as "whatever the psychologists work at" (Hildreth, 1933). Echoing this sentiment, clinical psychology has been defined as "whatever it is clinical psychologists do," a conclusion no longer considered frivolous or facetious. It is interesting to note that a similar resolution was made in the controversy over the proper interpretation of IQ tests and the definition of intelligence. Circular, but very operational, the definition of intelligence is often given as "that which an intelligence test measures."

This leads to the next question: Who is a clinical psychologist? Two answers might be as follows: (a) those who call themselves clinical psychologists (although most licensure laws restrict who may offer services to the public under that title) or (b) those who formally identify with some professional organization of that name. In the historical sense, one could define a clinical psychologist as a philosopher–physiologist–experimentalist who at least part of the time uses the clinical method. On the other hand, in view of the previous discussion, the obvious answer is "anyone who does what clinical psychologists do." Again, without being facetious, this definition has a certain utility.

Clinical Psychology Applied to the Armed Forces

As will be seen, in the U.S. Navy a number of individuals have "done what clinical psychologists do" without formally assuming that title. These have included line officers, nonpsychiatric medical officers, psychiatrists, and a variety of research psychologists with expertise in physiology and biochemistry; many of them are appropriately included in this book for the contributions they have made to clinical psychology at large as well as to the Navy.

Shortly after the turn of the century, it became apparent to psychologists and nonpsychologists alike that the "new science" was offering a more systematic and organized approach to questions about human behavior that had bothered people for centuries. Many of these questions could be placed under the general heading of predicting behavior, such as the following: Who would do well in school? Who would become mentally ill? Which criminals could be rehabilitated? Who would become a good employee? Who would make a good mate or parent? Who would become a successful sailor? Naturally, it was also recognized that if the reasons for certain behaviors could be discovered, they might be modified as well as predicted.

The activities of the Armed Forces of the United States are labor intensive, and their success depends almost entirely on the forces' ability to train and motivate men and women to act in predetermined patterns of behavior under routine as well as adverse or life-threatening conditions, including the willingness to be assertive, innovative, and flexible when required. Selection of personnel best suited for this process is obviously critical. This makes the Navy and the other services perhaps the greatest behavior-dependent and behavior-changing organizations in the world and obvious customers for whatever help the field of psychology can offer. It was inevitable that sooner or later the two groups would be teamed together in a common effort.

The Evolution of Clinical Psychology in the U.S. Navy

Before World War I

Before the United States engaged in World War I (April 6, 1917–November 11, 1918), the practice of what we describe as clinical psychology in the Navy was confined to the detection and treatment of the insane and the screening of recruits. As described elsewhere in this book, neither task was performed very effectively. At the turn of the century, psychology had not yet focused on the field of mental health and psychiatry was still in its infant stages. The American Psychiatric Association was founded in 1844 as the Association of Medical Superintendents of American Institutions for the Insane, a name that described the dominant function of its members until well into the 20th century. In 1892 (the year the APA was founded), the association changed its name to the American Medico-Psychological Association. Prior to this date, the term *psychiatric* had come into professional use, but it was rejected because the members thought its meaning could not be readily conveyed to those outside the profession; in 1921 its present name was adopted (Sabshin, 1983).

Early Care for the Mentally Ill

The care of the military insane was conducted at the United States Government Hospital for the Insane (USGHI) in Washington, DC, later known as St. Elizabeths. This hospital was created by Congress largely because of the lobbying efforts of Dorothea Dix, the famous advocate for the mentally ill. Originally planned to serve only military patients, it eventually served all branches of the U.S. government, including the Navy. All "White House" patients were sent there, including the would-be assassins of Andrew Jackson, as well as John Hinkley, Jr., who attempted to kill President Reagan. The responsibility for managing the hospital was transferred to the District of Columbia government on October 1, 1987, by an act of Congress.

In 1916, the name was officially changed to St. Elizabeths, a name used unofficially since the Civil War. During the Civil War, a number of wounded soldiers being treated for nonpsychiatric reasons were reluctant, when writing home, to say they were in an insane asylum, and they used the hospital's land-grant title instead. The institution was "a self-sufficient community with its own railroad, which it operated until 1967, a laundry, greenhouses, and a piggery." When the hospital was established, it occupied a "sprawling plot of pristine farmland. . . . between the Anacostia and Potomac Rivers" (Landers, 1987), in contrast with the decayed urban nature of that area today.

St. Elizabeths became known not only for its pioneering work in humane treatment of the mentally ill but also for psychodynamic methods of treatment initiated by its fourth superintendent, William Alanson White. It also became known for its research and the training of psychiatrists and other mental health workers, including, beginning in 1909, the training of Navy medical officers as "alienists," as psychiatrists were then sometimes called (Glass, 1966, p. 5). In fact, "St. E's," as the hospital is often called, became an important center for training Navy psychiatrists until its relations with the military ended in 1946. The training effort was then transferred to the United States Naval Hospital at Bethesda, Maryland, which had been commissioned in February 1942. Because it operated other training hospitals, the US Army apparently used St. E's much less than the Navy did and ceased sending patients there at the end of World War I.

As discussed further later on, the rate of admissions of naval personnel was quite high. For example, about 150 Navy enlisted men (there were few or no officers) were admitted in 1912 (Riker, 1913). Based on a total enlisted force of 48,283 that year (Taussig, 1915; US Department of Commerce, 1975), this is a rate of about 310 cases per 100,000 population.[1] This is in contrast to a rate of only 62.5 per 100,000 for the civilian population of New York State that same year (Malzberg, 1959). As will be seen, this extremely high admission rate undoubtedly resulted from the lack of proper screening in effect at that time.

Screening of Navy Recruits

Enlisted men entered the Navy via a network of recruiting stations located around the country. At each station a medical officer was assigned who was expected to conduct both physical and "psychological" screening. Few specific guidelines were available. Instead, medical officers were expected to use their own discretion and "common sense." Each had received orientation at the U.S. Naval Medical School in Washington, DC, but apparently there was a wide range of standards among physicians. In fact, the subject of psychiatry was seldom taught in medical schools nationwide; when it was included, it consisted

---

[1]Between 1901 and 1911, the US Army reported an insanity rate of 100–200 per 100,000 per year (Glass, 1961, p. 5).

of only a lecture or two. Lowndes (1912) deplored the fact that some medical officers made their decision concerning an applicant's ability to live and work aboard ship without ever having been on a sea cruise themselves.

In the years just preceding World War I, a number of Navy medical officers attempted to design improved methods of screening recruits. In 1907, Shepard Ivory Franz, then a civilian research psychologist at USGHI, developed a plan for routine psychological screening of psychiatric hospital patients (Franz, 1908, 1912), a procedure that has been described as the first of its kind in the country (Watson, 1953). In 1911 Heber Butts, a Navy medical officer stationed at the same hospital, published a scheme for screening Navy recruits that was rather comprehensive for that time. This included a detailed psychological and medical history and a variety of Binet-type questions administered verbally, designed to take 30–60 minutes (Butts, 1911a). Butts also attempted to validate his approach by applying it retroactively to the hospital records of 528 insane men from the Navy and Marine Corps. As a result, he found that nearly 54% of these cases showed a predisposition toward insanity that existed prior to enlistment, a finding consistent with the previously described comparison of the Navy admission rate with that of a civilian population. In describing his work, Butts gives credit to Franz for consultation and assistance, but an examination of Franz's original work by this author shows that the model Butts proposed for the Navy was essentially Franz's, with some adaptations by Butts. Unwittingly, this may have made Franz, primarily a physiological psychologist, a pioneer in the screening of naval recruits!

The deplorable state of affairs in screening recruits (or lack of it) was noted by the then-Surgeon General of the Navy, who wrote (Stokes, 1913):

> The continued increase in the number of cases of mental disease in the Navy is a subject for serious consideration . . . the general opinion of medical officers [is] that in the large majority the disease, or the tendency thereto, exists prior to enlistment . . . for those classed as feebleminded various tests, notably the Binet-Simon, have been under investigation by psychologists and educators with the purpose of evolving a method by which the mental development of an individual can be determined. . . . No value is claimed for this system in diagnosing mental conditions other than feeblemindedness . . . but it marks an advance in our methods and is worthy of further trial by medical officers on recruiting duty, who would do well to familiarize themselves with this method, that they may take advantage of its good features while bearing in mind its limitations. (pp. 417–418)

Efforts to Improve Screening

Apparently in response to this suggestion by the Surgeon General, a number of medical officers became very involved in attempting to adapt the Binet-Simon and Binet-type items to the screening process. These men and their published references included the following:

H. E. Jenkins (1915), Passed Assistant Surgeon,[2] Naval Disciplinary Barracks, Port Royal, South Carolina.

W. L. Mann, Jr. (see Jenkins, 1915), Passed Assistant Surgeon, Naval Disciplinary Barracks, Port Royal, South Carolina.

J. J. A. McMullin (1915), Passed Assistant Surgeon, Recruiting Station, Buffalo, New York.

A. R. Schier (1913, 1914, 1915, 1917), Acting Assistant Surgeon, USMC Recruiting Station, St. Paul, Minnesota.

G. E. Thomas (1915), Passed Assistant Surgeon, Naval Prison, Portsmouth, New Hampshire.

These men not only studied and applied the Binet-Simon scale, but also in a very creative way they designed a variety of shortened versions that they tried to validate on different Navy and Marine Corps populations, a very sophisticated approach for that time. Although not involved with the Binet approach per se, other medical officers also engaged in attempts to improve the process of psychological screening. These included Passed Assistant Surgeon Heber Butts (1910, 1911a, 1911b, 1912), Passed Assistant Surgeon R. Sheehan (1915, 1916), and Passed Assistant Surgeon G. A. Riker (1913), all of whom were trained at USGHI. In a very real sense, these medical officers became the first practitioners of clinical psychology in Navy uniform—a bona fide historical note![3] (There may be others who deserve inclusion in this group, but their work has not come to the author's attention.) As Lightner Witmer (1907) pointed out, clinical psychology is not the exclusive province of psychologists.

Of special interest is that these medical officers made careful study of the work of those civilian psychologists who were also pioneering the use of the Binet–Simon and in several cases worked with them personally. There is no indication of interdisciplinary rivalry or professional bickering, which provided a pleasant model of MD–PhD cooperation, one that unfortunately was not to be fully sustained over subsequent decades. These psychologists included Shepard Ivory Franz of the USGHI, Frederick Kuhlman of the Minnesota School for the Feebleminded, Grace Fernald of the Juvenile Psychopathic Institute in Chicago, Robert M. Yerkes of the Boston Psychopathic Hospital and Harvard University, and L. T. Sidwell and George Mogridge of the Iowa Institution for the Feebleminded. One of them, Henry M. Goddard of the Vineland Training School in

---

[2]The term "passed" in this title means that the officer has passed a qualifying examination for promotion to this rank. See the appendix on Navy ranks for modern-day equivalents of these titles.

[3]There is documentation that at least some of this group were trained psychiatrists; possibly all of them were.

New Jersey, even published a special article on intelligence in the *U.S. Naval Medical Bulletin* (Goddard, 1917).

Screening Immigrants at Ellis Island

Interestingly, during this period a fellow officer of the U.S. Public Health Service, Assistant Surgeon Howard A. Knox, was actively using psychological tests to screen "mental defectives" (a term used at the time to designate mental retardation) from among the immigrants at Ellis Island, New York. A number of items were borrowed from the Binet–Simon, especially nonverbal or low-verbal items appropriate for the immigrant population. Added to these were a number of performance tests, including his own Knox Cube Test, Healy's Frame Test, and the Seguin Form Board. On this basis, about 10% of the group was certified as "feebleminded," and a few were placed in the lower category of "imbecile." Presumably, these cases were refused admission to the country. Judging from Knox's (1914) written account, there were few or no norms used, and great latitude was given to the examiner. However, Knox emphasized that every effort was made to err on the conservative side and in favor of the immigrant. Subsequently, percentile norms were produced for various age groups for the Knox Cube Test, and it was produced for civilian use. It was also used to test active-duty recruits at least at one naval training station (Bisch, 1919).

World War I

O n April 16, 1917, the very day the United States entered World War I, a group of psychologists known as the "Experimentalists," a small elite group formed by Edward Titchener in 1904,[4] was meeting in Cambridge, Massachusetts, apparently by coincidence. Taking advantage of the fact that the group included Robert M. Yerkes, then president of the APA, they immediately formulated plans for the association to offer to the war effort the professional services of the entire APA membership. In a letter dated the same day, Yerkes wrote to the APA Council, asking permission to begin unilaterally to organize American psychologists. He stated (Yerkes, 1918):

> It is obviously desirable that the psychologists of the country act unitedly in the interests of defense. Our knowledge and our methods are of importance to the military service of our country, and it is our duty to cooperate to the fullest extent and immediately toward the increased efficiency of our Army and Navy. . . . I hereby request the council's authorization to appoint such necessary and desirable committee or committees.
>
> The duties of any group or groups of members appointed to represent and act for us would evidently consist, first, in gathering all useful information concerning the varied aspects of the actual and possible practical relations of psychology to military affairs; second, to cooperate, as circumstances dictate, with government agencies, with the National Council of Defense, with local psychological groups or individuals, and with such other agencies as may develop; third, to further the development and application of methods to the immediate problems of military selection.
>
> Already, many of us are working for national defense in our respective communities. [Author's note: The onset of war was not a surprise to the general population.] It is my thought that this action by our council

---

[4]Apparently, this was a 1917 forerunner of the Psychonomic Society, formed in 1959 by a group of academic purists in the APA in response to a felt need of scientific psychologists to distance themselves from applied psychologists.

should, far from interfering with individual initiative, tend to unite us as a professional group in a nation-wide effort to render our professional training serviceable. (p. 87)

Four days later, on April 10th, Yerkes began a 5-day tour of Canadian cities in order to draw on Canada's war experience in utilizing the psychological profession. (As part of the British Commonwealth, Canada had entered the war in 1914.) He conferred with a variety of psychologists, military physicians, military leaders, and political figures. There was universal agreement that psychologists and psychiatrists would be of great value in developing methods for the selection of recruits and in the reeducation and treatment of the victims of war. However, in spite of this general accord and firsthand knowledge of the need, it turned out that the Canadians had done very little in this area and could offer only broad suggestions.

The Psychology Committee of the National Research Council

At the request of the National Research Council (NRC), a psychology committee was organized. The president of the APA was named its chairman ex officio and was also made a member of the NRC. The committee consisted of Messrs. Cattell, Hall, and Thorndike from the National Academy of Sciences; Messrs. Dodge, Franz, and Whipple from the APA; and Messrs. Seashore, Watson, and Yerkes from the American Association for the Advancement of Science. At the first meeting of this committee, it was voted that

> WHEREAS, psychologists in common with other men of science may be able to do invaluable work for national service and in the conduct of the war, it is recommended by this committee that psychologists volunteer for and be assigned to the work in which their service will be of the greatest use to the nation. In the case of students of psychology, this may involve the completion of the studies on which they are engaged. (Yerkes, 1918, pp. 93–94)

The fact that students were considered more valuable to the war effort if they stayed in school and completed their studies was prophetic of the day when the military would subsidize the education and training of clinical psychology students.

A special meeting of the APA Council was held on April 22 (members of the APA today would undoubtedly envy the speed with which the group moved), and a number of committees were formed, several of which were eventually accepted as subcommittees of the Psychology Committee of the NRC. A description of the work of a few of the more important of these committees may be seen in the postwar report made to the APA (Yerkes, 1919).

The Committee on Psychological Examination of Recruits was chaired by Robert M. Yerkes of Harvard University (later of the University of Minnesota and Yale University). For this task Yerkes was commissioned a Major in the Sanitary Corps of the Medical Department of the U.S. Army, the Army version of today's Medical Service Corps. The original purpose of psychological screening in the military was stated in the plan to the Surgeon General:

> The Council of the American Psychological Association is convinced that in the present emergency American psychology can substantially serve the Government, under the medical corps of the Army and Navy,[5] by examining recruits with respect to intellectual deficiency, psychopathic tendencies, nervous instability, and inadequate self-control. (Yerkes, 1919, p. 89)

In keeping with the emphasis on testing for feeblemindedness existent at that time, it was the expectation that this would be the primary task of the program. However, long before the official trials of various methods of examination had ended, it was clear that the significance of psychological services would be much broader. In spite of some resistance from Regular Army officers, both line and medical officers quickly discovered that such testing was a new and important way of increasing military efficiency and decreasing the cost of training and maintenance. The work of mental testing and examination in the Army was done in 35 training camps, and a total of 1,726,000 men had been given examinations prior to January 1, 1919. The principal uses of the psychological examinations were in seven categories:

1. For the discovery of men whose superior intelligence warranted their consideration for promotion, special training, or assignment to positions of unusual responsibility.
2. For assistance in selecting suitable candidates for officers' training schools, non-commissioned officers' training schools, and other special training organizations.
3. For the guidance of personnel adjutants in the assignment of recruits so that organizations might be built in accordance with desirable intelligence specifications or, in the absence of such specifications, so that their different constituent parts, such, for example, as the companies of a regiment, should possess approximately the same mental strength, thus avoiding the risk of weak links in the Army chain.
4. For the prompt discovery of men whose low-grade intelligence or mental peculiarities render them of uncertain value in the Army, and the assignments of such individuals to development battalions for observation in military training.
5. For the discovery and recommendations or assignments to labor battalions men obviously so inferior mentally as to be unsuitable for

---

[5]Note how repeated references are made to helping the Navy, but it was usually the Army that responded.

regular military training, yet promising serviceableness in simple manual labor.

6. For the discovery of men whose mental inferiority unfitted them for any sort of military duty and whose rejection or discharge should therefore be recommended to military officers.

7. For utilization in connection with the organization of special training groups so that each group might be instructed or drilled in accordance with its mental capacity, thus avoiding the delay incident to dull or awkward individuals and enabling the especially able men to proceed rapidly and ultimately to take special forms of training in preparation for promotion or other forms of responsibility. (Yerkes, 1919, pp. 90–91)

Yerkes and his colleagues developed methods for the mental testing of large numbers of individuals that were practical and serviceable. The contributions made by this committee of the NRC and by the psychological personnel of the military profoundly influenced workers in psychology, education, the sciences, and industry. Civilian versions of the Army Alpha Test and Army Beta Test as well as the Woodward Personnel Data Scale introduced the new phenomenon of group testing and the large-scale use of the multiple-choice format. This program was so well accepted by the Army that it created an Army Division of Psychology in the Medical Department, and a school of military psychology was established at the medical training camp at Fort Oglethorpe, Georgia, to supply the needed personnel. During World War I, approximately 100 officers and 300 enlisted men received training in procedures in Army psychological examinations. After the war this work led to numerous publications. Readers interested in the history of psychological testing are referred to the voluminous psychological literature between 1920 and 1930 derived from these data, as well as to the formal report of the committee described in this chapter (Yerkes, 1919).

The Committee on Psychological Problems in Aviation—Including Examination of Aviation Recruits was chaired by Harold E. Burtt. This committee undertook the selection and development of mental and physiological tests that promised a priori evidence of aptitude for flying. In addition to determining which tests were predictive of flying ability, the committee also proposed to undertake the development of tests bearing on the mental and physiological state of the aviator during flight. Several visual, physical, and physiological tests were studied. This work resulted in the establishment of a group of research psychologists and medical officers in the study of aviation problems at the Bureau of Mines, Washington, DC, and a special psychology section was added to the Medical Research Laboratory at Hazelhurst Field, Mineola, Long Island, New York.

Edward Thorndike studied the records of over 2,000 fliers and determined the relation between actual success as a military aviator and such predictors as those based on age, social status, intellectual ability, business achievement, athletic ability, and a number of other characteristics. As a result, the Department of Military Aeronautics of the Army requested that Thorndike prepare and put into operation methods of psychological testing appropriate for selecting personnel for that department.

R. P. Parsons, a medical officer of the Navy, received help from the committee in giving screening tests to every candidate for flying status in the Navy. Again, it is of interest that, although the Army formally accepted the committee's program, in the Navy only an individual responded to the offerings of the committee.

The Committee on the Selection of Men for Tasks Requiring Special Aptitudes was organized under Walter Dill Scott, Edward L. Thorndike, and Walter V. Bingham. Although the original membership of the committee consisted solely of psychologists, many industrial and business specialists in employment, classification, and personnel assignment were called on to assist. (Thorndike and Bingham are familiar to many as pioneers in the field of personnel classification and selection, as was Scott in the field of industrial psychology.) The work of the committee proved to be tremendously important to the future work of civilian psychologists. They collected data on nearly 3½ million men and performed the following tasks:

1. Classifications for placement into such technical units as engineers, aviation, ordnance, and other staff corps were established.

2. All recruits were classified according to the occupational needs of the military.

3. An index of occupations and trades needed in the military was prepared and brought together in a book titled *Army Specifications*. (This was the precursor of today's *Dictionary of Occupational Titles*, a standard reference work in the field of applied psychology.)

4. Occupational titles were prepared showing the need for skilled workers in each type of platoon, company, regiment, or other unit. This enabled the Army to send to France entire units that were well balanced according to occupational needs. A system of practical trade tests was devised, standardized, and installed throughout the Army camps. At the time of the Armistice (1918), about 130,000 men who claimed an occupational skill had been trade tested.

5. Qualifications records were furnished for all officers, providing a list of occupational, educational, and military experience and a rating by superior officers. This system aided Washington as well as local commanders in assigning officers.

6. A uniform system of rating officers was developed as an aid in selecting candidates for commissions. Before the end of World War I, it was universally used in both America and France as a means of securing, every three months, a rating on an officer as an aid in determining promotion, demotion, discharge, and appointments to the Officers' Reserve Corps.

7. Definitions of duties and qualifications of no fewer than 500 different kinds of officers in the various arms and branches of the military were developed.

8. Methods of selecting aviators were investigated, an improved system of tests for aviation candidates was introduced, and a new program of selection was installed.

9. A plan was prepared and introduced for segregating, sorting, training, and using the partially fit.

10. This committee also cooperated with the Yerkes program in developing the intelligence test for enlisted men.

11. This committee was also to assist the Navy and Marine Corps in preparing and installing a complete personnel classification system program corresponding with the Army system. However, the Armistice occurred before the Navy could implement its own system.

12. The committee also developed a system for screening and placing individuals of special talent and ability who came to Washington to offer their services (the World War I version of the so-called dollar-a-year man[6] so well known in World War II). Approximately 10,000 men of this category were screened and placed.

The work of this special aptitudes committee began with the arrival of the first contingent of the draft, but the scope of its achievement was far beyond expectations, as the committee reported: "Neither the civilians or the Army officers who initiated this development dreamed of a scope that it would rapidly assume or the share it would have in effecting the speedy organization of a well-balanced Army trained and ready for the critical hours in France" (Yerkes, 1919, p. 104).

After 14 months of work, this committee was absorbed into the office of the Adjutant General of the Army and merged with the Central Personnel Branch, the latter being created expressly for that purpose. This organization continues today as an integral part of the U.S. Army.

The Committee on Pedagogical and Psychological Problems in Military Training and Discipline had as its goal the improvement of the procedures of

---

[6]During World War II, many prominent businessmen and civic leaders volunteered their services to the U.S. government. They received only a token salary—a dollar a year—hence the name.

military training and discipline. This group held a number of conferences, including one on psychological problems and the reeducation of disabled men. These conferences led the Surgeon General to authorize assignment of a psychologist, Major B. T. Baldwin, to Walter Reed General Hospital on April 17, 1918. This was the beginning of psychological service in military hospitals, an example that the Navy did not follow until December 1943. In the course of work at Walter Reed and other general and base hospitals where psychologists were assigned, the original program formulated in these conferences was considerably altered. One of the most important developments was the organization of the psychological service as an integral part of the educational work of the hospital. This new organization was known as the Educational Service of the Military Hospital and included practically all extramedical and extrasurgical activities carried on in the institution for the benefit of patients. In one of these instances even civilian agencies, such as the Red Cross, worked through the Education Department.

The Educational Service included a psychological and statistical division. The functions of the psychological services were defined as follows: (a) to have primary responsibility for psychological and educational surveys of individual patients; (b) to cooperate with other educational and medical officers in the study of special learning problems encountered under the curative workshop schedule; (c) to have cooperative responsibility for all measures intended primarily to direct and control the mental attitude of patients; (d) to have responsibility for all statistical studies of procedure under curative workshops; and (e) to have cooperative responsibility for all training and advancement of education staff and of teachers in training. The group also included social workers and occupational therapists.

This development contains two elements of historical interest. First, the emphasis was on education, as opposed to the modern-day emphasis on such psychiatric rubrics as psychotherapy, therapeutic milieu, and psychopharmacology. Second, the program was not confined to psychiatric patients but appeared to address the needs of all kinds of patients as they were rehabilitated to civilian life. It can be seen that the function of this group included many of the tasks later assigned to the Veterans Administration and that the membership of the group bore many similarities to the modern-day Medical Service Corps of the Navy as well as the Army. The Educational Service may also be viewed as a forerunner of the modern subspecialty known as health psychology, and Major Baldwin can be considered the first uniformed health psychologist.

This type of organization was put into service in 43 different hospitals, including 66 officers of the Sanitary Corps (i.e., psychologists, etc.). Originally, the occupational aides devoted themselves to teaching handicrafts. Although these activities seemed trivial to many, it developed that the most important single agency in directing and controlling the attitude of hospital patients was the Reconstruction Aide in Occupational Therapy. Approximately 1,000 of these aides, all of them women, were engaged in domestic and overseas hospitals when World War I ended.

A subcommittee of the Committee on Pedagogical and Psychological Problems was formed to address the problems of reeducation. The members were J. B. Watson (of behaviorism fame), K. S. Lashley, and S. I. Franz, the latter both noted authorities on brain mechanisms. This subcommittee gave assistance in the following directions: (a) systematic instruction of neuropsychiatric groups and the work of rehabilitation at St. Elizabeths Hospital; (b) the development and application of methods for reeducation of aphasics and paralytics; (c) conduct of investigations on the effect of injury to the brain, with special reference to the relation of experiments on monkeys to cerebral war injuries; (d) arrangement with the Medical Department of the Army in the preparation of motion pictures of animals and human subjects to illustrate varieties of incapacity; and (e) preparation of a program for reconstructional experimentations.

The Committee on Problems of Emotional Stability, Fear, and Self-Control set for itself the task of devising means that would aid in the prompt recovery and segregation of recruits whose emotional characteristics indicated unfitness for military service. Under the direction of R. S. Woodworth, this committee created the Personal Data Questionnaire (PDQ), the forerunner of dozens of paper-and-pencil personality inventories designed and published after World War I. Examined in large groups, participants were required to answer yes or no to a series of personal questions designed to show psychopathic or neuropathic tendencies or emotional instability. Men answering a certain number of these questions in an atypical way were referred for intensive psychiatric examination. Work on the PDQ was not completed at the end of the war, but several thousand copies of the questionnaire had been printed and several hundred used to develop the military norms.

A Committee on Morale succeeded in stimulating military interest and in acquainting the War Department with morale needs, which led to a number of actions by the Army, including officially adopting the need for a systematic plan for the "psychological stimulation of troops in promoting fighting efficiency." As part of this effort, a considerable number of men were trained in military psychology at the Medical Department Training Camp at Fort Oglethorpe, Georgia. At various times as many as 25 psychologists were engaged in this type of work, and several were placed on duty with a newly organized Morale Branch of the General Staff.

The Committee on Tests for Deception, using results obtained in laboratory experiments, combined four psychophysiological deception tests: association, reaction time, breathing, and blood pressure. These tests held up well in laboratory experiments, but then, as now, the lie detection process did not have the full confidence of the psychology committee; although a significant amount of research was produced, the tests were never used on a regular basis.

Other Committees. Additional committees included the following:

Committee on Psychological Literature Relating to Military Affairs: Madison Bentley, Chair.

Committee on Recreation in the Army and Navy: George A. Coe, Chair.

Committee on Problems of Vision Which Have Military Significance: Raymond Dodge, Chair.

Committee on Psychological Problems of Incapacity, Including Those of Shell-Shock and Re-Education: Shepard I. Franz, Chair.

Committee on Propaganda Behind the German Lines: James R. Angell, Chair.

Committee on Acoustic Problems of Military Importance: Carl E. Seashore, Chair.

Committee on Adaptation of Psychological Instruction to Military Educational Needs: Raymond Dodge, Chair.

In addition to the lines of service indicated by the titles of committees, special work was done by individual members of the Psychology Committee or its subcommittees, as follows:

For the Division of Military Intelligence, on methods of selecting and training scouts and observers, by John B. Watson and Madison Bentley.

For the Chemical Warfare Service, on psychological problems of the gas mask, by Raymond Dodge, John W. Baird, and Knight Dunlap.

For the Committee on Education and Special Training of the War Department, on adaptation of Army intelligence tests for use in the Student's Army Training Corps, by Lewis M. Terman.

For various military and civilian agencies, studies of special problems in learning, methods of instruction, and methods of selection for special tasks, by L. L. Thurstone, Herbert S. Langfeld, and Robert S. Woodworth.

Among these committeemen, at least four are identifiable as having made significant contributions directly to the fledgling profession of clinical psychology: Yerkes, Thorndike, Franz, and Woodworth.

The Status of Psychologists in the Military

At the beginning of World War I, there was no provision for including psychologists in uniform, nor was there any recognition on the part of the military establishment that psychologists could make a professional contribution to the war effort. In fact, most psychologists themselves were not sure of their role. The first committee formed was On Psychological Literature Relating to Military Affairs, but it was allowed to disband after its chairman concluded that "the psychological literature relating to military problems was not of great practical importance in connection with the emergency because most of the tasks presented to or discovered by the committee demanded engineering of the pioneer sort" (Yerkes, 1919, p. 87). However, it soon became apparent that there was no shortage of problems that could be addressed by psychologists, and members of the committee were incredibly busy and productive throughout the war. Many of the projects started were never fully completed before the Armistice (the United States was in the war for "only" 19 months), but they made valuable postwar contributions to the field of psychology.

Clinical psychology has often been singled out as being able to identify a public need for its services and then proceeding to meet it. It is interesting to note that in 1917 the entire profession played this role, experimental psychology included. Partly because of its much larger size, the U.S. Army availed itself more often of psychological talent than did the Navy. In addition, the various committees reported that the Navy bureaucracy was more suspicious and slower to accept the offerings of the committee, and that once cooperation was accepted, the Navy was slower to act and the red tape was more involved. Several large programs were recommended by the committee, especially in the fields of personnel selection and recruit screening. Apparently none of these formal programs was accepted by the Navy, but a number of projects were completed for them by individual members of the committee.

Most of the contributions made by psychologists, clinical and otherwise, took place under the auspices of the Army. However, many of them were to have a lasting impact on post-World War I psychology, scientific as well as professional, and helped shape a model of military psychology that was to be followed in large part by the U.S. Navy, thus justifying their inclusion in this book. Although dozens of psychologists were on active duty in the Army, the author was able to find only one psychologist member of the committee who was in naval uniform: Lt. Comdr. Raymond Dodge, then of Wesleyan University (Connecticut) and later at Yale University.

At the beginning of the war, there were no billets (duty assignments) for psychologists in uniform, but a number were commissioned and placed on active duty in order to implement their own recommendations. As a result, many members of the committee were in uniform, whereas others were hired by the military as civilian assistants and assigned similar duties. A few were recruited into the Army as enlisted men, with the promise of commissions; unfortunately these did not materialize. As a result, many resented what they perceived as a break in faith, which cast a pall over the relations between psychologists and the Army Medical Department. This situation had a negative influence on the development of clinical psychology during World War II.

One of the results of the collaboration between the APA and the NRC was that the NRC created a permanent psychological section, thus ensuring for psychology a place alongside the other prestigious organizations constituting that group. Another result was the sudden and almost complete changing of the entire field from a scientific to a professional mode, which demonstrated to an entire nation psychology's practical as well as scientific applications. As Yerkes (1919) wrote:

> The war activities of the Psychology Committee have revealed or created opportunities whose scientific and practical significance cannot be estimated. Two years ago mental engineering [author's note: a new term] was a dream of a few visionaries. Today it is a branch of technology which, although created by the war, is evidently to be perpetuated and fostered by education and industry. (p. 149)

As one reviews the history of professional psychology, a particular theme recurs: Because the public is relatively unaware of what the profession can offer, it has been necessary to identify a need, learn how to fill that need, and then market that skill. To the credit of the profession, the public has usually responded favorably, and by this process new services were added to the repertoire of the professional psychologist. This was certainly the role played by psychology in the Great War. In addition to educating the military and ourselves as to what needs existed and demonstrating our ability to meet those needs, the speed and high level of organization characterizing this response was amazing. In less than a month after the declaration of war by the United States, the APA, under the leadership of President Yerkes, had organized and energized a complete committee structure and begun actual work in the field.

The response of the U.S. Army was no less remarkable. Almost 2 million men and women were mobilized, screened, trained, and readied for duty in a matter of weeks and months. (Women served primarily as nurses and clerical assistants.) In reading the literature of that period, one can almost feel the sense of urgency. Because of this urgency, the Army eagerly accepted almost any offer of assistance from the civilian sector and used even untried methods to achieve total mobilization.

Applications of Psychology to Naval Problems

Unfortunately (or fortunately, depending on one's bias), the U.S. Navy's responses did not reflect the same sense of urgency. The numbers of recruits were not as overwhelming as those faced by the Army, and they accepted only literate volunteers; in addition, the Navy was not populated with noncareer people eager to try new ideas and with less respect for the traditional ways of conducting military affairs. The commonly held opinion that the Navy is far more tradition-bound and slower to try new ideas is reflected in the reports of the various psychology committees that offered their services. As Raymond Dodge (cited in Yerkes, 1919) said in his committee report:

> The military situations [in the Navy] that we had to analyze were not infrequently of confidential nature. In some cases the suggestion that the matters be referred to the committee for investigation met with quite emphatic disapproval. Moreover, the initial visual problem that we came upon [Dodge was the chairman of the Vision Committee] commonly turned out to be so intimately related to non-visual factors that they became the least important part of the investigation. So it came about that in spite of the enthusiastic cooperation of a committee, a partitioned investigation in our case proved impractical during war times and we had to work as individuals. In the early psychological war problems in whose solutions it was my privilege to participate, the conspicuous features were the failure of military authorities to appreciate the reality of the mental problems, even when they were the main problems of the situation, and the failure of military traditions to meet the new problems of human engineering in modern warfare. (p. 106)

Dodge (cited in Yerkes, 1919) also noted the following:

> The only serious difficulty within the path of scientific service was the initial lack of confidence of the authorities. When confidence . . . [was] established, their faith in our ability to turn the desired tricks became an embarrassment, and the only limit to service was one of human endurance. (p. 107)

As an authority in vision, Dodge was able, for example, to assist the Navy in designing tests for selecting and training gun pointers for members of the Armed Guard stationed aboard merchant ships. He was able to design a practice instrument that could simulate an actual gunnery condition and provide both a screening and training device for the sailors. However, Dodge (cited in Yerkes, 1919) still had difficulty with naval authorities:

> Four days after the receipt of the inquiry, I outlined the instrument that we could use later and I guaranteed the success. The second was a problem of salesmanship. Every gunnery officer who saw the instrument work was enthusiastic from the start, but it was months later before the initial wall of suspicion and red tape was passed. (p. 108)

In addition to his work with gun pointers, Dodge also assisted the Navy in setting up standards for screening and training men for the Listeners' School (a school that taught a process analogous to modern-day sonar) and similar procedures for selecting and training men for working aboard ship in the plotting room (where navigational charts and instruments are used to determine the ship's position and course). Dodge found himself working in areas quite removed from his field of expertise of vision but was nevertheless able to apply with considerable success his broad training in psychology, including human engineering and psychometrics.

The war ended just as the Navy was preparing to implement certain programs developed for the Army, such as mental screening and occupational classification, both of which were directed by senior PhD psychologists in Army uniform as well as civilians. The screening of recruits in the Navy, for example, was still conducted by medical officers; at one Naval Training Station (Hampton Roads, VA), at least, the psychological work was handled by a corps of psychological testers under the direction of a third-class Pharmacist's Mate who was described as "serving as the psychologist of the psychiatric division" (McDaniel, 1919). It is therefore apparent that the Navy had yet to view psychologists as being worthy of professional status.

Between the Wars

Because of the wartime–peacetime cycles that characterize the history of the United States, the military establishment suffers periods of feast or famine. With this apparently in mind, Dodge (cited in Yerkes, 1919) observed:

> The military danger in the next few years of peace is that with the passing of the present crisis, so few military officers will be capable of carrying on the mental researches. I fear that some other nation may take up the mental analyses where we left them when the emergency ceased, and may develop a very real military psychology that will be more deadly than . . . guns. Our efforts, however excellent, however valuable, are only the first crude beginnings of such a military psychology. . . . The months that I devoted exclusively to national service seem in retrospect a kind of scientific excursion. The shadow of sorrow at their close comes from the fact that with the rotation of military service the old chiefs with whom we worked and would have followed to the death if necessary are being replaced by strangers who know nothing of our limitations nor our scientific potentiality. (p. 109)

During World War I, individual units and officers of the Navy grudgingly conceded some of the contributions to be made by psychology and psychiatry, especially in helping to screen for the unintelligent recruit. However, unlike the Army, the Navy not only resisted the formal introduction of these two disciplines into uniform, but in 1918 the Surgeon General of the Navy flatly stated that after wartime there was no place for psychiatry in Navy medicine, firmly fixed on the usefulness of the general practitioner in the Navy, and failed to see the importance of any of the medical specialties (Wilkins, 1972). Presumably this bias would have extended to the field of clinical psychology.

Because of the self-contained isolation of most naval stations (e.g., shipboard), the concept of the medical officer as a generalist is obviously very appropriate. Of historical note is that this jack-of-all-trades approach probably gave rise to the Navy medical officer as the first uniformed practitioner of clinical psychology.

Improved Screening of Recruits

Between World War I and World War II, there was apparently minimal activity in the Navy in any area that could be defined as psychological except screening and testing. In 1923, the Bureau of Navigation (later named the Bureau of Personnel and now known as the Naval Military Personnel Command) established a training division and began the development of the General Classification Tests for selecting personnel for the various service schools. This was apparently a version of the Army Alpha Examination and was used on a servicewide basis. Beginning in 1923, all recruits arriving at naval training stations were given an intelligence test and tests of mechanical aptitude (names were not noted). In 1931, an intelligence test (the title was not given) was administered at the recruiting station level (Louttit, 1942).

Psychological testing in order to screen out less intelligent, emotionally unstable, or psychopathic individuals continued over the years but apparently with very little standardization. Furthermore, each recruiting and training station seemed to have its own mixture of tests, such as the Knox Cube Test and Binet-type items, depending on the inclination of the individual medical officer. Some attempt at standardization was made whenever an item was taken directly from the Binet test, and use was made of the age level assigned to that item. One medical officer suggested that the cutoff score should be at a mental age of "about 14" (Poppen, 1923). (For an 18-year-old, this would translate into an IQ of 78.) However, the medical officer was still allowed considerable latitude in making a final decision.

The psychiatric interview was not in routine use, although it was often advocated. A common perception of the interview technique at that time may be gleaned from the writing of one of its advocates (Jacoby, 1919b):

> Practical psychiatry has been defined as applied common sense. If the Medical Officer on recruiting duty will have a private interview with each applicant . . . he will form an excellent idea of the applicant's fitness or unfitness. . . . A very few minutes, not more than five in most cases, is all the time which needs to be consumed in this way. (p. 231)

As will be seen, this faith in the interview as a screening device was not well placed; for the Army it was to produce near-disastrous results in World War II.

Screening in the Naval Air Service

Because of their small size and the fact that their training was confined to very few bases, the aviation and submarine branches of the Navy had better psychological testing. The Naval Air Service began to recognize the potential of nonphysical variables that would predict success among aviators in training. In 1927–1928, for example, only about 50 percent of the officer applicants and far fewer of the enlisted applicants successfully completed the training course at Pensacola, Florida. Because the supply of applicants was more than ample, the attrition rate was not of great concern. However, in 1930 a systematic study of incoming students was begun that included a "psychological examination" (Sutton, 1930). This survey was continued until several hundred cases had been collected and the results compared with each subject's subsequent training and flying record. In spite of its pioneering mode, the technique was a vast improvement (DeFoney, 1931, 1933), and further improvements continued in succeeding years (see chapter 22).

Screening in the Submarine Service

In 1925, the Submarine School at New London, Connecticut, began to screen all applicants with the O'Rourke Intelligence Test, a multiple-choice group test developed within the Federal Civil Service Commission and adopted by the Bureau of Navigation in 1923. A significant decrease in the attrition rate was reported (Jones, 1926). However, like their colleagues in aviation, submariners were extremely reluctant to yield very much final decision-making power to outsiders (i.e., nonaviators or nonsubmariners). They were convinced that each branch of the service is unique and that the final selection of personnel could be entrusted only to those having personal experience with the conditions under which the selectees would be required to perform. As a result, the medical officer in each group could overrule the empirical findings of any psychological or mental examination, and the medical officer in turn could be overruled by a line officer of that branch.

In summary, it appears that until World War II clinical psychology in the U.S. Navy was practiced by general medical officers (some with psychiatric training), commissioned line officers (with no special training), and enlisted petty officers, who administered and scored tests.

CHAPTER 5

World War II

By the fall of 1939, Hitler had occupied Austria, Czechoslovakia, and Poland, and the winds of World War II were blowing. A Navy medical officer, Captain Dallas G. Sutton, the Navy's Chief of Psychiatry, was a participating member of the Roundtable on Psychology in the National Emergency held at the 1939 meeting of the American Association for Applied Psychology in Washington, DC. (As noted in chapter 22, Sutton had a background in researching the selection of naval aviators.) Largely because of his interest, provision was made early in 1940 for a small number of psychologists to be commissioned as line officers and detailed (i.e., assigned) for service in the Medical Department.

The First Active-Duty Psychologists

Reporting for duty in October 1940, C. M. Louttit of Indiana University was the first of this group on active duty (Louttit, 1941, 1943). As is suitable for "the first man aboard," he was in charge of recruiting other psychologists and presumably responsible for a new development. In the April 1941 edition of the *Psychological Bulletin*, the following announcement appeared:

> The Surgeon General of the Navy invites the attention of psychologists to the opportunity of becoming commissioned officers in the Volunteer, Special Service, Class H, of the U.S. Naval Reserve.
>
> Male citizens of the U.S. who are physically and otherwise qualified are eligible for appointment as commissioned officers in Class H-V (S) of the U.S. Naval Reserve. A candidate for appointment in Class H-V (S), U.S. Naval Reserve, must present the following credentials as to education and professional qualifications:
>
> (a) Certificate of, or evidence of, at least four (4) years of collegiate education; or a degree from an accredited institution of higher education in a subject or subjects which pertain to, or are related to, those specialties coming under the cognizance of the Medical Department of the Navy, the determination of which shall be made by the Chief of the Bureau of Medicine and Surgery.

(b) Evidence of license to practice their profession in a state or territorial possession of the U.S. where such is required.

(c) If the candidate has had special training, a certificate to this effect shall be included.

(d) Evidence of qualification in specialty, which shall be satisfactory to the Chief of the Bureau of Medicine and Surgery.

(e) In addition to the requirements listed above, candidates shall submit evidence of recent practical experience in their specialties as indicated:

For Ensign	(2) or more years
For Lieutenant (junior grade)	(6) or more years

(f) The rank in which candidates for Class H-V (S) are appointed will be determined by the candidate's age, academic seniority, and practical experience. [Author's comment: Note the implied preference for academics.] These must be appropriate to the duties of a specific mobilization assignment.

In addition to the above basic requirements, applicants for appointment as psychologists should have a certificate or professional degree from an acceptable institution and submit evidence of practical experience in actual individual counseling and examining, preferably with adults, in prisons, hospitals, college guidance, or other institutions. It is contemplated [that] the services of such officers [will be used] in examining recruits of the Navy and Marine Corps at Naval Training Stations, Marine Corps Depots, and Aviation Procurement Centers.

Psychologists desiring appointment as commissioned officers in Class H-V (S) of the Naval Reserve should communicate with the commandant of the naval district in which they reside, as listed below, requesting application forms and any further information they may desire regarding such an appointment. (Announcement, 1941, pp. 306–308)

This announcement was important for a number of reasons. It officially recognized clinical psychologists as a separate group with professional status, with skills in counseling as well as testing, and with adults as well as children. Furthermore, it offered psychologists a new opportunity for actual clinical work with patients, an avenue previously very restricted. Although it established a 4-year degree as a minimum, nearly all of the successful applicants possessed a master's degree or a PhD. In an apparent oversight, it limited applicants to ''male citizens of the United States.'' This was later rectified, and about 50 women did serve in this group before the war ended (Louttit, 1944). Unlike the situation in World War I, when World War II approached there existed a population of clinical psychologists, however unseasoned, to answer their nation's call, a call first made by the U.S. Navy; the U.S. Army did not routinely offer commissions to clinical psychologists until 1944 (Napoli, 1981, p. 100; Seidenfeld, 1966, p. 571). Given the importance of this event, it is noteworthy that the Navy was the pioneer.

In January 1941, the Surgeon General authorized the commissioning of clinical psychologists in the Medical Department. Louttit then recruited the late William

A. Hunt, who subsequently became chairman at Northwestern University and then Professor Emeritus at Loyola University of Chicago. Hunt, who reported for duty in April 1941, was the first clinical psychologist recruited in the H-V(S) group (see below). Louttit was technically a line officer assigned to the Medical Department. He was followed in June by Arthur L. Benton, who later became Professor Emeritus of Psychology and Neurology at the University of Iowa. These two "recruits" were indicative of the quality of the psychologists who entered naval service and went on to continue very distinguished careers after the war. Louttit himself was eventually transferred to the Bureau of Naval Personnel (formerly known as the Bureau of Navigation).

Psychologists were commissioned in the Naval Reserve in three categories (Bremner, 1943; Jenkins, 1942; Lewinski & Pennington, 1943; Louttit, 1941; Mitchell, 1944; Richards, 1944):

1. Hospital Volunteer Specialist (H-V(S)) to serve in connection with the Medical Department. Late in 1940 the Hospital Service Corps had been created in order to commission nonmedical professional personnel. As noted earlier, it included psychologists. Although numerous psychologists in this category were ordered to duties in naval aviation (Medical Department) and hospitals, most were assigned to assist in the examination and selection of recruits at naval and Marine Corps training stations. Women were designated by a "W" preceding the job code abbreviation.

2. Aviation Volunteer Specialist (A-V(S)) to assist in the selection and placement of personnel for flight training. They also functioned in a technical and advisory capacity to flight officers, flight instructors, and flight surgeons.

3. Deck Officer Volunteer Specialist (D-V(S)) to develop and advance ongoing personnel programs at naval bases and stations. Their duties were chiefly those of a personnel officer, who aided in examining, selecting, and placing trainees following their basic training. They were skilled in interview techniques and able to administer and interpret aptitude and intelligence tests.

The original intention had been to use only a limited number of psychologists as members of psychiatric examining units at naval training stations, but by February 1943, over 130 psychologists, including women, were serving in a variety of programs (Louttit, 1943); this number continued to increase until nearly 500 had donned naval uniforms by the end of the war. However, beyond a general mandate to "use psychological tests," their duties generally depended on the psychiatrist with whom they worked, and as they developed personal relationships and showed competence, their responsibilities expanded. Even when

37

their responsibilities were widened in 1943 to include duty at naval hospitals (Arthur L. Benton went to the San Diego Naval Hospital and Thomas W. Richards went to the Naval Hospital at Mare Island, California), it was on the basis of informal contact with individual physicians who had confidence in their work.

A similar situation existed with psychologists assigned to the aviation branch. They arrived at preflight schools, flight schools, and so on, unable to define their own place in the military organization or to find anyone who could. Because testing consumed only a few hours a week, they soon began to accept new duties. As J. G. Jenkins (1945), head of the program, observed:

> Almost to a man they discarded any worry as to whether a given task was appropriate for a Ph.D. or for a psychologist and began to weave themselves firmly into the local fabric. Psychologists on cadet selection boards had similar experiences, and in both cases they began to carve out for themselves a niche in naval aviation. (p. 632)

Clinical Psychology in the Army

Clinical psychology in the U.S. Army during World War II developed along a different path. Early in 1939, Horace B. English, then executive secretary of the American Association of Applied Psychology, opposed any use of clinical psychologists with the Army's Medical Department that did not grant them equality in diagnosis with physicians. He took this position partly because so much friction had existed during World War I between the Army medical officers and the psychologists. The latter were placed in the less prestigious Sanitary Corps and, in many cases, not commissioned in spite of the assurances relayed to them by Robert Yerkes, the senior psychologist. English was also instrumental in persuading the Adjutant General's Office of the Army to administer the psychological testing program rather than have it again placed under the Medical Department. Soon after the attack on Pearl Harbor, the Navy followed suit, placing its testing program under the Bureau of Naval Personnel. However, a number of persons did not agree with this separation from the medical establishment, and it diverted a number of uniformed and civilian psychologists who might otherwise have worked as clinicians into tasks more commonly identified with personnel psychology. Apparently, because of the early collaboration between Sutton and Louttit and the absence of friction between the Navy Medical Department and the psychological establishment in World War I, there was no similar bias to overcome in the Navy.

This historical situation very much impeded the development of clinical psychology in the Army and probably accounts for how the Navy was able to "one-up" the Army by beginning its program first (as today, interservice rivalry and a reluctance to engage in joint efforts was very strong). Napoli (1981) described the Army problem as follows:

> In the spring of 1942 no clinical psychologists were serving in Army hospitals under the supervision of psychiatrists. In part this was due to the psychologists' opposition to such service, in part to the limited role the army assigned to psychiatry. During the period of mobilization, when psychologists were developing tests for the adjutant general, psychiatrists were assuring the Medical Department that they could screen out most mentally unstable recruits at the induction centers. Thus the Army made no plans to use psychiatrists in hospitals, and it understandably saw no need for clinical psychologists there either. In June 1941 a committee of the National Research Council recommended that the Medical Department provide openings for psychologists, but the Surgeon General ignored the recommendation.
>
> As the size of the Army grew and more men entered combat, the number of neuropsychiatric casualties increased. It soon became obvious that the psychiatric interview at induction, which seldom lasted over three minutes, could weed out only the severely disturbed recruits. Psychiatrists now realized that they could not predict which otherwise normal men would crack under the strain of military duties. Psychiatric wards filled and the demand for clinical psychologists grew. In the spring of 1942 the surgeon general commissioned six psychologists in the Sanitary Corps as an "experiment" and assigned them to army hospitals. Although these men soon found useful work to do, they were not joined by any colleagues. The army's psychiatrists did not have sufficient influence to expand the program in the face of the hostility or indifference that other physicians showed to psychiatric problems and the strong objections that psychologists had to assignment in the Medical Department. Some personnel consultants drifted into hospital work, and enlisted men with psychological training were also pressed into service. But the army developed no unified program for the use of clinical psychologists until 1944.
>
> Only in the summer of 1945 did the supply of clinical psychologists catch up with the demand. By then 450 clinical psychologists were serving in the army. Two-thirds of this number worked in general, station, and convalescent hospitals, and others were assigned to correctional institutions and basic training centers. The Army's program for clinical psychologists, which in size and variety had no civilian counterpart, featured an unusual amount of cooperation and good feeling between psychologists and psychiatrists. Some professional rivalry arose, but many psychologists found that their subordinate position did not interfere with the performance of useful and rewarding work. Referring to its "symbiotic support of neuropsychiatry," Seidenfeld, the Army's Chief Clinical Psychologist, declared that psychology had "written an illustrious chapter in the Medical Department." (pp. 99–102)

However, Seidenfeld's enthusiasm omits mention of the fact that except for the six aforementioned psychologists assigned to the Sanitary Corps, all of the clinical psychologists commissioned were attached to the Adjutant General's Office (the personnel arm of the Army) and were only lent to the Medical Department. Even when the Army finally began to recruit enough clinical psychologists in 1945, they remained under the administrative control of the Adjutant General. This rift between medicine and clinical psychology remained unresolved until after the war ended. As William Menninger, Chief Psychiatrist of the Army at the end of the war, noted (Seidenfeld, 1966):

> The clinical psychologists proved their value to Army psychiatry. . . . their commission in the Adjutant General's Department was a handicap because it did not identify them with medicine. Even after their transfer to the Medical Administrative Corps, they occasionally were assigned to nonpsychologic duties by . . . commanding officers too lacking in perspective or knowledge to appreciate the value of their psychological skills. It is to be hoped that the War Department does not discard the present system as it did after World War I. (p. 577)

The Development of Clinical Psychology in the Navy

Navy clinical psychology was organized under the Neuropsychiatry Branch of the Bureau of Medicine and Surgery, and the Chief Psychologist reported to the head of that branch. Following his pioneering work in recruit screening at Newport Training Center (described later), William Hunt became the first Chief Psychologist in the Bureau of Medicine and Surgery under Francis J. Braceland, who later went on to a very distinguished career in American psychiatry. In numerous wartime and postwar publications, Hunt chronicled the development of clinical psychology in the Navy. One article specifically addressed itself to the war years: "Clinical Psychology in 1944–45" (Hunt, 1975). It is quoted at length not only because Hunt was close to this part of our history, but also because it offers some insight into one of the Navy's (and the nation's) most colorful clinical psychologists:

> While histories of clinical psychology are unanimous in attributing the tremendous development of clinical psychology after World War II to the beneficial influence upon the profession of the military experience, little is said of the specifics involved. I have chosen to write of the years 1944 and 1945 because it was in those closing 2 years of the War that the lessons learned from our clinical experience in the military began to be reflected in patterns of personnel practice and institutional and professional organization. In a very important way the seeds planted by the military experience began to germinate and make possible the subsequent postwar fruition.
>
> Our military service inevitably increased the breadth of our professional experience. Before the war most of us had operated within a somewhat limited framework in terms of patient populations, interprofessional contacts, and relations with the public at large. We were lamentably out of

touch with other professional cultures, as in turn they were out of touch with ours. I remember a long-deceased fellow officer, dean of a prominent Eastern medical school, who reassured me about my status as a psychologist: "I'm all for you fellows, Hunt. I've had telepathic experiences myself." Or my own insistence on equal standing among my medical colleagues and the resulting finding that it involved extra duty obligations and increased patient and institutional responsibilities.

There is one aspect of this education that often is overlooked. It took place not in a formal, authoritarian setting, but in a functional, working relationship. We learned by doing. The job was bigger than we were and we needed all the help we could get, from whatever professional or personal sources were available. Professional distinctions and professional politics were confined largely to the Washington level. In the field they faded before the immensity of the task. I remember one psychiatric chief of service who wrote me in the Bureau of Medicine and Surgery and asked that I send him two psychologists "to do psychotherapy. If you send psychiatrists," he said, "they'll be caught up in all sorts of extra medical administrative duties, but you psychologists as non-medical people are free of these, and can work with patients."

The Navy recognized the importance of this cooperative professional interchange when it first developed its concept of the Psychiatric Unit or team, which consisted of a psychiatrist, a neurologist or neuropsychiatrist, and a psychologist. These were conceived not as individual slots, but as an integrated team, the Psychiatric Unit. The conception was an excellent one for 1940, but after the outbreak of hostilities in 1941, while still extant as a concept, the 1-1-1 relationship of psychiatrist, neuropsychiatrist, and psychologist fell victim to the ensuing shortages in personnel and the ratio shifted as a function of availability at the moment, although the concept of a functional team remained.

Since I was to go on duty in the first of these units established (April 28, 1941) I felt somewhat uncertain about my duties and at my own expense traveled to Washington to interview Captain Dallas Sutton, the Navy's chief of psychiatry. Sutton informed me that I knew my job better than he did, that I should go ahead and do it, and that he would back me. He did add that in his opinion the most important task ahead of me was to get along with medical people. He added that of course they would have to get along with me but that he was afraid the brunt of the burden might fall on me.

As it turned out we shared the burden equally and I believe successfully, although there were moments of strain. I entered the ward room at Newport one day after lunch and found in progress a lively discussion about the appropriateness of my being called "Doctor." It continued with some disregard of my feelings. My friend, Cecil L. Wittson, the psychiatrist, was claiming that since I had a Ph.D. I was entitled to be called "Doctor," as Navy Regulations specified that professional people below the rank of Commander be called by their highest courtesy title. I pointed out, however, that many people held the doctorate in medicine, law, or philosophy, but that only a few held a full professorship in an academic institution. Accordingly, a strict interpretation of regulations would demand that I be called "Professor." I added that I felt it would

41

be foolish in a military organization to run around being addressed as "Professor" or "Prof" and suggested that we forget regulations and let the problem work itself out heuristically. It did, and from then on I was addressed as "Doctor" and swallowed my pride at this egregious insult to my professional rank.

The point that I wish to make is that we were engaged in a struggle for national survival and not in matters of professional pride. The little nuances of status only assume importance as the magnitude of the mutual task diminishes. If we in the mental health professions were actually to identify deeply with the betterment of the human race, there would be much less emotional investment in who will be riding on whose coattails when the saints come marching in. More of this deep mutual involvement in a common cause would have hastened our amalgamation in 1945, but it comes only occasionally within our profession. Cuts in research and training funds, threats to freedom of speech, limitations on animal and human experimentation drive us together, but the lesson of strength in unity erodes rapidly once the threat has disappeared.

Another beneficial aspect of the military was the encouragement of innovation. Encouragement is hardly the word. With the continuing short-ages of personnel and of time, innovation was necessary. The late Harold Hildreth and I were fascinated by the possibility of abbreviated intelli-gence tests, often of the one or two item variety, and developed several successful ones. They were only "screen" tests, of course, and any final decision rested on a more complete battery plus clinical appraisal.

There is not the time here to go into all the innovations that occurred, but necessity was not only the mother of invention, but a fruitful mother in every sense of the word.

Some of the innovations were in the use of personnel, and the enlisting and commissioning of women in the military helped immeasurably to advance the cause of feminism. We in the Navy's clinical program did our bit as well. The Navy had commissioned some female clinical psy-chologists, but they were assigned to duty in Naval Hospitals, as these were adjudged a more proper and civilized environment for women. Wittson and I wanted them assigned to the Training Stations, in the first place because we needed personnel, in the second place because we saw no reason why they couldn't function as well as males, and in the third place because we felt a male-female mixture might work out well dy-namically in handling recruits in the Training Station situation. We won our case, our WAVES arrived, and they justified our confidence in them.

When I arrived in Washington, however, I met another problem. I wanted to send female clinicians into the Marine training stations as well, and here I met a stone wall—for a bit. The rigors of life in a Naval Training Station were bad enough, but to risk our gentle ladies among those uncouth Marines was unthinkable. I prevailed, however, and off went one of my most trustworthy lady clinicians to live among the Marines. She went by way of Washington and some reinforcement. Nothing was heard of her for a month, and then I received an apologetic letter saying that she hoped we were not worried and that everything was going well. She had only one problem. Her office naturally was in the receiving building where the medical examinations were given, and as a consequence the corridors were frequented by nude young recruits. This posed a problem for her. If she showed too much interest it might reflect on the reputation of the [Medical Corps]. On the other hand, if she showed no interest at all, it might damage the ego of the young men. She said she thought she had achieved a proper balance. I closed the file. The situation was under control.

The matter of increased publication outlets for all that was developing in military clinical psychology still posed a problem. Basically clinical psychologists adjusted to military demands, but they were still professional people with a strong academic background and they needed the professional publication. The military services are not geared for this, and the professional societies were not in a position to offer it. There were paper shortages, ink shortages, printing shortages, and everything that one could think of to discourage the founding of a new Journal.

Into this breach stepped Frederick Thorne with his proposal for a Journal of Clinical Psychology. This sort of individual initiative was the only possible answer to the problem. I discussed the matter with my opposite number in the Army, Colonel Morton Seidenfeld, and we decided that a new clinical Journal would be of benefit to both the military and the private sector of clinical psychology. We therefore agreed to join the editorial board of the new journal. I have never regretted my decision.

Innovation requires justification and this leads to research. Most of it was applied. We aided in the validation of several screening tests, among them the Cornell and the Navy Personal Inventory. We kept process research on our own program going continuously, and we related our activities to the efficiency of the Training Station, demonstrating to the Commanding Officer the direct relationship between our selection activities and the Station disciplinary and sick call rates. . . . I am quite sure that the Navy's clinical psychology and aviation psychology programs were very influential in setting up the Office of Naval Research (ONR), the first of its kind and bellwether for the subsequent government funding of research in NIMH and NSF.

It must be remembered that at the time there was little support or funding for research per se as a separate activity, and none in the clinical psychology area. What was done was done as we did at Newport using local command support, wedging the time requirements into our duties, and scrounging for such odd material and financial support as local sympathy could rake up for us. This is why some of us who had a finger in writing job requirements for the military and later for the Veterans Administration adhered so assiduously to the model of the clinician as diagnostician, therapist, and researcher. It was the only way we could provide for research. In the absence of an organizational umbrella under which to shelter it, we had to place it in the care of each individual clinician by including it as one of his stated functions.

While I firmly believe that research provides the foundations of clinical practice, and while I feel that every clinician should have an understanding of the research process in order that he may evaluate properly the claims of every new technique or methodology that gets dumped on the market, I have never felt that every clinician should perform all three functions. Few can or care to, and the official model of the clinician as researcher as well as diagnostician and therapist has distracted and diverted many excellent clinicians from doing that which they do best and has produced much second and third-rate research. At the time it seemed the only way to protect the research function. Fortunately, research now can stand on its own feet.

Finally, I mention the contribution to the military as giving us a sense of identity and status, a sense of professional self-esteem and a resulting professional ego strength. In these times when patriotism is often considered "camp," it is difficult to realize that to most of us involved in it, World War II had many of the aspects of a holy war. The threat of fascism was very real, resistance to it seemed a moral obligation, and with the cold, calculated aggression of Pearl Harbor the only open alternative seemed not submission, but to answer aggression with aggression. Under these circumstances most of us took a genuine pride in making a real professional contribution to the war effort.

When 1945 was over we returned to civilian life and left a tradition that created a permanent place for clinical psychology in the military and assured our inclusion in subsequent government programs such as the Veterans Administration, the National Institute of Mental Health, the National Science Foundation, and others. In all these activities we carried the support and respect of those other professions . . . [that] had worked with us throughout the war. One more anecdote may illustrate this.

While seated at my desk at the Bureau of Medicine and Surgery one afternoon in August 1945, I was approached by my boss, Francis J. Braceland, then Chief of Psychiatry in the Navy. He told me that he had just lunched with some of the people responsible for the reorganization of the VA, that they wanted to include psychology, but that they had not heard of the APA. He told them firmly that they had better work through our professional organization and suggested someone call me. George Kelly had been demobilized recently and had accepted a position at the nearby University of Maryland. He agreed to spend half-time for a few months with the VA. Iris Stevenson from my office went down with him, and a number of us served as informal consultants on a non-pay status to help things get organized until James Grier Miller could take over after his release from the Army.

It was no accident either that when Robert Felix, the psychiatrist, was selected to head NIMH he selected as his staff assistant Joseph M. Bobbitt (a psychologist), who had worked with him in the Coast Guard during the hostilities. In all of the new government agencies that were being set up, relationships were being cemented that had started in the services. It offered an excellent power base for an expanding profession, and clinical psychology has made the most of it.

To aid and abet all this growth in 1945 we got our own journal, *Journal of Clinical Psychology*, a full year before the postwar publication boom began. At the time the APA was busy with its organizational problems and ill prepared for such a venture. No government source was available. Only individual initiative could have made it possible. I have always admired Fred Thorne's courage and foresight in undertaking the venture, and it has been a real pleasure over the years to see the Journal grow in stature and influence as it has realized the early hopes Fred had for it.

May the Journal and the profession continue to grow in the years ahead.
(Hunt, 1975, pp. 173–178)

This article highlights several items important to the history of Navy psychology. First is the emphasis placed on the fact that these years gave the clinical psychology group a sense of both professional and military identity. There has always been a sense of pride in being an officer in the U.S. Navy, and this proved to be no less true among the psychologists. Combined with the deep sense of patriotism that has always permeated American society, the knowledge that one is engaged in an exciting and worthwhile profession tends to produce a unique experience. As will be discussed further, the war experience also instilled in this group and those that followed them an intense loyalty to the Navy as they pursued their civilian careers—many of them in the Active Reserve.

Hunt also refers to the individual initiative so often required of the Navy psychologist. In another article (Hunt, 1945), he refers to the "rugged individualism" of this group, developed probably out of the natural tendency of any group to decentralize authority and emphasize individual responsibility where small units of men (e.g., ships' crews) often have to function independently in relative isolation for long periods of time. Anyone familiar with Navy psychology today will agree that this is still very much the case. The professional freedom allowed the individual psychologist is sometimes extreme, especially to those placed in the so-called Lone Ranger billets, where the psychologist is the only one of that profession and is the primary judge of what needs to be done and how to do it. This requires individuals to be flexible, creative, and able to live somewhat independently of the environment in which they operate. Above all, they must take advantage of opportunities and be assertive.

As we have seen, while he was still on active duty, Hunt was instrumental in founding the only journal of clinical psychology in the United States at that time (Witmer's *The Psychological Clinic* had ceased publication in 1935). Also, partly because of his personal intervention, the postwar organization of mental health services in the Veterans Administration was prevented from excluding the profession of psychology. Furthermore, he helped write the VA job description for psychologists, which put in place the now-traditional triad of diagnosis, therapy, and research. In addition, Hunt and others were able to later use the Navy experience to assure clinical psychology a place in the postwar plans of the National Institute of Mental Health and the National Science Foundation.

Clinical psychologists did not just leave the Navy after the war—"They sprang forth and landed running!"

The Emergency Committee on Psychology

As noted in a previous section, in 1917 the National Research Council had formed a Psychology Committee to assist in the war effort. This led to the formation of a permanent committee known as the Division of Anthropology and Psychology. Modeled after its World War I experience, this group organized the Emergency Committee on Psychology on November 3, 1940, in order to deal with "problems of human engineering in times of national crisis and defense." As before, the names of the committee chairmen read like a list of "Who's Who" in American psychology:

Gordon Allport, Harvard University, representing the Society for the Psychological Study of Social Issues.

R.A. Brotemarkle, University of Pennsylvania, representing the American Association for Applied Psychology.

Leonard J. Carmichael, Tufts College, Member-at-Large.

Karl M. Dallenbach, Cornell University, Chairman of the Committee, representing Section I of the American Association for the Advancement of Science.

Carl E. Guthe, University of Michigan, Chairman of the Division of Anthropology and Psychology, ex officio.

Walter S. Hunter, Brown University, Member-at-Large.

Walter R. Miles, Yale University, representing the American Psychological Association.

Carroll Pratt, Rutgers University, representing the Society of Experimental Psychologists.

Dael Wolfle, University of Chicago, representing the Psychometric Society.

Robert M. Yerkes, Yale University, Member-at-Large.

As in World War I, this committee decided that as a first step a bibliography on military psychology should be prepared. In 1917 the group assigned to this task was allowed to disband because there did not exist a useful literature base in this field. However, in 1940, not only did they find an extensive bibliography, but also, in the interests of time and expense, they were forced to issue a selected version (Pratt, 1941). This version even contained an extensive review of German military psychology, which, while filled with the Nazi biases on race and world conquest, was extensive and interesting.

In introducing this work, the editor, Carroll C. Pratt (1941), wrote:

> One of the advantages of this bibliography . . . was thought to be its educational value to large numbers of psychologists in this country who in all probability have never given much thought to the relation of psychology to military requirements. It may be assumed that most American psychologists have pursued their professional activities against a background nearly empty of any concern about war. (p. 311)

It appears that the prediction made by Raymond Dodge in 1919 of a postwar lapse of interest in military psychology proved true. This lapse came to hamper many of our efforts in World War II.

Unlike the situation in World War I, in World War II large numbers of psychologists were recruited directly into uniform, and their contributions were made while on active duty. In World War I the National Research Council had played a major role in marshaling American psychologists for the war effort. However, between the wars the NRC Psychology Committee had lost most of its liaison with the federal government, which established its own group—the Office of Scientific Research and Development (OSRD). In June 1942, at the request of the Navy, the OSRD formed the Applied Psychology Panel (APP), which funded and coordinated a wide variety of programs, usually in response to specific requests. Perhaps the most noteworthy accomplishment of the APP was its leadership in helping the Navy produce a highly successful personnel classification system based upon the Basic Test Battery, consisting of six new tests—General Classification, Reading, Arithmetic, Reasoning, Mechanical Knowledge, and Mechanical Aptitude.

From a historical viewpoint, this made the work of the NRC less important as a focal point for documenting the contributions of psychology to the war effort. Also, by this time Navy clinical psychology had its own identity, and in order to present its history in this volume it was no longer necessary to research the work of other organizations in order to trace its roots. For this reason the work of the NRC Psychology Committee in World War II is not detailed herein; in addition, during World War II its contributions as a separate organization were relatively sparse when compared with those during World War I (Dallenbach, 1946).

Psychologists' Role in the Military

The participation of psychologists in the military was considered an unequivocal success. At a 1945 conference on Military Contributions to Methodology in Applied Psychology, John Jenkins (1947), Captain (Hospital Specialist), USNR, wrote:

> It is time . . . to reflect on how well we have done by our country, by our profession, and by ourselves in the war years just past. The reflection becomes all the more pleasing as we are made aware of the contrast between 1941–42 and 1945. It may not be too much to say that most of us here at this meeting came into the military services through the servant's entrance. We were brought in, in an era of gloom and defeat, under the conviction that things were so bad that any available magic should be tried, even psychology. We have worked four years, more or less. Now we are going out the big front door, labelled as military specialists, while the band plays "Hail to the Psyche." Victory has replaced defeat; concrete realization of what psychologists can do has

replaced a vague hope that they might possibly do something; and a warm and cordial acceptance has replaced a suspicious and grudging admission to the military work-place.

As the capsheaf to the whole affair, we leave with the certain knowledge that military establishments are setting up permanent and lasting Sections and Divisions in our brand of military psychology. If ever a compliment was phrased in operational terms, surely that is it. Surely there can be no finer recognition of the worth of our performances than the establishment, within the framework of the conservative military structure, of functioning groups of our professional colleagues, commissioned to carry on what we have so well begun. (p. 1)

Until World War II clinical psychology remained in an embryonic state, being slowly fed meager scraps of nutrients held out by such parent surrogates as general psychology, psychiatry, philosophy, and education. With the rapid mobilization of the war years, not only did clinical psychology emerge from the womb but quickly passed through childhood and into young adulthood. Because of the efforts of those who donned the "blue and gold," clinical psychology in the U.S. Navy was also born, assumed its own identity, and poised for its own pattern of growth and adventure—however uneven.

Demobilization of psychologists after World War II was total. There were no commissions in the Regular Navy for this group, and there was an understandable urge to return to civilian life. Prior to the war there was a widespread recognition in the field of clinical psychology that it was essential to receive training beyond the master's level and to pursue coursework not included in the traditional PhD program. The availability of funds through the GI Bill and other government subsidies and the plentiful employment opportunities served to create a huge demand for training facilities. Universities rushed to serve this need, and clinical psychology programs flourished and abounded. Matured by their war experiences, over a million ambitious and goal-directed veterans descended upon colleges and universities. On every campus and in all areas of study, there existed an atmosphere of enthusiasm and optimism never before or since seen in American academia. In psychology more postwar degrees were granted in clinical psychology than in any other subspecialty. At the turn of the century there had been great hopes for the "new science" of scientific psychology—now great numbers of young people were looking forward to the "new profession" of clinical psychology, this author included.

CHAPTER 6

Enter the
Medical Service Corps

Although all of the psychologist members of the Volunteer Specialist Corps left active duty after World War II, arrangements were soon under way to make a permanent place for them in the organization of the Navy. Experience had shown that a variety of nonmedical administrative and professional specialties were needed. (Interestingly enough, this need had been documented in 1898, when Congress established the Hospital Corps, not only formalizing the enlisted structure but providing for twenty-five warrant officers; in 1912 and 1916 legislation enlarged this to include commissioned warrant officers (Erie, 1972)).

Establishment of the Medical Service Corps

In 1947 Congress passed the Army-Navy Medical Service Corps Act. As originally enacted, the Navy Medical Service Corps (MSC) was composed of four sections. The Administration and Supply Section was designed to constitute 60% of the Corps strength, the Medical Allied Sciences Section (including Psychology) 23%, the Optometry Section 5%, and the Pharmacy Section 10% (NAVMED, 1957). The original law also put a 2% limitation on the rank of Captain and specified Ensign as the rank of entry; however, those with a doctorate could enter with the rank of Lieutenant (junior grade).

When the Medical Service Corps was created in 1947, there were very few senior officers, even among the Administrative Section. In fact, among the first 255 permanently commissioned officers in 1947, none was above the rank of Lieutenant Commander. The original legislation did not provide for a Chief of the Corps, so between 1947 and 1954 the fledgling Corps was administered within the existing structure of the Bureau of Medicine and Surgery (BuMed) at the hands-on direction of Daniel J. O'Brian and Harry F. McCullah (each of whom retired as Commander, MSC, USN), using the facilities of the still-existent Hospital Corps. The medical establishment apparently did not view the MSC as having much autonomy, and O'Brien and McCullah reported directly to a medical officer. Not without justification, ·the early MSC was viewed by the Medical Corps as purely a support group of administrators and supply officers, having the lower status of paraprofessionals and being under the ultimate supervision of physicians. They resisted the idea of a separate corps with autonomy equal to that of the Medical Corps, but legislation in 1954 created the position of Chief of Corps. In that year Lt. Comdr. William C. Caulkins was administratively promoted to the rank of Captain and Chief of MSC (Gannon, 1979), and the Corps began to assume its own identity. (In 1955 Fay O. Huntsinger became the first board-selected Captain.) Most of the officers of the Hospital Corps were absorbed into the Administrative Section of the MSC, and today the former is limited to the enlisted ranks.

In the meantime, in 1948 two former line officers, James W. Bagby and Robert S. Herrmann, came on active duty as the first clinical psychologists in the Regular Navy. Bagby assumed duties as Head of the Clinical Psychology Section under the late George N. Raines, Captain, MC, USN, Head of the Psychiatry Branch of BuMed. This arrangement gave clinical psychology a unique opportunity to develop because it was one of the very few specialties in the medical department with its own organization, ability to recruit and assign its own officers, and promote its own development. Captain Raines was a strong administrator and very influential throughout the naval establishment. His support and protection for clinical psychology proved to be extremely important to this young group. He was also well recognized in civilian psychiatry, being one of the chief architects of DSM-I (*Diagnostic and Statistical Manual of Mental Disorders*), published by the American Psychiatric Association in 1952, which was considered to be a major achievement in psychiatric nosology.

In 1948 additional clinical psychologists started to come on active duty, some in a Regular status, some in a career-Reservist role, and others only to serve a 2-year commitment. Those who entered as Ensigns were usually commissioned as Regulars, while the career Reservists usually chose that status in order to keep a higher rank previously earned as a line officer. At the end of their obligated tour, a number of these integrated into the Regular Navy, while others remained as Reservists until their retirement. Only one who had also served in World War II as a psychologist joined the Corps—H. Barry Molish, who returned to active duty in 1950 (now Commander, MSC, USNR, Retired). With the advent of the Korean War in 1950, recruitment was increased; within 3 or 4 years the number of uniformed clinical psychologists was approximately 25, with about half in the Regulars.

This was a junior group; in 1950 the highest-ranking clinical psychologist was a Lieutenant Commander, and the majority of the Regulars did not reach that rank until the late 1950s and early 1960s. However, this was the beginning of the profession of clinical psychology as an integral part of the U.S. Navy; as will be shown, it has continued to grow and develop.

The Administrative Section

The Administrative Branch provided a golden opportunity for enlisted personnel and Warrant Officers to achieve commissioned rank and enter a new career path. A few of them had college backgrounds, but many had completed high school only after joining the Navy. Usually with the rank of Ensign, they were assigned to the School of Hospital Administration at Bethesda, Maryland, which had been commissioned in August 1945. Upon graduation they were assigned to a wide variety of medical department billets, including the Marine Corps and hospital ships. Because most of them had accumulated several years of active duty prior to their commissioning but had not obtained college degrees, most of them did not rise beyond the rank of Lieutenant Commander, the traditional ceiling for "mustangs," the nickname given to former enlisted men who became officers.

The Medical Service Corps has undergone impressive growth since its inception in 1947. The two branches are now called the Health Care Administration Branch (formerly the Supply and Administration Branch) and the Health Care and Science Branch (formerly the Allied Sciences Section). On July 1, 1949, there were 663 officers in the MSC (up from 622 in 1947), of which only 86 were in the Allied Sciences Section (Gannon, 1979). In 1987 there were approximately 2,400 officers in the Corps, with about 1,200 in each of the two branches. Compared with two men in 1948, there are now about 115 billets for clinical psychologists in Navy uniform.

As the Administrative Branch gradually included larger numbers of younger and better educated men and women, they began to establish themselves as accomplished administrators and managers. Today all enter the MSC with college degrees, and about 40% possess a master's degree or higher. In addition there are thirteen subspecialties, including automated data processing and other computerized tools of management.

As in the civilian sector, modern Navy medicine is enlarging its scope. It no longer focuses almost entirely upon acute conditions, as in disease, trauma, and combat injuries, but now involves total health care, including prevention, crisis intervention, and health psychology, as well as new methods of cost management, areas for which the MSC has assumed major responsibility. The MSC is swiftly moving from a supportive role toward becoming an equal partner in the medical department.

Specialties in the Health Care and Sciences Branch and their numbers now include biochemistry—40; microbiology—53; radiation health specialists—73; physiology—13; aerospace psychology—35; research psychology—15; entomology—31; environmental health—87; industrial hygiene—71; medical technology—86; social work—16; audiology—11; physical therapy—53; occupational therapy—9; dietetics and nutrition—45; optometry—122; pharmacy—136; and podiatry—17 (Angelo, 1985).

The Issue of Licensing

In the 1950s, every Navy physician was required to possess a valid license from some state. Because of the extreme shortage of medical officers in the 1960s, this requirement was not enforced, and for the first time in history osteopathic physicians (DOs) were given commissions to practice military medicine.

Studies by Congress and the Pentagon found that in 1986, 20% of all military physicians did not hold a valid state license and that 67% of all practicing physicians and nurses were not qualified or could not show evidence that their competency levels were current (Murphy, 1986). As a result, beginning in 1988 all military personnel providing health care service were required to maintain a license in some state or in Washington, DC, or be supervised by a licensed person of the same discipline. This means that all active-duty clinical psychologists will require the PhD (about 85% now have it). After completion of their internship and awarding of the degree, those officers will serve at least one year under supervision, and they will have two attempts to pass a state examination. Those who do not pass will be transferred to the inactive reserve. This should have important ramifications for the way interns in training are treated. In the past most interns not possessing PhDs have had to struggle to complete their dissertations while meeting the clinical demands of the internship and subsequent active duty. Unfortunately, the Navy has paid small attention to this need and provided little or no free time or support for the student's research. Since the services of a psychologist are thus lost if the degree is not completed during or soon after the internship, it is hoped that the Navy will provide active dissertation support for each PhD candidate. In the author's opinion, this lack of support has long been shortsighted and counterproductive on the part of the Navy, and it will be interesting to see the response. Properly conducted, this support could also provide a working relationship in a scholarly enterprise that could only enhance the quality of Navy psychology.

MSC Administration

In the early years the Chief of the MSC was drawn from the ranks of the Administrative Section, but in 1962, Captain Robert S. Herrmann became the first psychologist to head the Corps, and in 1978 Captain Paul D. Nelson became the second. To date they are also the only members of the Allied Sciences Section to hold that position. As of this writing (1987), the single billet for flag rank[7] (Rear Admiral) was reserved for the Director (formerly Chief) of the Medical Service Corps, and conceivably that position will again be held by a psychologist some day. A second billet of flag rank was created in 1988.

In 1987 the "graying of the MSC" was essentially complete. A number of its officers have assumed command of major installations, including the Navy's flagship hospital at Bethesda, Maryland, and a number of second-generation MSC officers are on active duty, including Robert D. McCullah, Captain, MSC, USN, a clinical psychologist and son of the aforementioned Harry F. McCullah. Of the clinical psychologists now in uniform, approximately 2% are at the rank of Captain, 20% are Commanders, 30% are Lieutenant Commanders, and 60% are Lieutenants, the latter including eight interns in training. Today the rank of entry is that of Lieutenant. In addition, a significant number are not only in the ranks of the retired but have also completed and retired from a second career in civilian life. The list of clinical psychologists who have served on extended active duty in the Medical Service Corps since 1948 is both long and impressive, as shown in Appendix 2.

---

[7]"Flag rank" means any of the four grades of Admiral. The term is derived from the fact that Admirals are allowed to fly their own personal flags (pennant-style blue flags with one or more stars according to the Admiral's rank).

The Korean War

On June 25, 1950, North Korea invaded South Korea, and once again clinical psychology in the Navy was faced with great change. By mid-1951, the 32 active-duty billets for clinical psychologists had been filled. This did not begin to meet the need, and the civil service program was expanded to include another 35 positions. The uniformed corps of clinical psychologists was placed in billets serving operational activities in the field, such as training centers, recruit depots, marine combat divisions, and naval hospitals overseas; civilians also worked in all but the last two locations (NAVMED, 1957). These civilian positions were never all filled, and as the number of uniformed personnel began to increase in the early 1960s, they were not replaced as normal attrition lowered their numbers. In 1987 none of the original civilian psychologists remained, and only two or three civilian billets have been retained. However, during their tenure they provided considerable stability and professional support for the then-budding collection of psychologists in uniform.

An interesting sidelight of the mobilization for the Korean War was the withdrawal of the Red Cross from its social casework in military hospitals, and a civil service program was instituted for psychiatric social workers in naval hospitals. This enlarged the team concept and provided some additional stability and professionalism to the work environment of the uniformed psychologist. In 1987 approximately 16 social workers were in uniform, and there were plans to expand their role in providing a wide range of clinical and related social services to Navy and Marine Corps personnel and their families (Angelo, 1985). The future of this small group may very well parallel that of Navy clinical psychology.

The Problem of Involuntary Recall

The official history of the Navy Medical Department (NAVMED, 1957) erroneously states that all of the psychology billets in the 1950s were filled by volunteers, but therein lies an interesting story illustrating some of the organizational dynamics that can operate in the military.

The Navy maintains a considerable number of Active Reserve units at all times. Members of reserve units, who are usually from the same community, drill regularly, maintain their military skills, and receive pay for their activity. In time of war or other military crisis, they are obliged to go on duty if the Navy so orders it—in other words, they are subject to "involuntary recall" by the Navy.

Although military logic dictated that these trained reserve units be called up when the Korean War broke out, the Bureau of Naval Personnel concluded that it would be bad public relations to call up entire reserve units because of the possible negative effect on the community, and it was decided that involuntary recall would be done on an individual basis instead. As a result, the Navy recalled a large number of individuals from the Inactive Reserve, most of whom did not drill regularly, had not maintained their military skills, and who drew no pay.

The effect on many individuals was devastating, including young clinical psychologists with families, those in the midst of early career development, and those in graduate school. Many of those recalled had served in World War II a few years earlier and were now working on obtaining an education and establishing themselves in civilian life. A number of "horror stories" emerged as a result.

Those most affected by the Navy's decision to recall individuals were the ones who faced recall as enlisted men. For example, one reservist in his second year of graduate school, recently married and with a child due in a few months, was given recall orders as a Third Class Petty Officer, the rank he had held in World War II, with the very low base pay of $78.00 per month. Since sea duty was expected, he was faced with the prospect of leaving his family behind to exist on a poverty-level income.

The man therefore asked the BuMed recruiter if he could be commissioned (i.e., achieve officer's rank) as a psychologist in the Reserve, which would reflect his current level of skills, bring better pay, and enable him to remain near his family. The recruiter told him that no commissions for psychologists were available in the Reserve, and that if he wanted to be commissioned as a psychologist, the man would have to join the Regular Navy, which implied a career in the Navy.

(Joining the Regular Navy usually means a minimum commitment of time, which varies as the needs of the service change. For example, from 1951 to about 1955 (the Korean War era), a Regular officer was not allowed to resign. This restriction was lifted, however, when the war wound down. Graduates of Annapolis are required to serve for 4 years after graduation, after which many of them resign or move into the civilian Reserves. A full career in the Regular Navy is usually thought of as being from 20 to 30 years, with 20 years being the minimum tour needed to receive a pension. Today, because of tight budgets, officers who can be spared are being allowed to resign at almost any time.)

Given the choice between leaving his family in poverty or being able to support them by joining the Regulars for an indeterminate number of years, the man joined the Regulars. Much later, this man learned that the facts had been misrepresented: Commissions in the Reserve did exist, and there had never been any recall program for psychologists.

One graduate student in the midst of his dissertation applied for and received a commission as a psychologist in a local naval reserve research unit, having been verbally assured by the local commanding officer, a mathematics professor at the university, that he would not be subject to recall (he had served 38 months in the Marine Corps in the Pacific during World War II). However, the student received an "unofficial" recall letter from the same BuMed recruiter mentioned above, and when he objected he was told that he could volunteer and be sent to California, or he could be involuntarily recalled and immediately sent to Korea. He "volunteered" and dropped out of graduate school. In a matter of months he was sent to Korea anyway and never did finish the PhD.

Former Reserve Line officers fared no better. (Line officers are usually trained in the traditional shipboard or aviation skills, as opposed to personnel in staff positions, such as the Medical Service Corps, the Civil Engineers Corps, and so forth.) The law at that time required that for 5 years following the end of World War II, all officers of the Armed Forces were subject to recall in time of emergency. The Korean outbreak occurred only months before the 5 years elapsed. A number of former Line officers who were studying psychology in graduate school were given the choice between accepting recall as Line officers, usually at their former rank of Lieutenant or higher, or accepting a commission as a psychologist at a much lower rank, that of Ensign. Because of the economic problem of supporting a family at the lower rank (and pay), many of these officers returned as Line personnel and left the field of psychology. Many did not return to graduate school.

Several Reserve officers who had transferred from the Line to MSC as psychologists received the same recruiter's offer of "volunteer and be stationed stateside or be involuntarily recalled and sent overseas without family." Unaware of the chicanery involved, most of them "volunteered" for recall. This particular recruiter was eventually given a medical discharge.

The Navy Management Style

In spite of the shady circumstances surrounding the birth of their organization, these 25 or so psychologists in uniform formed the nucleus for further development. About 15 of them were in the Regular Navy, and most of them stayed until retirement, as did a number of the career Reservists. Some of the Reservists left as soon as their tour was finished but remained in the Active Reserves. (The author resigned his Regular commission in 1960 and retired from the Reserves in 1986). These people broke ground in a number of new areas, including being the first Navy clinical psychologists to be stationed overseas or in a combat zone. They also made significant contributions to administration and research, each of which is discussed in a later section.

This group also had the distinction that nearly all of them had had active duty experience during World War II, both enlisted and commissioned. This fact of prior service tended to color much of the subsequent development of clinical psychology. These men knew the Navy, and they soon adapted to the traditional management style of "selecting the best man for the job and letting him do it." The task was usually defined only in the broadest terms, and, while guidance and support were given by BuMed (including, of course, admonitions if one got very much out of line), the individuals were allowed to design their own work styles.

The concept of the Lone Ranger was no accident. Chief Psychologists, then as now, have routinely resisted suggestions from the field to write a manual of job instructions. The fact that so many of the recalled psychologists displayed World War II campaign ribbons and knew their way around a parade ground or shipboard made it easier for them to establish working relationships with the line personnel of both the Navy and the Marine Corps. As previously described, compared with the Army and Air Force, the command structure of the Navy is far more decentralized. To put this in proper perspective, one only has to reflect on the fact that naval battles are conducted on the scene by local commanders, and the tradition is that once a ship leaves port the captain is the absolute authority. Army campaigns, however, are more often preplanned and directed remotely by rear echelon personnel (sometimes as far to the rear as Washington, DC).

There is an official military abbreviation, UNODIR, which stands for "unless otherwise directed." It is used to signal one's superiors that one is about to take a particular course unless told otherwise. (Aboard ship it was usually understood that the radios were then turned off so that a countermanding order could not be received, thus allowing the captain to do as he wished.) It is said that this abbreviation is used frequently in the Navy but almost never in the Army. As Grace Hopper (Rear Admiral, USN, Retired), the former mathematics professor who almost single-handedly ushered the Navy into the computer age, once said: "In the Navy it's often better to say 'I'm sorry' than to ask permission." At her retirement ceremony in 1986, she elaborated on this theme by saying: "The only phrase I've ever disliked is 'Why, we've never done it that way.' I always tell young people, 'Go ahead and do it. You can always apologize later' " (Hopper, 1986).

A personal anecdote illustrates this situation. When the author reported as the lone psychologist to the Naval Medical Research Laboratory at the Marine Base at Camp Lejeune, North Carolina, in 1952, he asked the commanding officer (CO) what kind of work he would be doing. The CO replied, "I don't know— go do what a psychologist does!" So he did . . . and in the next 3 years the issue was never raised again by either party.

This situation is said to be in sharp contrast with that in the Army and the Air Force, each of which has produced elaborate job descriptions for its psychologists. For example, while trying to recruit and train clinical psychologists near the end of World War II, the Army not only issued regulations as to what psychological tests could be used but also set up formal procedures for their requisition and methods for making special requests to the Surgeon General for tests not on the list. It is not surprising that many orders were unfilled 10 to 15 months after ordering—many orders were not filled until the war was over (Seidenfeld, 1966, p. 600).

Written transfer orders given to Navy officers usually refer only to assignment to a given location, with such general phrases as "for further duty" and "report to the commanding officer for further assignment," and so forth. This resulted in the opinion that Navy psychologists are, as Hunt said, "rugged individualists," whereas Army and Air Force psychologists tend to conform to a mold.

Serving Overseas

The Korean War marked the first time Navy clinical psychologists served overseas. Most of these billets were at naval hospitals in Hawaii, Guam, and Japan, but psychologists also served in combat zones with the Marine Corps. In November 1950, Allen E. McMichael became the first Navy clinical psychologist to serve in a combat zone. He served with the First Marine Division, and together with Sam Mullins, a Navy psychiatrist with experience in wartime England, developed a front-line psychiatry program of triage[8] and treatment. This program was modeled after lessons learned by the British and French in World War I, forgotten during much of World War II, and very nearly forgotten again during the Korean conflict—namely that most psychiatric casualties can be returned to duty if they are treated early, at the front lines. (This issue of "treat 'em and return 'em" is discussed in detail in a later chapter.) In 1953, William G. Cumming, Jr., became the first psychologist stationed aboard a hospital ship, serving on the USS *Haven* and the USS *Repose* off Korea as part of a research team studying the effects of head injuries. As part of his duties, Cumming also gathered data at the Battalion Aid Station established by McMichael and Mullins.

While the "great recall" disrupted the lives of many psychologists, who are the subject of our story, it should be noted that the disruption was even greater among our colleagues in the line, especially the Naval Air Service and the Marine Corps. In all of the services, more than 54,000 Americans were killed in action in the Korean War, many of them recallees who thought they had made their final sacrifice 5 years before.

---

[8]The sorting of battle casualties and allocation of treatment according to a system of priorities designed to maximize the number of survivors. It involves determining how severe each person's condition is and what the chances for recovery are.

The Vietnam Era

T he number of clinical psychologists in naval uniform stayed at approximately 30 until the early 1960s. At that time an informal program was started to recruit people already in graduate school and support them until they received their PhD and entered active duty. In addition, those psychologists with commissions in the Regular Navy were offered the chance to return to school full-time or part-time in order to complete their doctorate. This resulted in a slow but steady buildup; by the late 1970s, about 100 clinical psychologists were on active duty, including those rotating through the universities.

Clinical Psychologists Serving in Vietnam

The Vietnam War was unlike any conflict in our history. It escalated in relatively small increments, and it did not receive complete logistical support by the military for several years. However, by 1965 there were thousands of troops committed, and we were essentially on a wartime footing. There was no well-defined period that could be labeled "mobilization," and the Navy did not engage in what could be termed as a massive buildup. Consequently, there was no increase in clinical psychologists in response to the war, per se. Instead, the gradual increase mentioned above continued. As described in a later section, an internship program was initiated at the U.S. Naval Hospital in Bethesda, and in 1964 the program was officially approved by the American Psychological Association. In 1987 there were approximately 115 billets for clinical psychologists in uniform, and there is every indication this number will increase.

The First and Third Marine Divisions were engaged in Vietnam beginning in 1965, and one clinical psychologist was assigned to each division, rotating stateside until the end of hostilities. This assignment of psychologists in-country (i.e., to combat zones ashore) generated a situation not unlike the relationship between the war and the American public at large. Upon reporting for their Marine Corps assignment, these psychologists lost all official contact with the Clinical Psychology Branch in BuMed. In the words of one observer, "It's as if the East Coast Navy didn't even want to be bothered about Vietnam.'' This writer has been unable to find any written record of the names or work of these psychologists while serving with the Marines, and in 1987 none of them remained on active duty; apparently none of them served beyond their original commitment.

With few exceptions, the younger and relatively inexperienced men were assigned to Vietnam—usually unmarried, newly commissioned Reserve officers. After 3 or 4 months' orientation at Bethesda, Maryland, and 8 weeks at Camp Pendleton, they were given individual orders to the Division Medical Battalion in Vietnam. The mental health team usually consisted of one psychiatrist, one psychologist, and three or four enlisted corpsmen.

Among career-minded Marines, there is a general conviction that one should have at least a minimum amount of combat experience on one's record if one aspires to senior rank. However, there exists no similar standard in the medical departments of either the Navy or the Army. Apparently, then, it was not by chance that the younger Reserve psychologists and psychiatrists were assigned in-country billets. This situation is also said to have existed in the Army (Colbach, 1985). A number of these Reservists expressed the feeling that the Regulars were avoiding Vietnam and remaining in billets more conducive to their own career ambitions. Such a feeling was often cited as one reason such men eventually rejected the idea of applying for a commission in the Regulars.

The Marines and the Medical Department

Nevertheless, the Vietnam War carried on the tradition so firmly established in Korea of clinical psychologists' serving with the Marine Corps. The number and variety of such assignments continues to grow. The rigors of combat area billets notwithstanding, these duty posts have become among the most satisfying for psychologists. Throughout their history, Marines have come to depend upon the Navy Medical Department to treat them in battle, often at the risk of their own lives. Many hospital corpsmen have crawled under enemy fire to render first aid to wounded marines, and surgeons have labored under battle conditions in the field to perform life-saving surgery. In addition to the close bonds created by this history, the two groups have the luxury of not being involved in each other's politics, such as competing for promotions or ''turf.'' This has produced a kind of mutual admiration society that usually spreads out to involve all members of the Navy Medical Department and they are, as often as not, tendered an extra bit of respect and cooperation when attached to a Marine unit.

Anecdotally, this has led to many stories of how protective the Marines feel toward their Navy ''medics.'' For example, when on liberty, in an environment of heightened levity or chemical imbalance (e.g., a bar) Marines may engage in altercations between themselves, but should anyone attack or offend ''Doc'' (i.e., their corpsman), it is at one's own risk. Although historically Navy clinical psychologists may not have contributed greatly to this relationship, they usually benefit from it.

The Training Program
at Bethesda

A s the Korean buildup progressed, in the early 1950s, an orientation program for incoming clinical psychologists was established at the U.S. Naval Hospital at Bethesda. Under the direction of the senior psychologist, Elizabeth Broomhead, the psychology staff of the Department of Psychiatry undertook to polish the clinical skills of those reporting for active duty before they moved on to a permanent assignment. At that time only a master's degree was required, and the trainees varied widely in their level of preparation, ranging from those having only an MA and no clinical experience to those close to completing the PhD and having a year or more of clinical experience.

Each trainee was "adopted" by a staff psychologist and subjected to an intensive, individualized program. Depending on the background of each officer, the length of the program varied from 2 to 6 months. Because of the extended work days, a few of the trainees completed the 1,500 hours of internship then required by the American Psychological Association, although this was not a stated goal of the program.

During the tenure of William G. Cumming, Jr., at BuMed, a decision was made to upgrade the program to a formal 1-year, predoctoral program in clinical psychology. In 1963 Dr. Isidor Scherer was recruited to head the curriculum, and in 1964 it was accredited by the American Psychological Association. During its inspection in 1985, the APA committee termed it a "model program."

When Dr. Scherer retired in 1968, he was succeeded by Dr. Bruce Becker, a former Navy psychologist who had remained in the Active Reserve. Upon his retirement from civil service in 1984, Becker was succeeded by Dr. Melvin A. Gravitz. A former consultant to the programs at Bethesda and Walter Reed Hospitals, Gravitz was also experienced in working with a variety of government and military organizations.

At present the Bethesda internship program is the Navy's primary source for recruiting clinical psychologists. It also offers orientation programs for those newly commissioned officers not in the internship program. The majority of uniformed clinicians on active duty today are Bethesda graduates. As of this writing (1988), approval has been given to initiate additional internship programs at the naval hospitals in Portsmouth, Virginia, and San Diego, California. It therefore appears that the training of clinical psychologists will increase and keep pace with the expanding role of the profession throughout the naval establishment.

Women in
Clinical Psychology
and the Armed Forces

Women have been prominently represented in the field of clinical psychology since its very beginning. The reader may recall that 2 of the first 16 persons identified by Wallin as doctoral-level clinical psychologists between 1896 and 1910 were women—Clara H. Towne, a PhD from the University of Pennsylvania, and Grace Fernald, who received her doctorate from the University of Chicago (Wallin, 1961). Until World War II, clinical psychology was most identified with the psychological testing of schoolchildren, and since women dominated that part of the educational establishment, it was not surprising that their numbers would also increase in the psychological area as well. In fact, during the 1930s clinical psychology, like social work, was thought by many to be a field composed mostly of women.

Because of the influx of male veterans on to college campuses after World War II, the entire field of psychology soon became dominated by males. At annual meetings of the American Psychological Association, the near-absence of women members was very evident; it also resulted in very one-sided social events. However, this ratio has gradually changed: today (1990) the APA membership is 38% female, and both national and regional meetings are no longer primarily "stag."

Women in the Armed Forces

The introduction of women into the Armed Forces did not come easily. As summarized by one naval historian (Spector, 1985):

> During the First World War, the Navy had enlisted women to serve as clerks (yeomen) in the Navy and Marines, but this experiment was hastily discontinued at the conclusion of the war. At the beginning of 1941 the only military organizations in the United States which accepted women were the Army and Navy Nurse Corps. The nurses wore uniforms and were under military control, but they lacked military rank, equal pay,

retirement privileges, and veterans' rights. In short, they were considered simply as a kind of auxiliary.

With the outbreak of World War II and the passage of the Selective Service Act in the United States, there were demands from women's groups and other citizens that women be permitted to serve in the armed forces. Both Eleanor Roosevelt and Congresswoman Edith Nourse Rogers called for the establishment of some type of military organization for women. During the summer of 1941 the War Department began planning for a women's force "so that when it is forced upon us, as it undoubtedly will, we shall be able to run it our way."

The War Department's "way" was to establish a "Women's Army Auxiliary Corps." The key word was "Auxiliary," for the women's corps was to be in the army but not of it. "Auxiliary" status meant that the women GIs would have pay and benefits inferior to those of their male counterparts. It was not until late in 1943 that the "WAACs" became "WACs" with full army status, equivalent ranks, and equal pay.

Legislation to create an army and navy women's force finally passed Congress in the spring of 1942, despite the misgiving of congressmen who wondered who would be left to "do the cooking, the washing, the mending, the humble homey tasks to which every woman has devoted herself"? Mrs. Oveta Culp Hobby, a prominent businesswoman and civic leader from Texas, was appointed director of the new corps. The first 440 officer candidates were chosen from more than 30,000 applicants with something of the same care which was later devoted to the selection of the first astronauts. They reported to Fort Des Moines, Iowa, an abandoned cavalry post, in July 1942.

During the next year the corps expanded rapidly. By November 1942 the first WAACs were en route overseas in answer to an urgent call from President Eisenhower for skilled typists and telephone operators to serve in North Africa. By this time, the Women's Army Auxiliary Corps had expanded to three training centers, nine service companies, and twenty-seven Aircraft Warning Units. The War Department was beginning to talk about recruiting a million WAACs.

The Navy's turn came a few weeks later with the creation of the WAVES (Women Accepted for Volunteer Emergency Service) under Wellesley College's former president, Mildred McAfee. Over 80,000 women eventually served in the Navy, Marines, and Coast Guard, but federal law prohibited them . . . [to serve] outside the continental United States or aboard combatant ships or aircraft. In late 1944 that restriction was eased somewhat to allow WAVES to serve in Alaska, Hawaii, and the Caribbean. All the same, Admiral Nimitz refused to allow women at his headquarters; it was not until CINCPAC [Commander-in-Chief, Pacific] headquarters moved to Guam at the beginning of 1945 that WAVES were finally assigned to Pearl Harbor.

The unprecedented spectacle of large numbers of women in uniform, many of them serving in or near the combat zones, gave rise to amazement and disapproval among the more conservative male soldiers and civilians. An Arkansas radio evangelist told his listeners that WAAC recruits were paraded naked before their male officers. At Daytona Beach, Florida, where there was a WAAC training center, local citizens reported that these women "were touring in groups, seizing and raping sailors and coast guards-men." Large numbers of WAACs were reported as being returned home from overseas pregnant; it was widely believed that "WAACs were really taken into service to take care of the sex problems of soldiers."

War Department authorities pointed out in vain that illicit pregnancy among WAACs was almost unknown, and that their venereal disease rate was lower than in any known civilian community. The colorful stories continued to circulate throughout the war years. One war correspondent drily noted that if even some of the devoutly believed stories of WAAC promiscuity were true, each of the 200-odd women serving in North Africa in 1943 must have been shipped home pregnant several times. (pp. 393-394)

Women Psychologists in the Navy

During World War II a number of women psychologists served in a variety of administrative positions, working as officers in the WAVES, SPARS (Coast Guard), the Marine Corps, and the various Navy bureaus in personnel and training (Bremner, 1943). About fifty women served in the Volunteer Specialists Branch as clinical psychologists (Louttit, 1944). While they sometimes bore the brunt of crude remarks and off-color jokes usually aimed at their colleagues in the other corps, women psychologists were generally accepted, especially in the hospital setting.

During the Korean buildup one woman clinical psychologist came on active duty—Aimee W. Marrs (now Commander, MSC, USNR, Retired). However, for many years women were not otherwise represented among the uniformed group until 1973, when Patricia Crigler (currently Captain, MSC, USN) and Karen S. O'Hern reported for duty. In 1988 there were about 15 women clinical psychologists on active duty, a percentage considerably higher than that in the Armed Forces at large.

As of 1984 about 50% of all clinically related PhDs awarded in the United States went to women (Howard et al., 1986). While traditionally women do not gravitate toward the military as a career, it is apparent that they represent an excellent pool of potential recruits for Navy psychology. However, the "separate but equal" situation faded slowly. For example, in 1952 a separate section for women's medical specialties was established in the MSC for clinical dietitians, occupational therapists, and physical therapists. It was not until 1965 that these groups were "de-sexed" (Angelo, 1985).

One civilian woman made a significant contribution to Navy clinical psy-chology. The late Elizabeth Broomhead (introduced in Chapter 9), served as a WAVE officer during World War II and afterward joined the psychiatry de-partment at the U.S. Naval Hospital, Bethesda, in 1947 as the senior clinical psychologist. Until her retirement in 1971, "Liz" supervised the orientation of most clinical psychologists who came on active duty, including Robert Herrmann in 1948 and the author in 1952. She took a motherly as well as a professional interest in her then-young charges and became a friend and confidante of several generations of Navy psychologists and psychiatrists.

Recently a woman Navy clinical psychologist broke new ground. In January 1988, Lt. Erin Carlson, MSC, USN, was stationed on the remote island of Adak, Alaska, far out in the Aleutian chain. She was the first mental health professional of either gender to occupy that position. The Navy established an air station on Adak during World War II after the Japanese had invaded the Aleutians. It is a desolate location, described by Carlson as follows (1989):

> Adak is located approximately 1200 miles southwest of Anchorage, Alaska . . . and approximately 900 miles east of Petropavlovsk, USSR. . . . We are adjacent to the Aleutian Fault line, so there are frequent earthquakes, fortunately no severe ones so far. . . . There are two volcanoes, one to the west and one to the east of Adak. On clear days they are spectacularly beautiful! Adak is known as the ''Birthplace of the Winds.'' The average daily wind speed is 14–20 mph . . . gusts frequently exceed 50–60 mph and have been clocked at over 80–100 mph. The warm Pacific and cold Arctic air combine . . . to form active, variable weather patterns. The climate is characterized by precipitation, often in the form of horizontal rain, sleet, and snow due to the high winds. Winter is a sporadic series of snow and sleet storms . . . summer is rainy, foggy, and averages 42–48 degrees. The weather and harsh environment is a challenge all its own. There is one Main Road, there are no traffic lights. . . . Adak has one retail store—the Navy Exchange, and one grocery store—the Commissary. The ''garbage flight'' comes in on Tuesday with fresh vegetables, fruit, and milk. Other goods are flown in on Thursday or sent up from the lower 48 [states] on the barge, which usually takes 2–3 months. (pp. 42–47)

The base hospital included a 15-bed in-patient ward staffed by five nonpsychiatric physicians, but Lt. Carlson and one social worker were responsible for mental health services for all of the military and civilian personnel and their families. Excellent working relationships were established with the medical staff and the base chaplains. Prior to Lt. Carlson's arrival, several suicides and suicide attempts had occurred among the population, so one of her priorities was to identify those individuals, families, or both who were poorly suited for living in this unique and, for them, stressful environment. She also instituted efforts to have commands sending personnel to Adak to determine their suitability for the assignment beforehand.

The mental health workload ran the gamut. In addition to diagnosing patients and determining if they should be evacuated to CONUS (Continental United States), Lt. Carlson applied various treatment modalities, such as individual and group psychotherapy, stress management groups, hypnotherapy, and marital and family counseling. Alcohol abuse was a significant problem, and there were a number of cases involving spouse or child abuse, incest and molestation, and other signs of family dysfunction. In addition, after a few months into their tours, some people with no psychiatric history would show symptoms of anxiety or depression. Apparently the bleak, stressful environment, the isolation, and the strain of "living in a fishbowl" eventually took its toll.

Due in large part to Lt. Carlson's efforts, not only were mental health services provided to a very needful population, but also there was a significant decrease in the number of individuals and families who required an early return to CONUS. Obviously, this represented a significant contribution to the Navy in the form of cost savings and enhancement of the military mission. It was a demanding assignment that required of the psychologist a great deal of emotional fortitude and physical stamina. This author has learned from her superiors that Carlson performed her duties with skill and enthusiasm and has passed on to her successor a firm foundation upon which to build. As of this writing, February 1990, now-Lt. Commander Carlson is enjoying a postdoctoral year at the University of California, San Diego.

Sexism in the Navy

The role of women clinical psychologists in the Navy seems assured, with few episodes of sexism, but this is not true of the Navy at large. Although a 1948 law prohibits the use of women in combat billets, in 1987 the Navy enlarged the number of shipboard and other operational positions they may hold. In addition to their previous assignments to salvage ships, cargo ships, tugboats, repair ships, tenders, hospital ships, and some training aircraft, they may now serve on ammunition and supply ships that travel to and from combat zones, and they will also be included in the crews of some P-3 Orion reconnaissance planes. The Department of Defense has also announced that it will include women in the security guards assigned to overseas embassies and consulates, a move currently being resisted by the Commandant of the Marine Corps (Ford, 1988).

However, the issue of sexual harassment against women sailors is still a sensitive issue. In a recent Navy study, more than half of the 1,400 Navy women interviewed indicated they had been the victims of such harassment, including barriers to promotion or to assignment to the more desirable billets. As a result of this study, combined with pressure from Congress and publication of several embarrassing episodes in the media, the Secretary of the Navy has launched a campaign to sensitize male Navy personnel to the problem (Healy, 1987).

The role of women in America is an extremely important and volatile issue in our society generally, and it is no less so in the U.S. Navy. A number of Navy clinical psychologists have dealt with this issue either in individual counseling or in consulting with various commands. While it may be a personal choice, it is apparent that this area represents another important subspecialty in which Navy psychologists have an opportunity to offer their clinical and interpersonal skills.

CHAPTER 11

The Chief
Clinical Psychologists,
1944–1988

T he growth of clinical psychology in the Navy has been, of course, under the immediate direction of whoever held the billet of chief psychologist. This position was first occupied by William A. Hunt in 1944 when he transferred from the Naval Training Center at Newport, Rhode Island. At that time the title was that of Head, Clinical Psychology Section, Neuropsychiatry Branch, Bureau of Medicine and Surgery. In addition to detailing (assigning) personnel, Hunt also oversaw the dismantling of the organization at the end of World War II. As described earlier, he also used this position in order to play a key role in the postwar organization of clinical psychology in the civilian sector.

James W. Bagby and Robert S. Herrmann took charge of the section just prior to and during the Korean War, Bagby from 1948 to 1952 and Herrmann from 1952 to 1956. In the years 1956-1959, John E. Rasmussen filled the role of Head and was instrumental in creating the Naval Medical Neuropsychiatric Research Unit in San Diego. Herrmann returned from educational leave in 1959 and again assumed the post until 1962, when he was appointed Chief of the Medical Service Corps.

Following a 1-year tenure by John M. Laudenslager, the office was held for the next 11 years by William G. Cumming, Jr. It was during this period (1963-1974) that the gradual buildup began in the number of clinical psychologists in uniform, and an increasing number of active-duty psychologists were detailed back to school in order to complete the doctorate. Cumming also engineered the expansion and APA approval of the internship at Bethesda Naval Hospital. Loren D. Acord succeeded Cumming in 1974 for a 2-year term, during which time he initiated the Navy's Child (and Family) Advocacy Program.

In 1976, Robert D. McCullah followed Acord, at which time a number of organizational changes took place. The title of Head, Clinical Psychology Section was changed to Specialty Advisor in Clinical Psychology to the Surgeon General, and the position became a collateral instead of a primary duty. This dissipated the administrative strength clinical psychology had enjoyed under the old system.

Even though he was then assigned other duties that were equally or more time-consuming, McCullah continued to supervise and promote continued growth in the number of clinical psychologists and their participation in new programs, such as the Alcoholism Rehabilitation Program, the Health and Physical Readiness Program, postdoctoral fellowship training, and operational billets in the SEAL (Sea-Air-Land) program and with the Naval Investigative Service.

John F. House took over in 1982. In 1983 his title was changed to Specialty Advisor in Clinical Psychology to the Naval Medical Command, Washington, DC. (This command replaced the former Bureau of Medicine and Surgery, and the office of Surgeon General was moved to the office of the Chief of Naval Operations. The Naval Medical Command (NavMedCom) was thus reduced to a second echelon command. However, as of October 1989, the old system of BuMed as the primary medical authority in the Navy has been revived and all the former titles reinstated.) In addition to overseeing clinical psychologists in uniform as a collateral duty, House was also Head of the Psychology Division at Bethesda Naval Hospital and supervised the recruitment and training of psychology interns.

Frank A. Mullins, Jr., assumed House's duties in 1985. Prior to his departure in 1988, he administered the creation of a Department of Psychology at Bethesda Naval Hospital separate from the Department of Psychiatry and having status equal to that of other hospital departments.

In 1988 the role of Specialty Advisor in Clinical Psychology to NavMedCom and Head of the Department of Psychology at Bethesda Naval Hospital was assumed by James A. Scaramozzino.

Collectively and individually, this group has left its mark on the development of clinical psychology in the Navy. They developed a close and productive working relationship with the Medical Corps and the Medical Service Corps, broadened the range of the clinical and research activities of psychologists, expanded their relationship with psychiatry and the other medical specialties, generated an important role for psychologists with the operational forces (i.e., the "real" Navy), upgraded the training and professional qualifications required of their colleagues, and clearly etched a place for Navy clinical psychology in the mainstream of the profession.

As has the Navy at large, these leaders suffered the rise and fall of uneven budgets and unpredictable resources while plotting a course that has been ever forward and upward. Well done!

The Civilian Consultants

Most branches of the U.S. government employ civilian consultants for a wide variety of tasks, some of them long-term and others on an ad hoc basis. Such consultants have included a number of clinical psychologists and several experimental psychologists with expertise in clinical research. Since 1946 they have been a constant source of input into the Navy's psychiatric and psychology programs, and their influence has contributed significantly toward keeping the Navy's programs from becoming insular and out of touch with the mainstream of psychology. In addition, they have frequently acted as liaisons between the Navy Medical Department, major universities, and a variety of government agencies. Most of them have been permitted direct access to the Surgeon General and have not been required to travel a chain of command whenever they expressed their opinions, which they frequently did. This arrangement allowed for a viable and productive relationship that did much to foster the growth of clinical psychology in the Navy.

Although it was not an official part of their function, these consultants frequently provided uniformed psychologists with personal contacts in the field at large. In many cases younger psychologists who left active duty, the author included, benefited greatly from this personal association with such senior and knowledgeable people with whom they shared a common interest in the Navy as well as in clinical psychology.

Shortly after World War II, William A. Hunt, the first active-duty person to hold the title of Chief Clinical Psychologist, was appointed as a Consultant in Clinical Psychology to the Surgeon General, a position he held until 1964.

Walter L. Wilkins, the first clinical psychologist assigned to a Marine Corps base (during World War II), also served in this capacity (as Consultant) until 1960, when he became the first Scientific Director of the (then) Naval Medical Neuropsychiatric Research Unit at San Diego.

Because of incomplete records and the less-than-perfect recall of informants, the following list of other distinguished psychologists who served as Consultants may not be complete; apologies are extended to anyone not included. Also, the organizational affiliation indicated may no longer be current.

John T. Lanzetta, Dartmouth University

Kenneth MacCorquodale, University of Minnesota

Ivan N. Mensh, University of California at Los Angeles

John H. Rohr, Tulane University; later, Georgetown University

Eli A. Rubenstein, National Institute of Mental Health

Saul B. Sells, Texas Christian University

Denzel D. Smith, Office of Naval Research

Richard Trumbull, Office of Naval Research

One clinical psychologist has contributed uniquely as a consultant to the Navy Surgeon General—Joseph D. Matarazzo, of the Oregon Health Sciences University. He not only serves as an appointed Consultant in Clinical Psychology but also acts as the Medical School Liaison Officer at his school. In this capacity he recruits and advises students who wish to enter the Navy Medical Department, including those medical students being supported by navy scholarships. In 1973 he was appointed by then-president Richard M. Nixon as one of the charter members of the Board of Regents for the Uniformed Services University of the Health Sciences (USUHS). He was appointed by David Packard, the chairman of the board, to head two committees—the site selection committee (the facility is located at Bethesda, Maryland) and the faculty selection committee, the latter including the responsibility for writing the administrative rules under which the faculty would work.

At the University of Oregon, Matarazzo founded the first separate Department of Medical Psychology in a medical school in the United States. From this forum he has continually been active in the development of clinical psychology throughout the country, assuming a leadership role in a variety of major developments in the profession. However, perhaps his most noteworthy contribution to Navy psychology (and the other services as well) was his influence on the curriculum of USUHS. In addition to the creation of a separate and independent Department of Medical Psychology, the first-year curriculum mandated medical psychology as one of the four major subject areas.

Recruit Screening and Evaluation

Early Standards for Recruits

A military organization is no better than the quality of its personnel. No amount of guns, ships, and other instruments of warfare can compensate for a lack of motivation, morale, and training (MMT). In addition, the levels of MMT that can be generated are limited by the quality of recruits. This places an extraordinary burden upon the process of recruit screening. It has also provided a unique opportunity for the special skills of the clinical psychologist to make an extremely important contribution. In fact, the reader will recall that the task of screening recruits was the original reason envisioned for the enlistment of the first clinical psychologists in the Navy in 1940–41. Historically, as well as operationally, this task today is still one of the most important functions of that group.

Except in times of national peril or high unemployment, there has long been a reluctance to volunteer for enlisted service in the navies of the world. In addition to the inherent dangers of sea travel, living conditions aboard naval vessels were notoriously bad. Quarters were cramped, the food was poor, the pay was low, the separation from family and friends during long sea voyages was unpleasant, health care was minimal, and disease was a constant threat.

Screening Criteria Before World War I

From 1900 through the start of World War I, the U.S. Navy had considerable difficulty in fulfilling its enlisted quotas with qualified men. Quite literally, every volunteer who could pass what today would be a very superficial physical examination was accepted—no questions asked. In one large city only about one third could pass, and this was considered a tribute to the fine physical condition of the young men of Baltimore (Lowndes, 1912). Aside from underweight and insufficient height, the main causes for rejection were defective vision, disease of the heart (detected by history or stethoscope), defective teeth, flat feet, and varicocele (a varicose condition of the scrotum). Today neither of the last two conditions is considered to have any clinical significance for active duty.

Except for the existence of a few guidelines, individual medical officers were left to their own judgment to decide the fitness of an individual recruit. Not only did the competence of the medical officers vary, but also the length of their naval experience ranged from none to very senior. One senior medical officer advised his junior colleagues that "a man who is physically sound for life insurance is not always physically the man for the Naval Service" (Lowndes, 1912). In addition, the medical screening of applicants for the Marine Corps was frequently conducted on contract by civilian physicians, usually with no psychiatric training or firsthand knowledge of the requirements of military life.

In these early years there were no standards for intelligence or mental health. It was generally agreed that men of low intellect were not acceptable, but those rejected on this basis usually met the medical officer's personal definition of being "feebleminded," "dummies," or "imbeciles" (Butts, 1911a). In addition, it was generally agreed that the "psychopath" and the "insane" were not admissible. There were informal lists of undesirable traits and characteristics, such as "chronic alcoholics, morphine and cocaine habitues, vagrants and professional 'hoboes,' masturbators, sodomists, sexual perverts, cantankerous individuals, 'shut-in' characters, 'daydreamers,' liars, thieves, would-be suicides, former inmates of reform schools, penitentiaries, workhouses, and insane asylums, gamblers and stock market 'plungers'. . . ." (Butts, 1911b, pp. 295–296).

Theories of the Cause of Mental Illness

At the turn of the century, psychiatry as practiced in the Navy was no different from that in civilian life, and many naive and unsophisticated theories about mental illness existed in both groups. However, the documentation of these ideas is an interesting part of naval history—especially involving the "insane." As noted in an earlier chapter, these patients were all housed at the Government Hospital for the Insane in Washington, DC (USGHI), and an interesting survey of patients admitted between 1899 and 1910 provides a glimpse of some of the attitudes of the day. These insane patients were described as follows (Butts, 1910):

> The mental patrimony of many of the insane men of the Navy was squandered by their dissipated ancestors long before they entered the service; others began life well, but their mental capital was limited, and in the struggle for an existence it was nearly all expended prior to their entry into the service, so that they really enlisted as psychopaths. These psychopaths have, for the most part, been the shiftless, irresponsible men of the service. Prior to their enlistment an unduly large proportion of them have been professional tramps or hoboes, and after their entry into the service they became malingerers and general courts-martial prisoners. (p. 459)

This description illustrates the emphasis given in those days to heredity and "constitutional inferiority" as major factors in the etiology of insanity. Two other theories are also of historical interest—the supposed etiological role of masturbation and the use of physical stigmata as a diagnostic sign. In the aforementioned survey, "masturbation and sexual excess" was listed about 3% of the time as a factor in producing insanity. However, the survey author hastened to qualify this finding by writing that " 'masturbation' and 'sexual excess' are no longer considered causes of insanity, but *symptoms* of insanity." The most frequent etiological factor mentioned was alcoholism, followed by bad heredity, syphilis, sunstroke and heatstroke, malaria, head injury, and constitutional inferiority (Butts, 1910). The study also reflects certain ethnic prejudices common in that era, for example, "Greater caution should be exercised in enlisting men of Irish birth" (Butts, 1910).

The cases of heatstroke or sunstroke were described as having taken place prior to enlistment rather than as a function of the extremely hot temperatures experienced in the coal-run boiler rooms aboard ship. However, Butts (1910) goes on to note:

> There can be no doubt, however, that the heat of the engine and fire rooms has in a good many cases acted as the determining factor in producing insanity in psychopathic individuals. . . . The heat of the engine room may, I feel sure, be said to be a measure of cerebral resistance, the unstable, predisposed individual being affected much more quickly than a normal individual. (p. 467)

It was implied that nearly all of these insane persons bore the "anatomical stigmata of degeneracy," the most common of which were asymmetrical faces and craniums, misplaced or poorly formed ears, prognathism (projecting jaw) and opisthognathism (receding jaw). Photographs of these patients were offered as self-evidence of the relationship between insanity and these stigmata, and since the relation was so "obvious," the photographs were said "to illustrate the failure of the present system of enlistment to detect mental inferiority and that [the recruits'] undesirability for the service should have been apparent to any recruiting officer" (Butts, 1910).

Incidence of Mental Illness

There is ample evidence that the recruit screening process was indeed faulty. For example, as mentioned previously, the admission rate of enlisted men to USGHI in 1913 was nearly five times that of the civilian population. At a large naval training station, there were 2.3 times as many recruits showing evidence of nervous or mental abnormalities than were found in a survey of the civilian population, and in spite of some cursory screening at the recruiting station, feeble-mindedness was four times as common in the Navy as in the general population (Stearns, 1924). In the aforementioned survey of insane patients at USGHI, examination of their histories showed that in 53% of the patients, their psychotic symptoms became manifest within 6 months after enlistment and 74% within one year (Butts, 1910), suggesting that most were probably psychotic at the time of their entering the Navy.

Such data prompted the repeated suggestion that all enlistees be given at least a 6-month probationary period during which they could be discharged at no cost to the Navy if they manifest undesirable behaviors. In the years since, this suggestion has been made repeatedly by each of the Armed Forces but rejected on legal grounds, especially when applied to draftees.

The lack of adequate screening could also be seen in the naval prison system. In one study completed during the high enlistment rate during World War I, it was found that among those court-martialed and incarcerated, about half were found to show clear evidence of being nervously or mentally not fit for the service and two thirds of them were imprisoned during the first year of their enlistment, again giving rise to the conclusion that most or all of them had been unfit prior to enlistment (Jacoby, 1919a).

The Concept of Taking a History

Beginning in about 1910, the Navy medical literature began to include repeated pleas for the inclusion of a complete psychological and social history as a routine part of the recruiting process. This history would be taken preferably at the recruiting station, but both the medical and nonmedical personnel manning these stations unanimously agreed that they had neither the time nor the expertise to do so—apparently not realizing that most intelligent lay persons could be trained to conduct such interviews. At the very least, it was suggested that these histories be obtained during recruit training.

Today it must seem absurd to a trained clinician that such a history was not routinely obtained. However, it must be remembered that in those years psychiatric training was uncommon among most physicians and the field of psychiatry was not held in very high esteem by either other medical officers or line officers. Furthermore, the use of a careful psychosocial history was not routinely taught to alienists-in-training. In fact, psychiatry was not considered an integral part of the medical profession outside of the mental hospital. (The American Board of Psychiatry and Neurology did not hold examinations and award its first diploma until 1934.) During this period the work of Adolph Meyer, the "dean of American psychiatry," was only beginning to have its influence, and one of his most noteworthy contributions was the establishment of the comprehensive clinical history as the basic tool of modern psychiatry.

It is well known that William Alanson White, Superintendent of the USGHI, was in complete agreement with the teachings of Meyer, and because the Navy trained its medical officers at White's hospital, it may be assumed that it was this association that led to the plea for adequate history-taking repeatedly published in the *Naval Medical Bulletin*.

In addition to lack of training in any form of psychological screening, medical officers were allowed nearly complete freedom to process recruits according to their own methods. This resulted in great variety in the results between recruiting stations. It was suggested that recruiting medical officers be rated not by the total number of men examined, but by the number of men who produced useful tours of duty (Jacoby, 1919b). It is interesting to note that in 1931 (and repeated in 1939) there was an Army regulation stating that (Glass, 1966):

> If a man after having been enlisted at a military post or accepted at a recruiting station and forwarded to the designated place for enlistment be discharged or rejected, and it appears that the enlistment or acceptance was carelessly made or in violation of these regulations (and should have been discovered by the recruiting officer), the expenses incurred in consequence of the enlistment or acceptance of the man may be stopped against the pay of the officer responsible. (p. 11)

This author knows of no similar regulation in the Navy. In 1917 the situation was still uncorrected, leading the Surgeon General to deplore publicly the lack of history-taking or its being taken in such a perfunctory manner as to be useless (Stearns, 1918).

The Introduction of Binet-Type Testing

Beginning in about 1910, the work of Binet and Simon and their intelligence scale was generating interest in the possibility of applying it to the screening of naval recruits. It was generally recognized that the full Binet-Simon scale was too long and time-consuming, as well as requiring privacy and a skilled administrator in order to be practical for use at the recruiting station or the training center. However, the wide range of test items that constituted the Binet-Simon scale attracted a great deal of interest and, as in the civilian sector, prompted naval officers to experiment with shortened versions or different combinations of similar test items. (As described in an earlier chapter, this small group of medical officers was justifiably described as the first practitioners of clinical psychology in the Navy.)

Adaptations of Binet-Type Testing

Part of the problem was that the Binet-Simon scale was not standardized on adults, and the use of the mental-age concept was proving rather awkward to apply to populations other than schoolchildren. A rather sophisticated improvement for its day was the use of a point-scale instead of one marked off in increments of mental age. This system was first employed at the Psychopathic Hospital in Boston (Yerkes & Bridges, 1921).

In order to be useful for the Navy, it was decided that a mental test had to meet the following criteria (Thomas, 1915):

1. It should be fair in its requirements, and a definite minimum passing mark established.
2. It should be sufficiently varied to make evident one's intelligence, education, and training.
3. It should be so devised that but slight, if any, variations are possible in the results of the different examiners.
4. It should not consume much time.
5. It should be able to be administered by nonprofessionals. (p. 202)

The Butts Method

Perhaps the first attempt to systematize (as opposed to standardize) the psychiatric and mental screening of naval recruits was offered in 1911 by an alienist (Butts) at USGHI who, as previously discussed, adapted the work done by Franz, which had created the first model for regularly screening patients entering a mental hospital (Butts, 1911a). However, this consisted primarily of a long list of questions concerning the recruit's life history interspersed with a number of Binet-type items, such as memory for digits, interpretation of short stories, explaining the similarity between two different objects or concepts, and the interpretation of proverbs. This method took about an hour (much too long for recruiters), produced no objective score, and because the final conclusion was based on the clinical impression of the interviewer, would obviously vary greatly among examiners. However, it was one of the first attempts to systematically apply history-taking and mental examination to recruit screening.

The Schier Scale

Another of these early attempts was made by then-Acting Assistant Surgeon A. R. Schier, who adapted 10 separate tests and, based on initial trials, assigned each a point value according to its relative level of difficulty (Schier, 1915), thus producing a scale of 0–100. The tests used and their score values are shown in Table 1.

Schier then followed up 100 cases into recruit training (Marine Corps) and received ratings of their intelligence, aptitude for the service, and behavior, based upon their performance in training (method not specified). Based on these data, he devised a system of grouping and compared recruits' test scores with their performance records (Table 2). An examination of the overall service record of each man during recruit training also provided an interesting form of validation (Table 3).

In addition, the scale did not appear to correlate with level of education or ratings on General Behavior. Of interest is the fact that the recruits were placed into four categories, apparently reflecting the ubiquitous and traditional Navy scale of 1.0 to 4.0.[9] The average time of administration was 14.4 minutes.

The McMullin Scale

Although lacking the extended validation exhibited by the Schier method, a briefer scale was designed by Passed Assistant Surgeon J. J. A. McMullin (1915) as follows:

---

[9] A 4-point system is widely used in the Navy for evaluation, for example, the individual's performance record, the condition of equipment, and so on. The term "4.0" is Navy slang for anything considered to be of high quality.

Table 1

Marine Corps Recruit Screening Tests, Binet-Type, 1915

Test number	Description of test	Total possible points
1	Repetition of numerals (three sets of digits; each correct repetition, 2)	6
2	Drawing design from memory (one design drawn correctly, 3; both correct, 5)	5
3	Sentence building (if two or more sentences formed with three words, 2; if three words included in one sentence, 3)	3
4	Computation, orally (nine problems; each correct answer, 2)	18
5	Form-board puzzle (if blocks filled in correctly in 55 seconds)	10
6	Definition of abstract words (five words; each correct answer, 2; dictionary definition not required, object being only to determine if abstract meanings are comprehended)	10
7	Recognition of absurdity (four sentences; each correct recognition, 3)	12
8	Problem of diverse facts (two problems; each intelligent answer, 5)	10
9	Reading and report (cowboy story; if read and reported correctly, 3; changes, instead of word "purchase" use "bought"; instead of word "donned" use "put on")	3
10	Clock test (first answered correctly, 10; second answered correctly, 13)	23
		___
		100

Note. From "Review and Possibilities of Mental Tests in the Examination of Applicants for Enlistment" by A. R. Schier, 1915, *Naval Medical Bulletin, 11*, p. 223.

Table 2

Comparison of Recruits' Test Scores with Performance Record, Marine Corps, 1915

Groups	Points scored	Subsequent reports
A	75–100	Well above to average
B	60–75	Above to average
C	50–60	Average to doubtful
D	Below 50	Mentally deficient

Note. From "Review and Possibilities of Mental Tests in the Examination of Applicants for Enlistment" by A. R. Schier, 1915, *Naval Medical Bulletin, 11*, p. 223.

Table 3

Service Records of Follow-Up Group of Marine Corps Recruits, 1915

Disposition	Group			
	A	B	C	D
Deserters	9%	20%	42%	—
Promoted to squad leaders	20%	3%	—	—
Total loss, all causes	11%	33%	63%	50%

Note. Adapted from "Review and Possibilities of Mental Tests in the Examination of Applicants for Enlistment" by A. R. Schier, 1915, *Naval Medical Bulletin, 11*, p. 224.

The McMullin Scale (continued from p. 84):

1. Applicant repeats three sets of numbers, each set composed of seven digits.
2. Composes sentence containing three such words as buffalo, money, river.
3. Gives differences between the president of a republic and a king, or defines two abstract words.
4. Gives the opposite word to good, outside, tall, big, loud, white, light, happy, false.
5. Interprets code "mcoe licqkuy" (come quickly).
6. Draws two simple designs from memory after inspecting for 10 seconds.
   An average of 70 percent is required to qualify. Perhaps a minimum average of 75 percent would be a better standard. By way of control, this test was applied to 10 enlisted men on duty in Buffalo, all of whom passed with high averages.
   Two hundred applicants recently took this examination and 34 failed. In this series only two applicants were rejected because of their mental condition alone; the others who failed had some disqualifying physical defect, and the mental condition was named as a contributing cause for rejection. (p. 74)

CHAPTER 15

Recruit Screening in World War I

During the first few months following the entry of the United States into World War I, psychiatric boards were established by the Army in order to screen out the mentally unfit. However, their recommendations were not always followed by the commanding officers, and at one point a group of 8,640 cases was retained in service in spite of the opinion of neuropsychiatric officers that they should have been separated (i.e., discharged) (Miller, 1943). This situation provoked the following cable from General Pershing on July 15, 1918, a few months after the arrival of the American Expeditionary Force in France:

> Prevalence of mental disorders in replacement troops recently received suggests urgent importance of intensive efforts in eliminating mentally unfit from organisation's new draft prior to departure from the United States. Psychiatric forces and accommodations here inadequate to handle a greater proportion of mental cases than heretofore arriving, and if less time is taken to organise and train new divisions, elimination work should be speeded. (Miller, 1943, p. 168)

Not being faced with the same number of recruits as the Army and generally being able to require higher mental standards, the Navy evidently felt no need to respond to the problem with the same level of urgency. Although Pershing was not recognized as an authority in the field of mental health, his high position and reputation caused this cable to be quoted frequently by all the services when the need arose to argue for the improved screening of recruits.

The reader will recall that the Navy did not quickly respond to the pioneering work of Yerkes and his colleagues in World War I in developing the Army Alpha Test for screening recruits. Instead, they developed their own methods and, in typical Navy fashion, individual medical officers installed their own systems. The result was that there were different programs of screening and classifying recruits at the training center level. Two of the more interesting were developed at the Naval Operating Base at Hampton Roads, Virginia, and at the

Naval Training Center, San Francisco, California. Befitting the independence of each effort, both programs stated that "they hoped their efforts would be of help to other training centers."

Screening Methods at Hampton Roads

At Hampton Roads (Bisch, 1919), the task was defined as being twofold: (a) identifying the actual and potential psychoses and the functional and organic nervous diseases, and (b) identifying the feebleminded, including the "constitutional inferiors." In a display of confidence that may have been typical, unfortunately, of that era, Bisch wrote (1919):

> So far as neurological and purely psychiatrical [sic] examinations were concerned, recognized and unfailing [author's note: an appraisal not shared by modern medicine] methods were already at hand. When it came to the question of testing for mental inferiority, however, the problem at once became exceedingly complex because of the multitudinous number of psychological tests already in use, the fact that but few were standardized and therefore not of proved value. . . . It was therefore necessary either to devise new tests or to modify already existing standards. (p. 201)

Professing little confidence in the use of written group tests, Bisch selected four tests and had them administered individually but in an assembly-line fashion. These tests were:

1. Knox's Cube Test (developed for screening immigrants on Ellis Island) (Knox, 1914).
2. Repeating Digits Backward (taken from the Binet-Simon scale.)
3. Healy "A" Form Board.
4. Comprehensive Tests (four items taken from the Binet-Simon scale; later incorporated in the Wechsler-Bellevue under the subtest title of "Comprehension").

Five testing stations were placed in a large hall with an enlisted yeoman at each. The first yeoman would take a brief history (Figure 1), and each of the other four would administer and score one of the four tests. In addition, each of the four yeomen would rate the behavior of each recruit on a list of descriptive adjectives (Figure 2). The last tester would add up the total score for each subject and collect the history form and adjective checklist. Since each test took no more than three minutes, it was possible for each pipeline to produce one subject per three minutes. If the score(s) warranted it, the recruit was scheduled for a comprehensive psychiatric examination. Following the psychological testing, each recruit was given a routine neurological examination by a neurologist (Figure 3).

The forms used in this process are of historical interest in their use of wording

FORM I

No. _____

Name _____ Rate _____ Date _____

Birthplace _____ Race _____ Married _____ Children: m __ f __

Education: No. yrs __ City _____ Country _____ Grade __ Prep __ Coll. __

Occupation _____ Avg. Weekly Wage _____

Disease history _____ Venereal _____

Institution record _____ Alc. and Dr. _____

Physical defects _____ Stigmata _____

Neurological defects _____ Amentia _____

Inferiority _____ Crass ignorance _____ Illiteracy _____

Psychopathy _____ Psychiatry _____

Family history _____

_____

Summary _____

Disposition _____

Figure 1. Navy recruit screening card, brief history, 1919. (From "A Routine Method of Mental Examinations for Naval Recruits" by L. E. Bisch, *Naval Medical Bulletin*, 1919, *13*, p. 204.)

and phraseology. Not only do the forms reveal certain clinical biases of that era, they also use terms that would probably be considered pejorative in today's psychological climate (Bisch, 1919).

Each test was given a weighted score based on an arbitrary but logical decision concerning which test seemed most relevant to naval performance. Total scores were tallied for 2,000 recruits. A cutoff score was selected, below which a recruit would be given a more intensive examination, including the 1916 version of the Stanford-Binet and a formal psychiatric interview. The overall distribution of these scores approximated a normal curve, but the mean score was higher than in the general population—as might be expected among a group of wartime volunteers who were all English-speaking and literate. Of 11 cases selected for a full Stanford-Binet, 10 showed IQs below 60 and 1 an IQ of 81. By this method, fewer than 1% of the first 1,000 recruits tested were surveyed (i.e., discharged) from the service.

FORM II

(Reverse side)

REACTIONS DURING PRELIMINARY EXAMINATIONS

+	−		+	−		+		+	
		Composed			Childish		Irritable		Restive
		Willing			Oafish		Resentful		Nervous
		Cooperative			Stolid		Resistive		Variable
		Interested			Timid		Defiant		Suggestible
		Attentive			Bashful		Sulky		Distracted
		Cheerful			Sensitive		Shut-in		Anxious
		Stable			Reserved		Moody		Afraid
		Careful			Modest		Depressed		Fearful
		Deliberate			Frank		Despondent		Tearful
		Assured			Jovial				
		Apt			Suspicious		Effeminate		Nostalgia
		Energetic			Forward		Untidy		Uncleanly
		Rapid			Overconfident		Self-conscious		
		Systematic			Conceited		Self-depreciative		
		Thorough			Scornful		Sympathy-seeking		
		Efficient			Boastful				
		Intelligent			Boisterous		Abnormalities		
		Profound			Euphoric				
		Confidence gained quickly					Plea of unfamiliarity		

Special comments _____

_____

_____

_____

Figure 2. Navy recruit screening form, reverse side of preliminary psychiatric test sheet, list of "character descriptives," 1919. (From "A Routine Method of Mental Examinations for Naval Recruits" by L. E. Bisch, *Naval Medical Bulletin*, 1919, *13*, p. 206.)

FORM III
PSYCHIATRIC DIVISION
Detention Unit
Neurological status

Name _____ Rate _____ Age _____
Examiner _____ Date _____, 191 _____

Syphilis _____   Chancroids _____
Gonorrhea _____   Enuresis, D-N _____
Alcohol _____   Drug addiction _____
Convulsions _____   Fainting or dizziness _____
Sensory disturbances _____   Subjective symptoms _____
Institution history _____
Neurotic history _____
Test words: Slurring _____, Ataxia _____, Transposition _____, Elision _____
Speech defect: Stuttering _____, Lisping _____, Faulty articulation _____
Paralysis _____, Atrophy _____, Asymmetry _____, Spasms _____
Pupils: Right _____, Left _____, Irregular _____, Unequal _____,
    Reaction to light sluggish _____, Absent _____
Nystagmus _____   Strabismus _____
Hyperthyroidism: Enlarged thyroid ____   Persistent tachycardia _____
Exophthalmos _____   General nervousness _____
Tremor: Coarse _____, Fine _____, Face _____, Tongue _____
    Hands _____, Muscles _____, Intention _____
Patellar reflexes: Right _____, Left _____, Normal _____, Absent _____
    Diminished _____, Exaggerated _____
Babinski _____   Clonus _____
Romberg _____   Gait_____
"Stigmata of degeneracy" _____

Wassermann: (1st) Date _____, Result _____ (2d) Date _____, Result _____
Disposition _____

Figure 3. Navy recruit screening form, neurological examination, 1919. (From "A Routine Method of Mental Examinations for Naval Recruits" by L. E. Bisch, *Naval Medical Bulletin*, 1919, *13*, p. 207.)

This method correlated with years of schooling to the extent of .35, a significant correlation but in the lower range because the screening tests were so heavily weighted with nonverbal items (the use of the Pearson product-moment correlation was quite advanced for that time). The investigators had no way of realizing it then, but their use of a few Binet-type subtests probably correlated with the total Stanford-Binet score in the order of .60–.70 (Wechsler, 1955, p. 15).

Screening Methods in San Francisco

The screening program developed in San Francisco took on a different format. Stearns (1924) apparently did not have Bisch's aversion to group testing and selected the following test battery:

1. Trabue Language Scale C. A group of subjects is given a list of ten sentences with blanks representing words left out, and the appropriate word is chosen from a list and inserted. The number of missing words for each sentence ranges from one to seven, with an increasing number of words to choose from. Higher scores are given for the most appropriate word inserted, and fewer points for words that are acceptable but less appropriate.

2. Dissected Sentences from the Binet-Simon Scale. Each subject is required to rearrange a collection of apparently meaningless words into a meaningful sentence.

3. Cancellation Test. The subjects are timed to see how fast they can cross out all of the "Es" in a paragraph of reading matter taken from a newspaper.

4. Memory Span for Numerals. This is the traditional Digit Span test, but the subject is asked to write the digits down after hearing them repeated by the examiner to the group.

5. Healy Code. The subjects are shown, on a blackboard, a code in which letters are represented by a series of dots and crosses and then are timed on how well they encode a short sentence spoken by the examiner.

The collective number of points was adjusted so that a perfect score was 100. The tests were given to a sequential sample of 4,000 recruits and the curve, apparently relatively normal (but not so specified in the report), was divided into the following segments, which were assumed to represent the mental status of each recruit (Stearns, 1924):

Group I:	Below 65, inferior
Group II:	65-75, low average
Group III:	75-85, high average
Group IV:	85-100, superior

```
┌─────────────────────────────────────────────────────────────────┐
│ Name ─────────────────── Date ──────── No. ─────────             │
│                                                                   │
│ Age ──────── Civil cond. ─────────────── Rate ───────            │
│                                                                   │
│ Home ─────────────────── Enlisted ──────────────                 │
│                                                                   │
│ P.E. ───────────────── Appearance ──────────────                 │
│                                                                   │
│ School ───────────────────────────────────                       │
│                                                                   │
│ ───────────────────────────────────────────                      │
│                                                                   │
│ Occupation ────────────────────────────────                      │
│                                                                   │
│ ───────────────────────────────────────────                      │
│                                                                   │
│ Medical History ───────────────────────────                      │
│                                                                   │
│ ───────────────────────────────────────────                      │
│                                                                   │
│ Alc. ─────────────────── Arrests ───────────                     │
│                                                                   │
│ Symptoms ────────────────────────── Fitness 1-2-3                │
└─────────────────────────────────────────────────────────────────┘
```

Figure 4. Navy recruit screening card, life history, 1917–1918. (From "The Detection of the Psychopath and the Classification of Naval Recruits in Accordance With Their Intelligence" by A. W. Stearns, *Naval Medical Bulletin*, 1924, *20*, p. 158.)

The results were apparently not validated according to today's psychometric standards, but the author reported that these scores were compared with the subsequent performance in service school of an unspecified number of recruits and that "it was soon apparent that there was a tendency to fail on the part of the low men and to succeed on the part of the high" (Stearns, 1924, p. 161).

In addition to the test battery, a short history card (Figure 4) was filled out on each recruit. It is interesting to note that the history form contained none of the psychiatric jargon of the day, apparently in recognition of the paraprofessional level of the interviewers. The interviewers were given a full outline on how to evaluate each history, as set forth below. Note not only the terms no longer in use but also those concepts of suitability not appropriate today, such as "the association between divorce and psychopathy" (Stearns, 1924).

> As each question is asked, clues should be followed. The factors of special importance in forming an estimate of the individual seem to be:
>
> 1. *Age.* A considerable percentage of the 18-year-old boys are either 16 or 17 years old. This often means that they have run away from home or have enlisted fraudulently; also many of the bed wetters are in the

18-year-old group, so a little closer attention should be paid to the 18-year-old than to others. Also the men above 30 need a little closer inspection, because of the greater frequency in them of cerebrospinal syphilis and chronic alcoholism.

2. *Civil condition.* Men who are separated or divorced should have a little closer scrutiny because of the association between domestic difficulties and psychopathy.

3. *Relation between home and place of enlistment.* This is quite important, especially in younger applicants. It is unlikely that a boy under 20 would be applying for enlistment in a distant part of the country if his home life and social relations are normal.

4. *Appearance.* Under this heading general attitude and manner should be included. Although appearances are very deceptive, one soon learns to detect the dull, childlike reaction of the imbecile, and the dulled, apathetic reaction of the epileptic or dementia praecox case.

5. *School.* The grade reached in school and history of retardation is very important in detecting the feeble-minded and epileptic. The eighth grade usually, and high school always, rules out mental defect. Very few epileptics and psychopaths graduate from high school. One should not confuse the rustic with the imbecile, but differential diagnosis is necessary to make the distinction.

6. *Occupation.* A permanent, responsible job held by a man usually rules out nervous and mental diseases. The imbecile's activities are confined to unskilled labor, and his terms of employment are very short. The psychoneurotic, insane, and epileptic rarely hold a position long.

7. *Medical.* At least half the epileptics will admit attacks if properly questioned. The same applies to bed wetters. Practically all of the psychoneurotics give a history of previous ill-defined pains, dizzy attacks, or weakness.

8. *Arrests.* The relation between delinquency and nervous and mental diseases is well known. A history of arrests for minor offenses and of reform-school residence is easy to obtain.

As a result of the above analysis it is possible to place candidates for enlistment in three groups:

(1) Those obviously suffering from neither nervous or mental diseases, [composing] . . . at least 80 and probably 90 per cent of applicants.

(2) Those suspected to be suffering from mental diseases, [composing] . . . from 5 to 15 per cent of applicants.

(3) Those obviously suffering from nervous or mental diseases, [composing] . . . from 1 to 5 per cent.

As a result of this the definite cases should be rejected. The doubtful ones should be more thoroughly studied. Usually by consulting police records of the home town, insisting upon the references being bona fide and investigating these references, one can determine the desirability of the candidate. (Stearns, 1924, pp. 158–159)

In addition to the foregoing, Stearns utilized information on each recruit's occupational and educational history in a way that was quite sophisticated for that time. A list of 53 different occupations was created that covered the range from unskilled to professional. Each recruit was then placed on a four-point scale as follows (Stearns, 1924):

1. Industrial misfits, such as vagrants, criminals, or those continually shifting work.
2. Unskilled. Such as farmers, students, or day laborers.
3. Experienced. Those who, although they have not a trade and so would not be considered trained, have had enough experience at a given occupation to make them possibly worthwhile.
4. Trained. Embracing highly skilled individuals who have learned a trade or have a profession or business.

In addition to rating subjects on the four-point scale, the interviewer indicated the number code of the occupation or profession so that department heads of the station could search for recruits with skills they needed.

Educationally, each recruit was evaluated as follows:

1. Less than eighth grade.
2. Eighth-grade graduate.
3. High-school student (level unspecified).
4. College (level unspecified).

This allowed for each recruit to be given a threefold rating. For example, a rating of 4-4-4.15 would be a person of superior mental ability, with a college background, trained in a skilled occupation or profession (in this case the digits .15 refer to the profession of chemist on the aforementioned occupational list).

This scoring method was used to help decide if recruits were to be kept in the service, what type of training school might be offered to them, and to what types of jobs they might be assigned. Even though this system was predictive of the multivariate and statistical approaches developed after World War II, the decision was still made on a clinical or commonsense level.

These programs were developed by individual medical officers, and this author has no knowledge how long they were retained after the originator was transferred. Stearns, for example, was a Reserve medical officer during World War I, but at the time of publishing the details of his program, he had left active duty and was employed at the Boston Psychopathic Hospital.

Return to the Status Quo

At the end of World War I, the Surgeon General of the Navy advocated return to the status quo, that is, not using medical specialists and using the medical officer as a generalist. As he stated, "There would be no place for psychiatry in Navy medicine" (Wilkins, 1972). This and other readings strongly suggest that the relatively sophisticated models of recruit screening developed at Hampton Roads and San Francisco soon fell into disuse and that formal screening was again left to the common sense of individual medical officers until the advent of World War II.

Supporting this conclusion is the fact that the early screening programs designed by Hunt and Wittson at Newport Naval Training Center in the months prior to the attack on Pearl Harbor were designed apparently "from scratch." In the professional literature subsequently produced about the World War II screening program, this author found absolutely no references to the work done in World War I described above. It appears that the Newport Center programs were another example of "reinventing the wheel."

After about 1925, there are apparently no references to recruit screening in the professional literature, but an examination by Louttit of the annual reports of the Bureau of Navigation to the Secretary of the Navy and the Surgeon General allows for the somewhat tenuous conclusion that in 1931 the General Classification Test (GCT), which was being used to select recruits for service schools, was being used not only for screening recruits from the service at the training station level but also was in use at recruiting stations. The use of a group intelligence test (presumably the GCT) and taking a short history at the recruiting stations apparently continued until World War II (Louttit, 1941, 1942).

The fact that the Navy was not availing itself of state-of-the-art techniques for personnel screening and vocational placement was pointed out by a Naval Reserve officer while on training duty in 1934. Writing in the *U.S. Naval Institute Proceedings* (NIP), Lt. Comdr. Preston S. Lincoln observed "that as recruits reported for duty aboard ship they were assigned to fill vacancies by each division officer utilizing the 'hunch system' and without even examining the man's record" (Lincoln, 1936). Lincoln also pointed out that Johnson O'Connor, an engineer with the General Electric Company, had developed, in cooperation with Massachusetts Institute of Technology, Harvard University, and Stevens Institute (Hoboken, NJ), and validated a series of tests for personnel selection and placement, including clerical ability, manual dexterity, engineering aptitude, and executive ability. Lincoln also pointed out that the Navy had ignored previous notes of these tests in the 1932 issue of NIP, but also observed, "The Navy is a highly conservative organization, and it may well be that, regardless of these tests, many officers will continue to . . . select men by the 'haphazard method.' " (In civilian life the O'Connor tests remained in wide use in personnel selection and vocational guidance work until the 1960s.)

Recruit Screening
in World War II

A s previously described, C. M. Louttit was the first Navy psychologist on active duty during the prewar buildup, reporting for duty in October 1940, and subsequently William Hunt reported in April 1941 to the Newport Naval Training Station. These two men represented the Navy's initial effort to apply psychological knowledge and training to the program of psychiatric screening. Although this arrangement established the mechanism for bringing clinical psychologists aboard, recruitment was slow, and no formal guidelines had been established for the conduct of their work.

The Psychologist's Role Defined

On January 2, 1941, the Surgeon General officially described the psychologist's duties as follows (Louttit, 1941):

> The clinical psychologists attached to the training station will examine those recruits where scoring on intelligence and achievement tests at recruiting stations and on entrance to the training stations have shown irregularities or discrepancies. He shall also examine recruits with instruments designed to indicate temperamental and emotional characteristics. By these means he will not only aid in the elimination of the unfit but also advise in the matter of selective placement. (p. 226)

This was elaborated on in a follow-up directive on February 1, 1941 (Louttit, 1941):

> It must be remembered that clinical psychological examinations must go beyond the mere securing of numerical scores. Such scores have meaning only insofar as they are interpreted in the light of the examinee's personal reactions, his history, and his attitudes. The psychologists selected for work with the Medical Corps will have had considerable training and experience in interviewing, counseling, the interpretation of social histories as well as of strictly psychological tests. Therefore, their findings should prove a valuable supplement to those of the psychiatrists. (p. 226)

The reader will recall the previously mentioned Navy tradition of describing a job in the broadest terms, assigning the best person available for the job, and letting the individual decide how best to do it—a procedure that apparently was followed in assigning clinical psychologists to the naval training centers.

Development of Abbreviated Screening Tests

As the war approached, enlistments began to increase, and after Pearl Harbor a flood of recruits entered the training centers. Immediately upon arrival, these people had to be logged in, provided with eating and sleeping facilities, and given a complete physical examination, the latter including a brief psychiatric screen. The process was done in assembly-line fashion, with the recruits proceeding from station to station. The flow was quite uneven, and the staff would combine normal working days with long periods of 16- to 18-hour shifts, 7 days a week. About 15 minutes was allowed for the psychiatric screening, including any testing. This placed a premium upon speed as well as validity. Priority was given to the development of shortened versions of intelligence and personality group tests.

As we saw earlier, during World War I, a number of short intelligence tests had been designed for recruit screening, many of them using a collection of items taken from the Binet-Simon scale or the Stanford-Binet scale. In similar fashion, in World War II groups of items were taken from the Wechsler-Bellevue Test of Intelligence, which also included many Binet-type items. The Kent E-G-Y, a series of 1-minute tests designed for busy clinicians, was adapted also. The result was a number of brief (5–10 minutes) paper-and-pencil tests, as well as individual tests of intelligence that were not only useful but correlated with the Wechsler-Bellevue in the range of .65 to .96—the higher correlations, of course, derived from those scales that had the most number of items from the Wechsler-Bellevue (Hunt & Stevenson, 1945).

This use of abbreviated intelligence tests had a long history, but the idea of brief personality tests had been considered untenable. However, the exigencies of war did not recognize the presumed limitation of the statistical requirements for such instruments, and work in this area also proceeded. The dynamics of this process are described by Hunt (1975):

> One day Cecil Wittson came into my office and demanded to know why, if we could abbreviate intelligence tests, we could not do the same for personality inventories. I gave him all the usual arguments about the number of items necessary for validity and reliability, etc., but he refused to listen, and thus the Navy Personal Inventory II was born.
> At the time Walter Shipley, my successor at Wheaton College, was working on a contract to develop a biographical inventory for the Office of Scientific Research and Development [OSRD] that used a large number of items originally collected by Carney Landis. It showed some promise, but was a cumbersome thing of well over a hundred items. His OSRD

committee refused him permission to work on a brief test on the ground that it was an impossible task, so over one holiday weekend on his own time and assisted by two of my ex-students at Wheaton he selected his 17 most discriminating items, threw in 3 buffer items and presented us at Newport with a 20-item neurotic inventory, which we proceeded to validate and standardize. This last was a relatively easy task, since the flow of men through the Training Station was large and we had the confidence and support of the command. The OSRD committee at first was aghast, but the inventory stood up under use and Walter Hunter later was to claim it as one of the OSRD's outstanding accomplishments. (p. 175)

As described elsewhere, the psychiatric screening program of the U.S. Army was a disaster. Not only were psychiatric casualties described in the Army literature as "weak," of poor character, or malingerers or cowards, but also they were summarily discharged with no attempt at treatment or further screening. Thanks to the early use of psychiatrist-psychologist teams and the luxury of a mostly volunteer and literate population, the Navy was able to dodge this particular "bullet." In addition, thanks to the efforts of Hunt and Wittson and their colleagues, a definite amount of empirical evidence was generated to support the efficacy of the Navy screening procedures.

Validation Studies at Newport

Early in the screening program at Newport, an attempt was made to validate the process. Each recruit was given a three-minute interview by a psychiatrist and placed in one of three categories:

1. No evidence of psychiatric condition—the recruit was passed on to active duty.
2. Evidence of psychiatric disability—the recruit was admitted to a hospital ward for further observation.
3. Some evidence of psychiatric disability but not severe enough to warrant admission to the observation ward.

These "suspect" cases were passed on to active duty. A follow-up was conducted in which 227 of them were compared with two random samples of "normals" from the first category (Wittson, Hunt, & Stevenson, 1945). The results are shown in Table 4.

A preferred method of study would have been to compare the "normal" groups with recruits who otherwise would have been discharged as psychiatrically unfit but who were allowed to go on active duty instead. However, this might have unduly jeopardized both the welfare of the men and the war effort. On the assumption that psychopathology existed on some sort of continuum, the "suspect" group was chosen instead. The results not only supported this assumption but also indicated that a 3-minute psychiatric interview was not without some

Table 4

Comparison of Service Records of Suspect Group and Normal Control Group, Navy Recruit Screening Program, 1941–1944

Evaluation measures	NP suspect group I (N = 227)	Normal control group I (N = 227)
Number of medical surveys with neuropsychiatric (NP) diagnosis	7	2
Average yearly attrition rate (percentage)	1.0%	0.3%
Percentage having Petty Officer status	80%	90%
Percentage in service schools	30%	59%
Percentage failing in service schools	11%	8%
Number of days lost through AOL* and AWOL**	1,155	636
Number of days disciplinary sentence	4,401	1,841

Notes. *Absent over leave. **Absent without leave. The recruits in this study were processed in September, 1941, and followed for a period of 38 months. Adapted from Tables 1 and 2, "A Follow-Up Study of Neuropsychiatric Screening" by C. L. Wittson, W. A. Hunt, & I. Stevenson, 1945, *Journal of Abnormal and Social Psychology, 41*, p. 80.

validity. Not only was the subsequent discharge rate more than three times that of the "normals," but their rate of achieving petty officer status or doing well in service schools was much lower, and their AOL/AWOL (absent over leave/absent without leave) rate and disciplinary rate was much higher. These results, of course, do not reflect the number of "false positives" released into the fleet, that is, those screened as being capable but subsequently receiving psychiatric discharges. This latter rate averaged about 3%, whereas those discharged during training averaged about 3.7% (Hunt, Wittson, & Hunt, 1952).

Validation Studies at Three Training Stations

In a postwar study of the overall effectiveness of screening conducted during the war, Hunt, Wittson, and Burton (1950) compared the psychiatric discharge experiences of three naval training stations—Great Lakes, Illinois; Newport, Rhode Island; and Sampson, New York. At Great Lakes the screening unit received full cooperation from the command and was allowed to discharge as many men as it saw fit. At Newport the discharge rate was held to approximately 4% of the incoming recruits. At Sampson the command was not sympathetic toward screening, and discharges were held to a minimum. Unlike the previously described study, this encompassed the entire screening process, including the hospital admissions and those referred by the training commanders.

Several samples were taken between January and July 1943. For purposes of illustration they are combined by the author and averaged in Table 5.

Table 5

*Comparison of Psychiatric Discharge Rates of Recruits at Three Naval
Training Stations, 1943*

Screening unit	Number	% Discharged during training	% Discharged subsequently
Great Lakes	5,532	5.0	2.65
Newport	5,032	3.7	3.0
Sampson	6,811	0.85	3.95

Note. Adapted from "An Investigation of Naval Neuropsychiatric Screening Procedures" by W.
A. Hunt, in H. Guetzkow (Ed.), *Groups, Leadership, and Men*, 1951, Pittsburgh: Carnegie Press.
Copyright © 1951 by Carnegie Press. Adapted by permission.

As noted, there is an inverse relationship between the number of men discharged during training and the subsequent loss of manpower due to psychiatric
discharge. However, the relationship is not linear. For example, Great Lakes
discharged 26% more men than Newport but produced only a 12% differential
in subsequent discharges. Newport discharged 335% (i.e., 3.35 times) more than
Sampson, but its subsequent discharge rate was only 24% less. Apparently, as
more men are discharged during training, there is less return in terms of attrition
rate, and there may be a point of diminishing returns.

Psychological Screening

In keeping with the relative independence of each medical officer, the screening routine varied somewhat between training stations, but the procedure was
essentially the same. If the number of screening personnel was adequate, each
recruit was given a short psychiatric interview—usually by a psychiatrist but
frequently by a psychologist (once accepted by the psychiatrists as competent).
They were placed in three categories: "pass," "suspect but pass," and "hold
for further study." At Newport the "hold" group was usually admitted to a
hospital ward, whereas at San Diego they were placed in a holding company.
This practice was later discontinued; the recruits were placed in regular units
and the commanders were given special instructions to evaluate carefully their
performance.

Recruits who showed clear symptomatology were usually placed on a hospital
ward for study. Those who were merely suspect were placed in training, but the
company commander was advised to evaluate them carefully. This decision was
usually based upon the initial short interview, but very often the overwhelming
number of recruits prevented giving each recruit even this much time. Therefore,
short-form psychological tests would be inserted into the intake process and used
as a method of deciding which recruits should be interviewed. For example, at
the San Diego Training Center, they developed a Personal Data Sheet (PDS),

which was an abridged version of the Thurstone Personality Schedule—which in turn was a version of the Woodworth Personal Data Sheet developed by Yerkes' group in World War I. It consisted of 25 questions relating to personal adjustment, such as "Do you get discouraged easily?" and "Do you ever feel that someone is trying to do you harm?" (Gerstle et al., 1943)

As the recruits stood in the receiving line awaiting the physical examination, they were seated on the floor and given the PDS to check off. In addition, they were asked to write on the form whether or not they had been a patient in a mental hospital, whether or not they wet the bed at night, and to list any arrests and the reasons therefore. While they were still in the receiving line, their papers were checked over, and on the basis of their replies and ability to complete the task, a certain number were singled out for psychiatric interview. In this fashion a draft of 75 men could be processed in about 10 minutes and the interviews limited to about 35% of the group.

Those assigned to the hospital or passed into training under special evaluation were further processed by additional interviews, psychological testing (according to the skills and time available), and, if not passed into active duty, processed for presentation to the Aptitude Board. Although the data presented to the boards may have varied between training centers, the process between centers was very similar. The Aptitude Board consisted of a line officer, a nonpsychiatric physician, one or two psychiatrists, and a psychologist. The board prepared its findings and made recommendations for discharge to the commanding officer, who had the final word, barring intervention from higher authority, which rarely occurred. Like other training centers, San Diego mentioned use of parts of the Wechsler-Bellevue and the Kent E-G-Y tests but also mentioned the Bernreuter Personality Inventory and "various psycho-physical measurements such as the dynamometer and spirometer." Also noted was the fact that "one of the psychologists is an experienced Rorschach examiner and use is made of this method in selected cases" (Gerstle et al., 1943).

Continuing Validation Studies

Hunt and Wittson continued to seek ways to validate the screening process in spite of the fact that wartime conditions precluded the use of ideal experimental designs. In one study, they interviewed 944 cases of naval personnel sent for interview because of symptoms picked up by enlisted personnel conducting vocational aptitude placement exams. On the basis of a brief interview, the recruits were diagnosed and placed into three classes: (a) mild symptoms, treatment not indicated; (b) moderate symptoms, shore duty but not sea duty indicated; (c) severe symptoms, hospitalization indicated. Years later the subsequent naval careers of 932 of the 944 men were studied, and the percentages of psychiatric discharges in each category within 1 year were computed. The results were as follows: mild diagnosis (N = 527), 6.5%; moderate diagnosis (N = 367), 20.2%; severe diagnosis (N = 38), 89.7% (Wittson & Hunt, 1951). Hunt referred to this technique of experimental design as *historicoexperimental*; today the preferred term might be *quasi-experimental*. This penchant for research exhibited by Hunt and Wittson exemplifies the unique contributions psychologists can make to the clinical process.

The apparent success in the use of the short psychiatric interview in screening Navy recruits cannot be easily generalized to other populations or other situations. It must be remembered that only broad classifications were used—mild, moderate, or severe—and no attempt was made at a psychiatric diagnosis. In addition, the population contained a wide spectrum of the general population, including a certain number of borderline retardates, illiterates, and psychotics. When this technique was applied to a population consisting of healthy volunteers with a record of good previous adjustment and achievement (e.g., graduation from high school), the results were essentially negative. For example, the psychiatric interview, even of an hour's length or more, failed to differentiate between candidates for the Office of Strategic Services (OSS) during World War II (OSS Assessment Staff, 1948), the prediction of success as a pilot (Holtzman & Sells, 1954), the prediction of success for officer candidates in the Marine Corps (Wilkins et al., 1955), or prediction of success in the Peace Corps (Fisher et al., 1967). In the 1960s, the Navy also discontinued the use of the short interview for the selection of submariners or personnel for special missions, such as Operation Deep Freeze, the Navy's project in Antarctica.

In addition, a distinction must be made between "screening" and such terms as "diagnosis" and "personnel selection." Even though it may seem rather callous, the military is interested only in the number of people effectively screened; it is not concerned with the welfare or treatment of the individual at the point where screening occurs. This permits the issue of "false positives" and "false negatives" to be evaluated in statistical rather than humane terms. Also, as will be shown, the efficacy of the short screening interview was found to be more illusory than real.

Postwar Screening

Following World War II, there was a severe reduction of personnel in the Armed Forces, including the discharge of all Navy clinical psychologists. Predictably, the psychiatric screening of recruits essentially ceased to exist. However, beginning in 1948, the screening routine developed at Newport was reinstituted at the training centers. The fact the Newport screening routine was adopted was hardly an accident. Hunt and Wittson had resumed their previous collaboration as consultants to the Surgeon General, frequently visiting Great Lakes and the other centers to consult concerning the screening process. (Hunt had joined the faculty at Northwestern University and Wittson was eventually at the University of Nebraska Medical School in Omaha.) Rumor has it that they did not react kindly toward deviations from their Newport model.

When the Korean War suddenly erupted in 1950, the screening process was once again on a wartime basis, with long lines of recruits being handled by an understaffed group of psychiatrists and psychologists.

The Search for an Actuarial (Statistical) Approach to Screening

The process of screening remained relatively unchanged until the advent of what, in the opinion of many, was one of the most important developments in personnel selection in decades—the successful application of the actuarial (i.e., statistical) approach created under the direction of Dr. John Plag of the (then) Navy Medical Neuropsychiatric Research Unit in San Diego. (The history of this important unit is discussed in a later chapter.)

Clinical vs. Statistical Prediction

The question of whether human performance should best be predicted by the mechanical application of statistical tables or by some method of quantitatively or subjectively examining each applicant is an old problem. Meehl (1954) had labeled this the issue of "clinical vs. statistical prediction" (the latter was sometimes referred to as actuarial prediction); his book presents an excellent summary and discussion of this issue.

In the clinical method, it is common for one or more persons to survey an application or interview an applicant and to then make several observations about the applicant's qualifications. No rules of procedure are necessarily followed, and it is not required that the same variables be considered or viewed in the same way in each case. Such a method is considered by its proponents to be more sensitive and capable of taking into account all of the variables, and to humanize the procedure by testing each applicant as a true individual. However, other persons may regard such a method as inaccurate and uneconomical. Most selectors can be classed as being more or less in one camp or the other, and both sides are likely to make a strong case for their approach to personnel evaluation and selection. As Meehl points out, it is customary to apply honorific adjectives to the method preferred, and to refer pejoratively to the other method. For instance, Meehl (1954) writes:

The statistical method is often called [by its adherents] operational, communicable, verifiable, public, objective, reliable, behavioral, testable, rigorous, scientific, precise, careful and trustworthy. Those who dislike the method consider it mechanical, atomistic, additive, cut and dried, artificial, unreal, arbitrary, incomplete, dead, pedantic, fractionated, trivial, forced, static, superficial, rigid, sterile, academic, oversimplified, pseudoscientific and blind.

The clinical method, on the other hand, is labeled by its proponents as dynamic, global, meaningful, holistic, subtle, sympathetic, configural, patterned, organized, rich, deep, genuine, sensitive, sophisticated, real, living, concrete, natural, true to life, and understanding. The critics of the clinical method are likely to view it as mystical, transcendent, metaphysical, supermundane, vague, hazy, subjective, unscientific, unreliable, crude, private, unverifiable, qualitative, primitive, prescientific, sloppy, uncontrolled, careless, verbalistic, intuitive, and muddleheaded. (p. 4)

In spite of the fact that the short screening interview seemed to correlate with the successful completion of an enlistment, its validity and utility became increasingly suspect, partly because of the work of Meehl and partly because of the results of Dr. Plag's doctoral dissertation, which was done on recruit screening while he was serving as a civilian staff psychologist at the Great Lakes Naval Training Center.

Evaluating the Psychiatric Interview

In 1960 Plag and his colleagues undertook a series of studies in order to better define and quantify the nature of the screening process. In the first study, a comparison was made between the ability of the screening interview and that of a combination of age, education, and a measure of verbal intelligence (GCT) to predict which men would complete a successful enlistment. A group of 1,903 recruits were given psychiatric interviews and rated in three categories—below average, average, or above average—by the examining clinicians. During training they were not examined again, although those who proved unsatisfactory were discharged by routine administrative methods conducted by nonpsychiatric personnel. At the end of two years the subjects were rated on measures of military efficiency. The measures of a successful enlistment were: 1) attrition or in-out; 2) pay grade achieved; 3) semi-annual performance marks; 4) presence of disciplinary action; and 5) division officer ratings. Because there are differences in the quality of recruits at different times of the year, a separate analysis was performed on those entering training in May of 1960 and those in August of 1960.

The psychiatric screening interview ratings produced an average correlation with the various criteria of .15 ($p < .001$), with a range of .06 to .20; the combination of age, education, and GCT score produced an average R of .26 ($p < .001$), with a range of .17 to .32. In addition, when the correlation of the interview score was added to this R, it contributed no significant increase (i.e., no unique variance). It was therefore concluded that the Navy's brief psychiatric intake interview was of little practical value in prediction (Plag, 1964b).

Evaluating the Psychiatric Screening Process

Another study was conducted to test the psychiatric screening process as a whole and its efficacy in separating unsuitable enlistees (Plag & Arthur, 1965; Plag et al., 1970). A group of 134 recruits who had been designated by an Aptitude Board to be separated were "smuggled" back into training, subsequently graduated, and transferred into the fleet. Only a few persons were aware of the transfer: the members of the Aptitude Board and the Recruit Evaluation Unit, the company commander of the unit to which the recruit was referred following the negative evaluation (not the recruit's own unit), the local commanding officer, certain officials in Washington, DC, and the researchers.

Special care was taken that the subject, his peers, and all personnel at those commands to which he was assigned after graduation did not know of his status as a research subject. The local clinicians were also unaware of it until they had prepared the lengthy examinations and documentation required for presentation to the Boards. The board members included line officers, nonpsychiatric medical officers, a psychiatrist, a psychologist, and a legal officer. They conducted a full review of each case, but, in keeping with the research protocol, returned each man to duty. Although several subjects failed training several times and were returned to the board, they were returned to another unit and eventually graduated. At the end of 2 years, those remaining on active duty were given psychiatric follow-up examinations and evaluated on their level of effectiveness. Identical examinations were conducted with a group of control or non-Aptitude Board subjects who were matched man-for-man with the experimental subjects on the basis of a series of variables such as age, GCT scores, and education. Each matched pair was interviewed by the same psychiatrist, who was unaware of which man belonged to which group. Both groups were also rated on a series of 15 behavioral items relevant to military adjustment. At the end of the 2-year period, 72.4 percent of the "unsuitable" recruits remained on active duty, whereas 85.8 percent of the control subjects survived this period of service. The overall adjustment ratings given by the interviewers to the "survivors" were not significantly different from those given to the controls, and only 3 of the 15 behavioral ratings were different (Plag, 1963).

At the end of 4 years, 54.5 percent of the experimental group had completed a successful enlistment and were judged effective enough to be recommended for reenlistment if they so desired. This overall rate of effectiveness was significantly less than the 72.4 percent effectiveness for the fleet as a whole.

These findings indicate that the process of psychiatric screening (which includes input from several sources) has some predictive validity. However, among those men who, in the opinion of experienced and well-trained professionals, including the collective wisdom of psychiatrists, psychologists, line officers, and in many cases peers, were all rated as unsuitable and predicted to fail, about 72% were able to render 2 years of satisfactory service and about 55% produced 4 years of effective service. Discharge of these men would have meant a large loss of manpower, as well as unnecessarily stigmatizing them with a psychiatric discharge, which could have negatively affected the rest of their lives. If some method could be devised to neutralize the potentially harmful effects of the 45% who were unsuccessful, the remaining 55% would represent a tremendous savings to the Navy in both money and human resources. Psychiatric screening can indeed be a mixed blessing.

Why the Psychiatric Screening Process Fails to Predict Performance

The reason for the failure of the process to correctly predict the performance of so many individuals may not lie in the accuracy or inaccuracy of the psychiatric evaluation made at the training center but in the application of this evaluation to the future—or as a predictor. The fact that the 2-year survivors were not psychologically different from the control subjects suggests that they had matured since they entered as raw recruits. In our society, the 17- to 20-year-old age group is in a developmental stage of rapid change, and for many of them the Navy can be a very maturing influence, especially in wartime. In World War II and later in Korea, it was common to hear stories of "fuzzy-cheeked kids" suddenly assuming positions of leadership and responsibility, performing heroic deeds under fire, or both.

This capacity for change was illustrated by an examination of 76 of these 2-year survivors. Plag and Arthur (1965) offer three hypotheses to account for this ability to adjust to Navy life after an apparent failure during training and provide an illustrative case for each:

Subject A

The first hypothesis, namely that the good fleet adjustment of some sailors results from emotional growth subsequent to training, is illustrated by the following protocol of Subject A. During recruit training, this enlistee was described by his company commander as being unable to carry out instructions, being unreliable, disobedient, overboisterous, argumentative and as being poorly motivated for the naval service. The summary of his aptitude board report is as follows:

Subject A presents himself in the interview as a self-centered, pouting and resentfully defensive 17-year-old recruit. He is and has been poorly motivated for service. His enlistment was apparently predicated on his reaction to his mother's marriage two months ago. School history, as revealed by the recruit, indicates that his adjustment there reflected the disruptions that were going on at home. Thus, it is noted that he failed the fifth grade shortly after the divorce and he failed the ninth grade when his mother began to contemplate marriage seriously. He finally quit school when his mother did get married. The recruit has no insight into this relationship. He lacks the necessary maturity and self-sufficiency to function effectively in the Navy. It is recommended that he be discharged as temperamentally unsuitable for further training.

On psychiatric re-examination two years later his adjustment was summarized as follows:

His general adjustment has been very good. He shows good morale, describes a resilient attitude to authority which allows him to "let things happen and take them as they come." His relations with petty officers and peers have been mutually friendly. His quarterly marks average 3.6–3.8. He made third class in approximately one year and eight months and has had no disciplinary action.

He attributes his success to "going to sea right away. I had a lot of growing up to do and at sea you've got to do it." Apparently he was on a ship with good morale, and quickly he identified with the camaraderie of the men of the [name of ship]. This identification had its roots in his early identification with his real father who "was this kind of seaman—he had a man's sense of responsibility and I tried to be like him."

In the phase-two examination, when describing the personal or environmental factors responsible for changes in adjustment, the psychiatrist stated:

His ego assets are fairly good, for he recognized the realistic needs of the situation in boot training and "realized I had to give up my carefree ways." This capacity for assessing situations, planning and concerted work toward self-realization and productivity has continued. For example, he liked the Mediterranean cruise and the good liberty and good times, but knew that he would have to get into a school within a given period of time or he would simply have no opportunity to better himself. He tried for and received schooling and has gone on to do good work. . . . Perhaps the "acting out" quality of his behavior in boot camp could have been dealt with in an intellectually insightful way. However, I feel certain the real determinants were related to his self-esteem. He seemed quite aware of the character of his behavior and where it was taking him.

Subject B

The second hypothesis indicates that differences between fleet environments and recruit training standards are large enough that some enlistees who cannot measure up in recruit training are able to adjust satisfactorily to shipboard life. The following protocol of Subject B is illustrative. Upon presentation to the Naval Aptitude Board for discharge from service, he was described as being unreliable, objectionably dirty and untidy, unable to keep up with his company in training and poorly motivated for the naval service. The summary of his aptitude board report read as follows:

Subject B is a dull, passive and ineffectual 20-year-old recruit who lacks the necessary general adequacy, initiative and drive to function effectively in the Navy. It is recommended that he be discharged as temperamentally unsuitable for further training.

Upon re-examination two years later, the summary of the subject's adjustment read in part:

Subject man appears to have made a fair adjustment. He states he has felt well, suffers no neuropathic traits. His mood has been stable, and he has probably been a reliable performer. He has had one incident of nonjudicial punishment which was dismissed with a warning. He manifests no evidence of excessive dependency; his demands are modest; and he is even-tempered. He has re-enlisted for a period of six years partly out of a liking for the Navy and partly because of a lack of opportunity in civilian life. He has intellectual limitations but passed the exam for commissaryman third class. Because of quota limitations, he was not promoted and is now designated as a cook striker, which suits him. He apparently recognizes his limitations, but these do not depress him. His steadiness is probably his greatest strength.

In reviewing the subject's prior service and recruit training adjustment, the examiner stated:

He is a small-town Southern Negro with old-fashioned Southern Negro attitudes. His mother is a domestic and his stepfather is a handyman. Neither of his parents was used to success or expected much—they were not competitors and were not, apparently, aggressive. The subject is a product of this environment and is, himself, passive, compliant and steady, but limited culturally and intellectually.

He has fitted in well with an authoritarian system where the rewards for conformity, obedience and average work output are food, a place to sleep, security, small but regular income, and where modest needs for diversion are met. Subject man got off to a slow start in boot camp, but as he says, "caught on to things gradually" and has done fairly well.

The adjustment of most of the subjects comprising this group were rated by the examiners as being in the average to slightly below average range. These enlistees were able to adjust satisfactorily to shipboard life despite the fact that their performances were not qualitatively much different from those shown in recruit training. In other words, it would appear that training commands sometimes maintain standards which are either higher than those encountered in the fleet or irrelevant to duties in the fleet. For example, difficulties in passing tests, problems in marching and drilling and difficulties in passing inspections on the recruit training level may be quite irrelevant to the degree of competency an enlistee achieves in his occupational specialty aboard ship.

On the other hand, it is possible that some of the subjects comprising this group made satisfactory fleet adjustment, despite their performance inadequacies in recruit training, simply because they were assigned duties such as chipping paint and mess-cooking—tasks frequently viewed as requiring no more than a minimal level of performance effectiveness. In other words, had these enlistees been placed in positions of greater responsibility, perhaps they would not have been able to maintain acceptable fleet adjustments. As one examiner stated, regarding a subject in this group:

Although there are no emotional differences between this enlistee's present and past adjustment, I feel the man has gotten along in the Navy so far because during the first four years the service can support a dependent, somewhat compulsive, low or below average I.Q. person such as the subject. Whether or not this is desirable from the Navy's point of view is another matter.

Subject C

The last hypothesis, about the behavior of the 13 subjects in the third group, postulates that some enlistees experience an acute and unfavorable emotional reaction upon entering recruit training which is inconsistent with their pre-service level of adjustment. In retrospect, these cases would more appropriately have been labeled "situational maladjustment." The enlistees in this group differed from those in the other two groups in that their preservice histories were not markedly pathological. Subject C is a case in point.

While in training, Subject C's adjustment was characterized by very poor performance, difficulty in passing weekly tests, poor motivation and unreliability. He gave a history of disrupted home life, school failure and an extensive juvenile delinquency record. His aptitude board report concluded with the following summary:

Subject C relates in a passive manner and shows many dependency features. He has always had difficulty in relating to authority and peers. He shows little enthusiasm or motivation. His chronic disciplinary behavior promises to continue and he is not considered to be suitable for the naval service. His discharge is recommended.

After two years in the fleet, the phase-one follow-up examination revealed the following:

His adjustment in most respects has been satisfactory. He has been on report five or six times for minor offenses such as being away from his place of duty, etc., but he has had no court martial. . . . He appeared to be a moody, easily annoyed person who often is unhappy. His motivation is adequate. . . . He appeared to have definite schizoid and passive-aggressive personality traits but these are not severe enough to preclude military service.

In the phase-two evaluation, the examiner remarked:

His adjustment is about the same as it was prior to recruit training and better than it was during recruit training. During this interview he indicated that his civilian adjustment was somewhat better than that revealed in the aptitude board report. . . . He claimed he came to the attention of the civil authorities only on a few occasions and apparently there was nothing serious enough to warrant action. . . . His poor performance in boot camp apparently was largely situational and transitory in nature— he has since shown that he is capable of better performance. . . . He apparently exaggerated his defects in relating his civilian adjustment while in boot camp—probably due to the fact that he was dejected and unhappy and wanted to be discharged from the Navy.

The graduation from training camp of a number of men who had been declared unfit by a team of mental health professionals produced a number of interesting anecdotes. For example, one psychiatrist at a Recruit Evaluation Unit (REU) felt so strongly that one recruit should not be graduated that the psychiatrist demanded his objection be recorded in writing. Two years later this same officer received a letter from the former recruit, thanking him for the chance to find himself and to realize potential he did not know he had—and that he was succeeding on active duty and was eligible for promotion!

Constructing the Odds-for-Effectiveness Tables

Given the above findings, Plag and his colleagues concluded that the use of statistical or actuarial data for screening recruits could serve a real need, especially if used in the recruiting process before the individual was sworn in and the Navy had assumed an obligation. Using the simplified criterion of successful enlistment—the sailor performed well enough to be recommended for reenlistment at the end of a 4-year tour of duty—the researchers followed a group of 1,776 male recruits and correlated the level of their service with the following preservice predictors: age (.16); education (.32); number of school grades failed ($-.17$); number of expulsions from school ($-.19$); family stability [divorced parents] (.14); number of arrests ($-.11$); AFQT score [Armed Forces Qualification Test—a short paper-and-pencil test of literacy administered at the induction center] (.22); and length of duty obligation (.16). These variables produced a multiple correlation (R) of .38 ($p < .001$).

In order for these findings to be translated into usable form, the various beta weights assigned to each predictor were computed and translated into tabular form, which would quickly provide the odds that any person with a given combination of predictors would successfully complete enlistment. For political reasons as well as statistical parsimony, the number of predictors was reduced to four: AFQT score, years of school completed, number of expulsions or suspensions, and arrests. Each recruiter was given a simple table to follow in order to determine the odds-for-effectiveness of each applicant. For example, if a recruit scored between 41 and 53 on the AFQT, completed 12 + years of schooling, had 0–1 expulsions or suspensions from school, and had one arrest for an offense other than traffic violations, the odds would be 83 out of 100 that he would successfully complete a 4-year enlistment. In times of surplus applications, a recruiter could arrange them in descending order according to their scores, processing the people at the top of the list until the monthly quota was reached. These individuals would then be given the physical examination; if any were disqualified, the recruiter would then accept the next lower person on the list (Plag & Goffman, 1966a, 1966b, 1968).

A survey of all Navy recruiting offices in 1968 demonstrated the feasibility of obtaining effectiveness scores. On the basis of this survey, it was determined that the selection ratio was favorable enough to have permitted the rejection of as many as 4,500 applicants annually (Plag, 1970). Early in 1969, the odds-for-effectiveness tables were officially adopted as a method of screening at recruiting centers.

Although the author lacks documentation of the financial effects, it is widely believed that the use of these tables saved the Navy several million dollars in the first year of use, and that they have continued to do so. Since the tables permitted more accurate estimates of 4-year attrition rates, the Navy was able to lower the quotas necessary to retain the required number of men on active duty.

Time and social forces tend to change the predictive value of the variables used in the tables in the original research, but in a modified form these tables remain in use in 1987. On the basis of AFQT score, age, and education, all applicants must receive a score of 70 in order to be eligible—that is, have a 70% chance of succeeding. Arrest records and drug use are analyzed based on interview data at the recruiting station and other records. The 70% level is considered nonwaiverable. A recruiting officer may give preference to high school diploma graduates, for example, but only if the 70% level is reached.

Changes in the Screening Process

These research findings resulted in a modification of how recruits were screened at training centers. With the realization that incoming populations would now receive a maximized level of preenlistment screening and that a lot of manpower was being needlessly lost because of the inappropriate use of the psychiatric interview as a predictor, the recruit screening teams shifted to a mental hygiene or preventive medicine format. Instead of screening individuals, the Recruit Evaluation Units (REUs) began to respond to referrals made by company and division commanders or self-referrals. A decision is then made to hospitalize the subject, discharge or return him or her to duty with instructions to the company commander to observe the recruit carefully, and, preferably, make regular reports to the REU. If enough mental health personnel are available, an attempt is made to counsel each recruit referred or to offer brief psychotherapy or group therapy. Line personnel are also asked to encourage such recruits to adapt and successfully graduate from training. However, since the professional staffing levels may fluctuate and the attitude and support of local commanding officers varies, the success of this effort may differ among time frames and training centers.

The magnitude to which this revised method of screening is still statistically superior to those used in the past cannot be decided by examining the usual figures. Not only have there been wide differences in the numbers produced by different training centers, but they have also fluctuated within a given center as the level of training of the professional staff and their numbers change, sometimes on a monthly basis. Individual centers also engaged in the transient use of diagnostic fads. For example, during the same months in 1943–1945, the incidence of psychoneuroses among total discharges at Great Lakes was 24%, compared with 10% at Farragut; the discharge rate for mental deficiency was 40% at San Diego, compared with 20% for Great Lakes and only 2% at Farragut; in the same month Great Lakes was discharging only 2% for psychoneuroses, whereas San Diego discharged 60% in that category (Hunt & Wittson, 1949). Given the large numbers of recruits at each center being drawn from large geographical areas, it hardly seems likely that these differences are diagnostically accurate; they are probably the result of variations in the clinical style or expertise of each professional staff. There is no evidence that the situation is different in 1988.

In addition, local commanders would often place ceilings on psychiatric discharges, sometimes because of their perception of the needs of the Navy and sometimes because of some notion that the nature of these statistics reflected upon them personally. It must also be remembered that the vast majority of the routine statistics gathered are recorded by relatively untrained enlisted personnel, and every experienced researcher is familiar with the fact that sometimes this source of error is huge.

It is fair to say that the process has come a long way since 1900, when psychiatric screening was essentially nonexistent. In 1918, General Pershing sounded the alarm bell when he sent the message that it was vital to the war effort that "urgent efforts be given to eliminate the mentally unfit." Today, the work of Plag and his colleagues has completed the cycle of "Pershing to Plag" and has given the Navy access to state-of-the-art techniques for the recruiting and screening of personnel.

CHAPTER 18

The Marginal Recruit

Since the early days of the 20th century, Navy medical officers have expressed the idea that certain recruits who do not meet the usual standards of mental ability could be enlisted and assigned to menial tasks, such as labor battalions ashore or coal passers aboard ship. This would allow the talented person to be assigned the more demanding jobs and would avoid wasting a bright person on a simple task. In times of critical shortages of manpower this principle has clearly been used, but usually in the guise of lowering the standards rather than enlisting personnel labeled as inferior, thus ensuring that all recruits passed the standard. Since these personnel were not labeled as below standard and were folded into the mainstream of Navy life, it has been difficult to measure the consequences of enlisting substandard personnel.

Marginal Performers in World War II

However, the lowering of standards, especially mental standards, has not been without cost. For example, several groups of sailors with "low intelligence" (IQs about 70 or the 5th percentile) who trained at Newport Training Center during World War II were judged capable of performing in the fleet and were graduated and later compared with a control group. It was found that the low-score group had about six times as many hospitalizations (24% versus 4.4%) and almost four times as many disciplinary actions, usually involving being AWOL or AOL (45% versus 12.2%) (Hunt et al., 1952). Other groups of low IQ men also showed four times the number of discharges for psychiatric, medical, and disciplinary reasons than a control group (17% versus 4%). Further, if they combined low intelligence with some form of psychiatric condition but were still deemed suitable for duty, their discharge rate was five times higher than that of a control group (21% versus 4%) (Hunt et al., 1954). It should be pointed out that about 83% of the low-IQ-only group and about 79% of the low-IQ-plus-psychiatric-symptoms group completed their enlistments; however, it is not known at what level of proficiency they performed.

Marginal Performers in the 1960s

In 1966–1968, another attempt was made to utilize substandard personnel. As part of then-President Johnson's War on Poverty program, the military establishment was required to accept 40,000 such individuals in 1967 and another 100,000 in fiscal year 1968. About 85% of these were mentally substandard, while the remainder fell below physical standards. Each of the services was directed to accept a proportion of its enlistees from the marginal personnel pool. The Navy was required to increase its mentally below-standard group from about 3% to about 15% of the total number enlisted (Plag, Wilkins, & Phelan, 1968).

The below-standard group was defined as falling in Group IV on the AFQT, or scoring between the 10th and 30th percentiles. A group of those who completed recruit training was followed during a 4-year enlistment and compared with a control group consisting of those who scored average, or at the 50th percentile on the AFQT. About 72% of the Group IV population received satisfactory discharges compared with 79% of the average group; about 65% of the Group IVs completed "effective" tours (were recommended for reenlistment), compared with 75% of the average group. There were no significant differences in rates of court-martials or in psychiatric or physical illness (Plag, Goffman, & Phelan, 1967).

The differences in the 1960s studies were not as large as those reported in the World War II studies, but the populations were quite different. The 1940s groups studied by Hunt et al., were of much lower IQ levels—most of them at about the 5th percentile—whereas in the 1960s groups, more than 70% were above the 25th percentile. It would thus appear that Group IV personnel, as a group, can approach, but not equal, the efficacy of an average sailor, and the differences between the groups increase as the mental standard is lowered.

Consequences of Using Marginal Performers

The Navy apparently fared much better than the Army. The Navy was better equipped to distribute more broadly the Group IVs throughout the fleet and minimize the negative consequences of the ineffectives and still receive at least some benefit from the work of those who were effective. The Army apparently did not fully implement its plans to give special training or schooling to this group, and many of them were assigned to the same units and sent to Vietnam, often in support units unloading ships and performing similar work (Colbach, 1985). Not only did this group produce a number of examples of poor performance, but when compared with the general Army population in Vietnam, they were referred ten times as frequently to a mental hygiene unit. They did not differ from other troops in types of diagnoses or severity of illness but were generally referred by their unit commanders for being ineffective or a "problem" (Crowe & Colbach, 1971).

Even though the general statistics concerning Group IV personnel have a positive side, the actual use of these men in the field produced many horror stories. In Vietnam, the low ability of many of them was very evident. When unloading supplies, they often misread labels and mislaid critical supplies. Many of them seemed less able to withstand the stress of combat and were less adept at protecting themselves. Numerous stories were told of individuals who were killed probably because they had not learned their lessons well or were not quick enough to follow complicated (for them) orders in combat. A number of them were dyslexic (that is, could not read well and often could not tell right from left), at least one anecdote relates how a man was instructed to run 200 yards and then turn left, only to turn right—into a mine field. A common complaint to the mental hygiene unit from field commanders was, "Get this guy off my back before he gets us all killed!"

Aboard ship a man with low aptitude would usually be given simple tasks, and many of them could do a job if it were carefully explained to them. However, even though such people were generally as well-meaning and responsible as the average crewman, the complaint was often made that a capable man would have to be used to supervise one who could not be trusted to work alone because of his lack of aptitude.

Marginal Performers With Psychiatric Problems

Attempts to utilize personnel described as substandard because they qualify for a psychiatric label but who are still considered qualified for duty have met with similar results. For example, a study was made of a group of World War II naval recruits judged to be "marginal" because they qualified for a psychiatric label but who were considered capable of rendering some level of military service. During a 3-year follow-up, 22% of them were hospitalized for various reasons, compared with about 4% in a control group, and 34% incurred disciplinary action, compared with only about 12% for the control group (Hunt et al., 1952).

In 1968 it was found that among a group of patients returned to duty from the psychiatric sick list, only 43% subsequently met a 4-year criterion for effective service (Plag, Goffman, & Bowen, 1968).

Those most likely to return and produce an effective tour of enlistment tended to be those with completion of more years of schooling, whose illnesses were acute and nonrecurring, and whose histories were devoid of suicidal tendencies (Plag, Goffman, & Bowen, 1968).

Enuretics

Another marginal group is the enuretics (i.e., bed wetters). In a military situation, especially in the close quarters on shipboard, enuresis creates a morale problem and sanitary problem for the group as well as for the individual.

In a time of comfortable surplus of manpower, the frequent bed wetter is generally not accepted by the Armed Forces. Many recruits conceal evidence of their problem when they enter the service; many of them are discovered during training and discharged as unsuitable for duty. In addition, enuretic recruits are considered to possess a variety of personality and emotional problems that decrease their likelihood of successful service (Ditman & Blinn, 1963). While the success rate of enuretics is generally lower than that of nonenuretics, it has been shown that in the Marine Corps (Harris & Firestone, 1957) and in the Navy (Plag, 1964a), about 70% of them are capable of producing an acceptable tour of duty. Generally, about 700 to 800 men are discharged from recruit training in the Navy each year because of enuresis.

The Practice of Clinical Psychology in the U.S. Navy–Then and Now

Introduction

Clinical psychology is often described as a method of applying the knowledge of psychology to a wide array of human problems and needs; so wide an array, in fact, that one can only guess when the limits of application will be approached—if ever. Furthermore, there are no rules or steadfast guidelines to this process. It is limited only by the vagaries of the game and the imagination of the players.

With this in mind, it can be said that some of the most interesting and imaginative applications of psychological knowledge have been made in the U.S. Navy. Sometimes these applications are rather traditional and routine, but at other times they are unique and innovative and take place in spectacular and adventurous environments. Occasional disagreements with the naval establishment notwithstanding, rarely do Navy clinical psychologists not describe their work as exciting.

Types of Clinical Assignments in the Navy

Among Navy clinicians, there are five broad categories of assignment:

1. Direct clinical service, such as in hospitals, clinics, and training centers.

2. Administration of a psychological service, such as a training program or an alcohol treatment program. This billet may also include some direct service.

3. Administration of a nonpsychological program or unit within the Medical Department; this position could also be held by a nonpsychologist.

4. A clinical psychology billet not assigned to the Medical Department, such as working with the operating forces (e.g., SEALs, the Naval Academy).

5. Cross-assignment to the Research or Aviation Psychology Branches of the Medical Department. The assignment of a clinical psychologist to one of these branches is unusual and normally lasts for only one or two tours of duty, although a few individuals have permanently shifted their specialty designation to one of these groups.

Types and Distribution of Billets for Clinicians

In any given fiscal year, the Navy receives authorization for a finite number of officer billets. Depending upon the needs of the Navy, these billets may be shuffled among the various commands and corps. Thus, for example, when the Line Navy felt a need to provide psychological services to their Sea-Air-Land teams (SEALs), they were able to convert one of their officer billets into one for a clinical psychologist. Sometimes on-site commanders have perceived the need for a psychologist, and they have requested one. In other cases the psychologists themselves saw the need and succeeded in making a case to the command in question—which, of course, placed them in the position of having to produce accordingly. To the author's knowledge, they have done so in every case. The practice of moving personnel according to changing needs is another instance of the Navy tradition of "doing with what you've got."

One outstanding characteristic of Navy clinical psychology is the wide variety of billets one can occupy, not only in the different skills required but in the populations served and in locations all over the world. This section describes some of these activities.

The U.S. Navy has a long and fascinating history. It follows, therefore, that the clinical psychologist frequently operates in a historical context—sometimes being influenced by this history and sometimes contributing to it. Wherever appropriate, the historical background is described. Some of these billets have been established for decades, whereas others have been created in recent years. Still others have been improvised on short notice in response to a sudden need of the Navy and may be terminated once the need has ceased or receives a lower priority.

One of the drawbacks of this system is that many psychologists are assigned to positions that reflect the most pressing need of the moment, and since there are fewer personnel available than there are existing or potential billets, the result is often "robbing Peter to pay Paul." This may produce gaps in the continuity at any one location, and the reader should be aware that on a year-by-year basis, some of the billets described may not be occupied. When psychologists occupy positions that have been vacant prior to their arrival, the lack of continuity often means that they have to create their own job description. As will be seen, this has produced some very imaginative and exciting tours of duty, but ones that sometimes bore little resemblance to the work done by predecessors and successors.

Administration and Management

As one rises in rank in the Navy, it is to be expected that one's opportunities for administrative responsibilities will increase. For example, at this writing (1988) a clinical psychologist, Captain Robert McCullah, is Director of the Career Development Division, which plans and directs career development for each of the several corps of the Medical Department, such as the Medical Corps, Nurse Corps, Dental Corps, Hospital Corps, and so on. Captain Patricia Crigler, one of the first uniformed women clinical psychologists in the MSC, is Head of the Health Promotions Division of the Medical Department, which is responsible for coordinating a variety of health programs.

Clinical psychologists have served as administrators in such locations as the Medical Research Laboratory at the Submarine Base in Groton, Connecticut, and as Executive Officers of medical battalions attached to divisions of the Marine Corps. Several of these officers have received special training at the fiscal and supply school at Bethesda.

It is apparent that Navy clinical psychologists are therefore participating in one of the newest subspecialties in the field of psychology, health care administration. Many of them will go on to a second career after their retirement from the Navy, and it can be predicted that some of them will continue to make valuable contributions as administrators. For example, upon his retirement in 1968 as Chief of the Medical Service Corps, Captain Robert S. Herrmann served for the next 13 years as Assistant Superintendent of the Colorado State Hospital in Pueblo.

Not all psychologists look with favor on a career in management, and the Navy has shown that it can accommodate those who wish to remain in close contact with patient care, research, or teaching. However, management is a career that is becoming increasingly open to both civilian and military psychologists. Surveys among members of the American Psychological Association have shown that each year an increasing number are working as full-time managers. As one writer notes: "Perhaps the best-kept secret in psychology is the extent to which the practice of management has evolved as a truly significant and increasingly expanding professional arena for psychologists to explore'' (Kilburg, 1984, p. 614). In recognition of this fact, the Society of Psychologists in Management was formed, holding its second meeting during the APA convention in 1986.

Clinical psychologists are the largest subgroup of these managers and, when combined with a number of counseling and industrial psychologists, constitute more than half of those APA members reporting themselves as occupying positions primarily in management (Kilburg, 1984).

In 1956 William Hunt questioned the role of the clinical psychologist in management:

> It is a proud, and indeed a very necessary thing to be an administrator in a clinical setting, but it can separate one from the practice of the profession. . . . Let us not rush into administration unless there is something demonstrably suitable in it for one with a training background of a clinical psychologist. It is not enough merely to ask—can the psychologist do it? . . . we must follow it immediately with—should we? (Hunt, 1956, p. 58)

In 1988 the answer would be, ''Yes, Bill, we can—and yes, we are!'' (Whether we should is for the reader to consider.)

Direct Mental Health Services

Hospitals and Clinics

Historically, direct mental health service for naval personnel began with treatment of the insane at the U.S. Government Hospital for the Insane (USGHI) in Washington, DC, as we have seen. Between 1900 and 1946, those psychotic patients who could not be discharged into civilian life or transferred to a state hospital in their home state were usually sent to this facility. Eventually more than 50 percent of these patients were discharged as recovered or improved (Butts, 1910). Treatment techniques generally followed those of civilian practice except for the fact that the population was composed largely of young males. There is every evidence that when psychiatric patients were treated in Navy hospitals, they were dealt with in a humane and respectful fashion, including at the USGHI. Unfortunately, when they were discharged to civilian hospitals or those run by the Veterans Bureau (renamed the Veterans Administration in 1930), they were often sent to abysmally inadequate facilities, including the traditional "snake pits," which characterized most public mental health hospitals until after World War II.

The situation did not change until the postwar years, when the Veterans Administration (VA) was revitalized under the leadership of General Omar Bradley. Federal monies were poured into a program of national mental health reform, with the VA providing much of the early leadership.

Conditions in State Mental Hospitals

The inhumane conditions surrounding the treatment of insane patients were graphically exposed in a book aptly entitled *The Shame of the States*, written by Albert Deutsch in 1948. For example, Deutsch makes the following observations about the conditions at the Philadelphia State Hospital for Mental Diseases in Philadelphia, Pennsylvania, the historical home of American psychiatry:

> Four hundred patients were herded into this barn-like dayroom intended for only 80. . . . Most of the men had to stand all day or sit on the splintery floor. There was no supervised recreation, no occupational therapy. Men in all grades of mental disorder, many of them disturbed or violent, were thrown together indiscriminately. I saw many black eyes and bruises, inflicted either by some patients or by brutal attendants. Only two attendants were on this ward; at least 10 were needed. The hogs in a near-by pigpen were far better fed, in far greater comfort, than these human beings. (Deutsch, 1948, p. 50)

He goes on to describe their sleeping quarters, as follows:

> Hundreds of . . . patients slept in double-deckers under leaking, crumbling ceilings. Many slept (if they could) in crowded basement wards. Many incontinent patients occupied double-deckers. The discomfort to those in the lower beds can be imagined. Bedbugs and cockroaches swarmed about the place. Supply shortages forced large numbers to sleep on case-less pillows, on straw-filled mattresses, sometimes without blankets. (Deutsch, 1948, p. 51)

These conditions in public mental hospitals throughout the nation were more the norm than the exception, and to be admitted to some of them was equivalent to a death sentence. According to Deutsch (1948), the American Psychiatric Association has established a set of minimum standards for mental hospitals, including the number of staff required, professional abilities, nutrition, and proper treatment plans, and in 1948, he claimed, not a single state mental hospital in the United States met, or had ever met, even these minimal standards!

Treatment Techniques Before the 1950s

It must be remembered that treatment of the insane did not include psychotropic drugs until the 1950s, and under the best of conditions the tools available for treatment were quite limited. Dynamic psychotherapy, group therapy, milieu therapy, and behavior therapy did not enter the mental hospital scene until after World War II; occupational therapy does appear to have been in limited use prior to that time. The basic techniques included hypnotic drugs, such as chloral hydrate, hyoscine hydrobromate, and codeine; the frequent use of cold packs (in which the patient is submerged in clothes soaked in cold water); and the continuous bath (see below). However, these techniques were directed more at patient management than treatment. Rest and good diet in a supportive and protected environment, supplemented by the mysterious but often positive effects of the mere passage of time were the primary agents of treatment. Training programs for physicians and staff were sparse or nonexistent throughout the country.

Hospital Care for the Mentally Ill in the Navy

However, it may be said with some pride that the Navy Medical Department treated its psychiatric patients more humanely and with greater care than did civilian public hospitals. A good overview of the Navy program may be gleaned from an outline of a proposed training program for ward personnel published in a 1913 edition of the *Naval Medical Bulletin* (Riker, 1913).

We can not consider our work complete with the construction of a suitable place for the reception of insane patients, as we have not competent nurses to look after them, therefore we must instruct members of the Hospital Corps in the proper care of such cases, and this instruction should form a part of the regular course of teaching.

Primarily, only men of excellent physique and whose reliability is beyond question should be selected for this work. The course of instruction to be followed is outlined below:

The responsibilities of the work are to be explained, pointing out that the patients they will have to care for are not responsible for their words and actions and that any violence on the part of a man nursing such cases, except in self-defense, is not only cowardly but contradictory to the profession they follow. The care of keys and keeping doors locked to prevent the escape of patients is second only to violence, as runaway insane patients may commit suicide, homicide, or die from exposure, so let us begin our course of instruction with—

(1) Violence to the patient, except in self-defense, will not be tolerated, and where a patient is known to be very violent an extra hospital corpsman shall be on hand when the patient's room is entered, in order to assist and prevent undue injury to the patient.

(2) Master keys opening all doors of the psychopathic department shall be carried by hospital corpsmen on duty and are to be firmly attached to the trousers by a heavy key ring and chain; the keys for windows, water and electric light control cabinet shall be kept in the Hospital Corps room; the doors at both ends of the passageway are to be kept locked at all times, also the doors opening into the bathroom, Hospital Corps room, and unoccupied patients' rooms; patients under no circumstances should be allowed to enter the Hospital Corps room, even for a moment, as they are liable to snatch articles that might be used for assault, and, though the culprit may be apprehended immediately, there always remains the struggle to regain possession of the article.

(3) Accurate accounts of all incidents occurring in the ward shall be noted, no matter how slight, including the time meals are served, the amount taken by each patient, when patients are allowed out of their rooms, stating time of unlocking and locking doors, the amount of outdoor exercise taken, bowel movements, baths, medication, comments of patients, and special notes when restraint has been used, including exact length of time.

(4) Report any sudden change in a patient by telephone to the officer of the day; also inform him of any injuries, including slight scratches, as these patients are very prone to infection. Never under any circumstances place a patient in restraint unless this officer is informed. Should

a patient who has been quiet and orderly suddenly become violent, confine him in his room and inform the office of the action.

(5) It is seldom necessary in properly equipped hospitals with well-trained attendants to use restraint jackets, but in the naval service they must be used very frequently, as we travel with our patients on trains or we are compelled to use restraint on board ship; therefore we must include in our course of instruction a description of these jackets and the manner of putting them on. A very simple, as well as effective, jacket can be made of No. 7 Navy canvas, having the body of the jacket extend from the neck to the waist and lace up the back. The sleeves are made without an opening for the hand, and about 2 inches beyond where the tips of the fingers come they are closed entirely and the canvas is extended into a band about 2 yards long and 2-1/2 inches wide. The jacket is slipped on the patient and laced up the back. The arms are then folded. Drawing the long-tail end of the sleeve of the right hand under the left arm, it is carried across the back to the right side, passing between the right arm and chest, then across the front of the right arm, about the middle, and around to the back again, where it is to be tied with its fellow of the opposite side that has been passed in a similar manner but in the opposite direction.

(6) There should be at least 2 hospital corpsmen on duty during the day and 1 at night, with a reserve man prepared to be called upon sleeping in the Hospital Corps room. Under no circumstances should hospital corpsmen on duty leave the ward without being relieved, and requests for medicines or other things are to be telephoned to the main building. The visiting of hospital corpsmen or of other patients should be prohibited, and only near relatives of the patient should be admitted as visitors. The ward must be kept as quiet as possible at all times.

(7) All patients must be given a cleansing bath at least twice a week, and the hospital corpsmen must be present at all times with patients while bathing or in the bathroom. Under no circumstances will the patient be allowed the possession of control water keys. Patients on admission should be stripped, given a bath, placed in bed, and a purge administered. If very destructive, a union suit of canvas made to lace up the back can be used, otherwise he will be given pajamas. The shoes of all patients are to be kept in a closet, and only when patients are taken out for exercise shall they be allowed to wear them. Mess gear entering and returning from the psychopathic ward shall be accounted for and a report made to the chief nurse upon the completion of each meal, whether or not there are any missing pieces.

(8) No drugs or chemicals of any description are to be kept in the psychopathic ward. When medication is ordered, the single dose that is prescribed is to be sent from the main hospital and administered in the presence of the hospital corpsman. Soiled linen is to be returned to the linen room each day and clean linen received in its place. Mattresses are to be covered with rubber sheeting and bedpans or metal chambers to be used in most instances. Patients using the toilet must be closely watched.

(9) As the insane are very prone to masturbation, sodomy, and other sexual perversions, a strict watch must be kept in order that two or more

patients do not have the opportunity of committing these offenses. Patients with filthy habits, such as smearing fecal matter over the floors and walls of their rooms, may be given an enema once or twice daily and watched until the desired effect has been produced. Then remove the bedpan immediately.

(10) All except suicidal patients should be locked in their rooms at night. Suicidal cases are to be left with their doors open and frequent observations of these patients shall be made by the hospital corpsmen on duty.

(11) The temperature of rooms for the treatment of the insane must be kept fairly high, as these patients are much below normal in vitality and are therefore very susceptible to colds, pneumonia, and like diseases.

(12) One of the most valuable assets we have in modern psychotherapy is the continued bath for the treatment of excitements. To give this bath, the tub previously mentioned is filled with water to the overflow point. The patient's body is then smeared with vaseline and he is placed on the canvas sling in the reclining position, the water covering the entire body up to the chin. The bath is continued for several hours; some patients, however, are so much benefited by this treatment that they are allowed to remain in the tub for several days or a week. Greatly excited cases may fight and splash about, but they usually quiet down in a short time and often sleep while under the treatment. Of course, it is necessary to have a hospital corpsman in constant attendance. The temperature of the water should be about 70°F, and it is kept at this temperature by adjusting a constant flow from the water mixer.

In concluding this outline of instruction I might say that persons who are caring for the insane, if interested in their work, soon become able to anticipate the actions of their patients and, from a change of mental attitude, will divine their intentions while they are being formulated. In this way clever attendants are often able to prevent catastrophes. Some of my readers may think the course suggested too elaborate to justify its adoption in the service, but when we review the statistics of the Navy for the preceding year and find that there were about 150 cases of insanity, not including 22 suicides, a fair percentage of which it is reasonable to assume were mentally deranged, they will agree with me that the number is sufficiently large to warrant the expenditure of time and money in order that these unfortunates may be given the same chance of treatment and recovery that the surgical case enjoys. (Riker, 1913, pp. 77–86)

As sparse and unsophisticated as this scenario may appear to the modern reader, it must be said that it still represented the cutting edge of programs for treatment of the insane. Even the emphasis on nonviolence toward the patient and the insistence on good hygiene was in sharp contrast to the disgraceful and inhumane treatment offered in the average public mental hospital of that time.

Naval hospitals did not have separate psychiatric departments, and neurological patients (as they were called) were housed with general medical patients. However, under the workload of men returning from World War I, some hospitals did begin to establish separate wards, such as the U.S. Naval Hospital at New

York (Sheehan, 1920). Throughout the 1920s and 1930s, it was often suggested that the Navy Medical Department should establish separate pavilions for these patients in the form of self-contained units separate from but connected to a naval hospital, but this suggestion did not receive much attention until the advent of World War II (Helgesson, 1943). While liberal use was made of occupational therapists, physical therapists, and social workers (usually provided by the Red Cross), no psychologists were used in naval hospitals until 1943.

The Role of Psychologists in Navy Hospital Care

Disbanded in 1946, uniformed clinical psychologists did not reappear on the Navy hospital scene until the early 1950s, when the Korean buildup occurred. Since that time, of course, they have been regularly stationed at hospitals and other direct-treatment facilities, such as a mental hygiene unit at a training center.

In most naval hospitals, the psychologist's work was confined largely to psychological testing as an adjunct to the diagnostic or treatment activity of the psychiatrist. However, in keeping with the tradition established in World War II, individual psychologists soon established broader working relationships with the medical establishment; as they demonstrated competence, they were involved in individual and group psychotherapy as well as providing diagnostic information on neurological patients and occupational consultations on general medical patients. Research was rewarded but not necessarily encouraged—but several hospital-based psychologists took advantage of the opportunity and published from time to time. Some of these publications were coauthored with internists and pediatricians as well as psychiatrists. Mental health care was offered to dependents only if the workload permitted, but frequently the psychologists would have the choice of working with children and families of servicemen in addition to their other duties. As usual, local conditions and individual relationships as well as the personal preferences of the psychologist determined the scenario in which one worked.

Various Roles of Psychologists in the Navy

For those psychologists assigned to Navy or Marine Corps training centers, the primary task was usually recruit screening. As described in detail earlier, the recruit screening format developed by Hunt et al. during World War II was continued until the late 1960s. Every recruit was given a short personal data questionnaire and a 3- to 5-minute interview, and those not passed were marked for further study or discharge. However, when research showed that screening of equal validity could take place at the recruiting station level by the application of actuarial methods, the Recruit Evaluation Units shifted into a mental hygiene format, and only those recruits referred for cause were examined. This allowed the clinicians to spend more time with individual recruits and permitted a certain amount of counseling and short-term therapy. This not only offered the promise of salvaging those recruits who benefited from the use of crisis intervention, but also it permitted the psychologist to exercise a broader array of skills and to pursue individual interests, such as studying a particular clinical group.

However, direct mental health services have been provided not only by those psychologists assigned to direct service billets. Even when assigned to an operational billet, Navy clinical psychologists usually perform at least a consulting function to other units or individuals. For example, when this author was assigned to a research laboratory, he maintained what amounted to a small part-time clinical practice for the benefit of colleagues and dependents, including consulting with local civilian school authorities concerning children of dependents. This frequently led to formal or informal consultations with local commanders on psychological matters dealing with morale and the proper handling of individual psychological problems with line personnel—enlisted and commissioned. One psychologist assigned to a Marine division in Vietnam was asked to assist the psychological warfare section of the division. Although not specifically trained in that specialty, he was able to make several suggestions that led directly to an increased number of defections among North Vietnamese soldiers.

Psychologists stationed at smaller naval hospitals often find themselves to be the only such professional in an otherwise active naval environment, such as a nearby naval base to which several thousand persons may be assigned. Clinical psychologists may find themselves going aboard ship to offer consultation to a medical officer, giving stress-reduction classes to the crew, advising on morale problems, or advising a sailor away from home on what advice to give his wife on seeking help for a child having school problems. Not infrequently Navy psychologists find themselves in the combined role of clinician, industrial psychologist, personnel psychologist, and social worker.

One psychologist assigned to a marine base hospital found himself consulting with the local Provost Marshal, a person responsible for monitoring the behavior of 30,000 Marines and dependents. In addition to his routine duties, this psychologist soon found himself to be the local authority in such areas as lie detection, the psychology of highway accidents, criminology, the role of psychopathology in criminal behavior, the proper manner in which to resolve marital disputes, and child and spouse abuse! (Fortunately, the problems of drug and alcohol abuse were handled by other colleagues.)

In 1987 hospital billets existed not only in the continental United States but also at several overseas locations, such as Naples, Italy; Rota, Spain; Roosevelt Roads, Puerto Rico; Yokuska, Japan; Okinawa; Hawaii; Guam; and Subic Bay, Philippines.

Emphasis on Short-Term Therapy

When patients are admitted to a naval hospital, the primary consideration is whether they can be returned to active duty within a reasonable amount of time. Among psychiatric patients, this naturally places a premium upon methods of short-term treatment. This may include group therapy, short-term psychotherapy, and a regimen of medication. Usually, if a patient can be returned to duty within 90 days on either restricted or unrestricted status, an attempt is made to do so. If the prognosis extends beyond that time frame, a medical discharge is seriously considered, either directly to civilian status or to a VA hospital.

The Navy psychologist thus has little opportunity to engage in long-term psychotherapy. However, within the mental health field there is disagreement about whether long-term psychotherapy, especially formal psychoanalysis, is a valid form of treatment, whether in or out of the military setting. It is therefore likely that clinical psychologists in the Navy will continue to have only limited opportunities to engage in this form of psychotherapy. On the other hand, the military setting has traditionally provided the Navy psychologist with the opportunity to become expert in the short forms of therapy, such as behavior modification, hypnotherapy, and cognitive therapy, each of which is in the forefront of psychotherapy throughout the mental health field today.

The Issue of Sexuality

The issue of sex has historically been of interest to the field of mental health, but both the Navy and civilian populations have frequently been ambivalent in their sexual attitudes. For example, until the advent of penicillin in the 1940s, it was a court-martial offense to contract syphilis or gonorrhea, in addition to which a person could be discharged without veteran's benefits or medical care. At least until the 1930s, the admission of the practice of masturbation was cause for refusing a person entrance into the Navy. In fact, as described earlier masturbation and excessive sexuality (an undefined term), were considered to be part of the etiology of insanity or symptomatic of insanity. At the turn of the century, these views were not unusual. In psychoanalytic theory, Freud considered excessive masturbation to be the primary cause of hysteria, especially in women (Masson, 1984). Freud (1896/1950) also maintained that masturbation caused neurasthenia, writing:

> Pure neurasthenia . . . which produces a monotonous clinical picture of exhaustion, sense of pressure on the head, flatulent dyspepsia, constipation, spinal paraesthesias, and sexual weakness, admits of only two specific aetiological factors, excessive onanism [i.e., masturbation] and spontaneous emissions. (p. 146)

However, should the reader think that this point of view vanished soon after 1900, one need only examine the first edition of the *Diagnostic and Statistical Manual of Mental Disorders* (DSM-I), published by the American Psychiatric Association in 1952, which states, "Symptoms of psychophysiological, autonomic, and visceral disorders are due to a chronic and exaggerated state of the normal physiological expression of emotion, with the feeling, or subjective part, repressed.'' Among the undesirable effects listed were acne, headaches, hiccoughs, hypertension, upset stomach, and obesity (DSM-I, p. 29). This document was formally accepted by the medical departments of the Armed Forces. However, this thinly disguised reference to the effects of masturbation was not repeated in the second edition of the manual, DSM-II, in 1968.

No doubt because of their history of being isolated at sea for long periods of time, sailors have always been credited by the public with a heightened sense of sexuality. In song and story, the theme of ''A girl in every port'' and ''There Ain't Nothin' Like a Dame'' (from the famous musical *South Pacific*) have been part of American folklore. In actual fact, naval personnel are a cross-section of the general population, and they harbor the same array of sexual attitudes and display the same collection of biases, prejudices, myths, and misinformation. However, they are subject to some unique forces. Naval personnel are often confined to small spaces in close proximity with others, with very little privacy, which strains the ability of some individuals to avoid expressing sexual ideas or acts that their shipmates would find threatening or unacceptable. This produces a variety of sublimations in order to siphon off some of the pressure, such as the overuse of sexual epithets. Heterosexual prowess is not only a frequent topic of conversation, it is often absurdly exaggerated and expressed in humorous fashion, whereas references to homosexual behavior are sometimes hostile and derisive to the point of homophobia.

Attitudes Toward Homosexuality

Homosexuality was considered to be a psychiatric condition until December 1973, when the American Psychiatric Association ''cured'' it by voting to eliminate it from its DSM. In some states it is still a crime punishable by imprisonment. Until 1973, homosexuality was a court-martial offense in the Navy, and long prison terms were not unusual.

Commanding officers have differed in their approach to the issue of homosexuality, depending on their interpretation of existing regulations and, very often, their personal biases. Some would prosecute a person vigorously and insist upon maximum punishment. If the act was not blatant and had not attracted an undue amount of attention, another commander might allow the person to be quietly discharged, considering it to be for the good of the service. On one large base familiar to the author, the commanding officer created a small task force on homosexuality and located it unobtrusively in an unmarked building. When its investigators had gathered overwhelming evidence on a suspect, the individual would be given the choice of a quiet administrative discharge or face certain prosecution and conviction. Needless to say, that particular command was able to deny that a ''homosexual problem'' ever existed within its ranks.

If a homosexual patient who had been admitted to a psychiatric unit had not come to the attention of the legal authorities, it was not an uncommon practice to arrange for a medical discharge under such rubrics as anxiety neurosis—not an inaccurate diagnosis considering the threat under which the person lived. Because homosexual orientation in itself is no longer a court-martial offense in the Navy, gay men and lesbians are now often given an administrative discharge. Nonetheless, homosexual conduct (as opposed to orientation) is still a felony under the Uniform Code of Military Justice, and homosexual persons still encounter harassment at times. Thus, the issue of sexuality and homosexuality in the Armed Forces is far from being resolved.

Traditionally, the courts have given the military wide latitude to conduct its own internal affairs, including regulations that prohibit the enlistment of persons of homosexual orientation and provide for their discharge upon discovery. But in February 1988, the U.S. 9th Circuit Court of Appeals held that the U.S. Army could not discharge individuals who have simply a homosexual orientation but who are not charged with homosexual conduct. It was said that "this would mean (if upheld by higher courts) that while the government has the power to regulate conduct, including homosexual conduct, it does not have the power, without very compelling justification, to exclude or discriminate against people because of their sexual orientation" (Stewart, 1988).

The court ruled that sexual disposition toward one's own gender was analogous to one's race or religious beliefs and was therefore protected against discrimination on the same basis. Since naval regulations are worded similarly to those of the Army, this decision obviously affects both branches. However, on February 26, 1990, the Supreme Court upheld the right of the Defense Department to discharge gay men or lesbians even if there is no evidence of actual homosexual acts (Savage, 1990). Nevertheless, there are numerous other similar cases still pending in the lower courts, so the matter is far from settled. The issue of sexuality in the Armed Forces (and society in general) will probably continue to be very much a gray area and pose thorny problems for military commanders.

Decriminalizing homosexual orientation in the military and most segments of civilian life has produced an interesting clinical phenomenon. Formerly, service personnel could be severely punished if they were found to have homosexual tendencies, even if they did not engage in actual homosexual conduct, so they would often struggle against these impulses, even to the point of successful self-denial. This form of repression would sometimes lead to what was termed "homosexual panic," in which individuals might dissociate and run around aimlessly, physically attacking those who might try to restrain them, attempting to harm themselves, or both. Sometimes such persons would merely fall into a heap, crying and yelling curses at no one in particular. After sedation and a day's rest, they would usually be amnestic for the event. With the threat of punishment or exposure no longer as great, the frequency of these panic states has approached near-zero, and most younger mental health workers have never witnessed this condition.

The Need for Knowledgeable Counseling

In spite of the assumption that we live in an age of sexual enlightenment, the sexual knowledge of the average sailor or officer, like their counterparts in civilian life, is disturbingly low and permeated with an array of prejudices, fears, and misinformation. Large numbers of Navy personnel are not only sexually inexperienced but have little knowledge of the mechanics of procreation, sexually transmitted diseases, or the simplest social skills in interacting with the opposite sex.

Navy clinical psychologists today are clearly faced with the responsibility of having expertise in the field of human sexuality. Not only must they have a working knowledge of the psychodynamics of sexuality in order to treat and diagnose patients, but they must also be prepared to counsel young men and women in the normal conduct of sexual behavior and to provide accurate sex information. The epidemic of AIDS, the most recent threat to the continued health of naval personnel, highlights the importance of this task.

An additional task is the need for the Navy to help personnel cope with episodes of rape and sexual abuse among families. Also, there is an increasing awareness that personnel staffing emergency rooms of naval hospitals, clinics, and military police stations need quick access to the services of a mental health professional in order to help them, in turn, to assist the victims who pass through their doors.

The average psychologist or physician who leaves training with only a superficial knowledge of human sexuality will be especially lacking in those areas needed to give adequate guidance for dealing with both the mundane and sometimes seemingly bizarre aspects of sexual behavior. This presents both a challenge and an opportunity for the clinical psychologist in Navy uniform.

Health Psychology

One of the more recent and perhaps one of the most far-reaching applications of psychology in the Navy is in the field of health psychology. The military created one of the first models for health psychology during World War I, which was based at Walter Reed Hospital. However, beginning in the 1970s, the field has become greatly expanded and formally established as part of professional psychology. Health psychology is a division of the American Psychological Association, with more than 2,700 members (in 1987); it also publishes its own journal. Sometimes subsumed under the broader title of behavioral medicine, health psychology is defined as (Matarazzo, 1980):

> . . . the aggregate of the specific educational, scientific, and professional contributions of the discipline of Psychology to the promotion and maintenance of health, the prevention and treatment of illness, the identification of etiologic and diagnostic correlates of health, illness and related dysfunction, and the analysis and improvement of the health care system and health policy information. (p. 815)

The principles of health psychology have long been practiced in clinical settings, especially in mental health (Weiss, 1982). With the advent of separate departments of psychology in some naval hospitals, this effort is becoming more organized and visible in such fields as internal medicine, neurology, physical medicine and rehabilitation, surgery, pediatrics, and so forth. However, the concepts of health psychology have been carried well beyond the confines of the hospital.

In the Navy, health psychology is organized in the Health Promotions Division. At this writing, it is headed by Patricia Crigler, Captain, MSC, USN. At this time the program has the following subdivisions:

Health information. Information is gathered on a wide variety of health subjects, such as nutrition, stress management, how to avoid back injury, how to manage and cope with sickle-cell traits, and so forth. This information is then disseminated to local commands for further distribution.

The physical readiness test. This is a test of physical fitness that all naval personnel are required to perform. In keeping with this requirement, local commands conduct such activities as regular jogging and calisthenics. Because several senior personnel have precipitously died attempting to meet these standards (as has happened among civilian groups), the program is under constant review and new age-group norms are being considered and empirically evaluated. (Because many psychologists have had training in evaluation research, this is another opportunity to contribute.) Once in place, these new norms may provide important benefits to nonmilitary groups.

Alcohol and drug rehabilitation. As described in the next section, this is an extensive program being conducted throughout the Navy.

Family advocacy. This program deals with child and spouse abuse, rape, and sexual assault. This is a large program that coordinates and monitors individuals in treatment so that they are not transferred to places where treatment is not available, and it ensures that treatment is completed. A central registry is maintained, which at this writing (1988) contains the names of about 11,000 clients. Support is also given to hospital social workers who conduct liaison activities with the families of patients and assist in discharge planning.

Weight control and eating disorders. Under current regulations, individuals face mandatory discharge if they are not able to meet certain height and weight standards. In the past the responsibility of controlling weight was left to the individual. Now, as in the case of alcohol abuse, plans are under way to offer the same kind of clinical and psychological help to those having difficulty maintaining or losing the required weight. It is hoped that the Navy will not discharge good workers simply because they do not look good in a military uniform without having first attempted to correct the problem.

Smoking cessation. As in the case of alcohol and the "happy hour," the Navy is attempting to remove the age-old tradition once heard aboard ship of announcing that "the smoking lamp is lit." As in the civilian sector, the health costs of smoking are tremendous.

Morale, recreation, and welfare. This section coordinates all of the physical facilities in the Medical Department that provide support to the objectives of the Health Promotions Division, such as clubs, bowling alleys, and so forth. Access to good recreational facilities can obviously be important to the morale and operating efficiency of a military unit and helps prevent the manifestation of a variety of health-related conditions.

Alcohol and Drug Abuse—Alcohol in Navy Life

As in civilian life, alcohol and drug abuse is a major problem in the military, including the Navy. Consumption of alcohol has been associated with the sailor's way of life for centuries. Nonmedicinal alcohol was banned from U.S. warships during the administration of Woodrow Wilson, but the image of sailors indulging to the point of inebriation and the display of rowdy conduct while sailors are on liberty or shore leave has remained part of Navy lore. Inexpensive liquor has remained readily available at base stores and at officers' and enlisted clubs. In addition, the almost daily exercise of "happy hours" at every shore base of any size, the frequent and traditional celebration of promotions (otherwise known as "wetting down" parties), holidays, the completion of missions, or, for that matter, any excuse at all served to create an atmosphere in which regular drinking was condoned (Kolb & Gunderson, 1975).

In spite of this, Navy personnel were expected to hold their liquor, and they were disciplined, sometimes severely, for alcohol-related misbehavior. In addition, a medical diagnosis of alcoholism could be used as a reason for separation, sometimes with a less-than-honorable discharge. As a result, many people denied or hid their alcohol abuse and did not seek treatment.

Eventually, the Navy realized the tremendous waste of personnel and other resources involved in the abuse of alcohol. Not only was the health and well-being of numerous individuals affected, but it directly threatened the military mission of the operating forces. One of the earliest documentations of this fact was in the frequency of automobile accidents among the military. During one year of the Korean War (1952), over 4,000 Navy and Marine Corps personnel were admitted to the sick list due to alcohol-related private automobile accidents, which was about the same number of admissions due to enemy action (McGuire, 1954). In essence, the Marine Corps had the equivalent of an entire regiment knocked out of action as a result of these alcohol-related collisions.

Navy Alcoholism Treatment Programs

Today the Navy no longer considers alcohol abuse a disciplinary offense and has established an extensive treatment program in an attempt to salvage personnel with a potential for contributing to the naval mission for the duration of their tenure. A history of alcohol abuse, per se, is no longer the threat it once was to the career of an individual who successfully completes a Navy alcohol rehabilitation program, and promotion boards are forbidden to view such treatment negatively.

In 1987 the Medical Department operated about twenty-two treatment units, all of them located as separate departments at naval hospitals. Under control ,of the line are four alcohol rehabilitation centers, located at Norfolk, Virginia; Jacksonville, Florida; Miramar Air Station, California; and Pearl Harbor, Hawaii. The medical facilities include about 450 beds, as well as outpatient programs. About seven of these departments are headed by clinical psychologists, an equal number are under the direction of psychiatrists, and the remainder are managed by nurses and other allied health personnel. Currently, between 8,000 and 10,000 persons are treated annually in these programs.

In addition, the Navy line also operates short outpatient programs for those cases considered less serious, known as "dry docks" and Alcohol Safety Action Programs (NAVASAP). The latter were established primarily to deal with those convicted of drinking-and-driving offenses, but they also accept other cases of relatively minor severity. (Dry dock programs were replaced by referral to outpatient or NAVASAP programs.)

In 1987 the director of the Medical Department's Alcohol Rehabilitation Branch was a clinical psychologist, Lt. Comdr. Charles D. Hazelhurst; in 1988 he was succeeded by another clinical psychologist, Lt. Comdr. Ralph E. Bally.

The Medical Department's Approach to Treatment

The treatment programs under the Medical Department use the traditional "shotgun" approach developed many years ago at the U.S. Naval Hospital at Long Beach, California, which received considerable media attention because of two famous patients—former First Lady Betty Ford and Billy Carter, brother of the former president. The treatment duration is currently 42 days. Group therapy on a daily basis is usually the backbone of the program, typically consuming 9–10 hours a week. In addition, the patients are exposed to a wide array of speakers, daily AA meetings, films and other educational materials, and lectures on family dynamics and parenting. If possible, the family is introduced to a local Al-Anon group, an AA-type support program for family members of alcoholics. Frequently these activities include local nonmilitary patients. Antabuse, an anti-alcoholism agent, is sometimes used, but no drug therapy is included. The program is entirely educational-cognitive. There is minimal emphasis on one-on-one dynamic-oriented therapy, but the group sessions often work in depth. Any medical problems that arise, including the need for detoxification, are handled by an adjoining or nearby medical facility and are not considered part of the program. All patients are ambulatory and relatively healthy.

The primary treatment persons are Alcohol Counselors, usually enlisted peers or paraprofessional civilians who are themselves recovering alcoholics and graduates of a similar program. Some are given on-the-job training, whereas others have a certificate in alcohol counseling issued by a post-high-school institution. The primary role of the clinical psychologist is to train and supervise these counselors and, if one is in charge, to conduct administrative affairs, promote the organizational health of the program, and to conduct liaison activities with the local military and civilian populations.

The TRISARD Program for Alcohol Treatment

One of the most interesting alcohol treatment programs is the Tri-Service Alcohol Rehabilitation Department (TRISARD) at the U.S. Naval Hospital at Bethesda, Maryland. One reason for establishing this program was to provide treatment for senior personnel located in the Washington, DC area, a group that, in the opinion of some, was thought to contain an alarming number of problem drinkers. However, it also serves all active-duty personnel on a first-come, first-served basis. The head of this department is currently a Navy psychiatrist, although any qualified Navy mental health professional may hold this post. The 60 operating beds are allocated as 25% Army, 25% Air Force, and 50% Navy. Because of its "flagship" status, Bethesda-TRISARD is unusually labor intensive, having approximately twice the staff-to-patient ratio of other naval hospital departments.

Evaluating the Effectiveness of Rehabilitation Programs

Because of their training in scientific psychology, psychologists assigned to an alcohol rehabilitation program will find themselves confronted with an interesting social-scientific phenomenon—namely, addressing the question of whether alcohol rehabilitation programs really work or are really cost-effective. Outcome evaluation research in any field is difficult, but the field of alcoholism rehabilitation is politically and socially very sensitive. A highly vocal and visible segment of the public decries any attempt to statistically measure the effectiveness of these programs or to accept their value on any basis but faith. However, the Navy is in the enviable position of being able to evaluate these programs if it so desires. The treatment population is plentiful, completely under military control, nearly 100% available for treatment follow-up, and capable of generating clear-cut measures of outcome, that is, job and social performance.

A study of the pioneering program at Long Beach Naval Hospital has already produced some provocative findings. A group of 87 patients treated at this facility was matched person-for-person on a number of relevant variables with 87 patients who were admitted to a general medical service of a naval hospital with a primary diagnosis of alcoholism and who received only basic medical treatment, if needed. On a 1-year follow-up, they were categorized as "definitely improved," "slightly improved," and "unimproved." In spite of the fact that the Long Beach group had intensive, multimodal treatment for up to 90 days, there was no significant difference between the results of the two methods of treatment (McGuire, 1981).

The inferences to be drawn from this study are that either (a) a broadly based, intensive program is no more effective than a short-term admission to a general medical service and therefore not as cost-effective, or (b) the patients helped by one program are not the same type of individuals helped by the other, thus the treatment effects are masked.

A recent article in the prestigious journal *Science* (Holden, 1987) that reviewed the issue of whether alcoholism treatment programs are effective concluded there is no evidence that, among other things, long-term treatment is better than short-term treatment programs, or that costly in-patient programs are better than short-term outpatient programs. Research that compares the effectiveness among the different kinds of Navy programs previously described supports the conclusion reached by numerous studies on civilian populations, namely, that the success of any alcohol rehabilitation program depends more on the characteristics of the patient than of the program (Gunderson & Kolb, 1980).

As a trained scientist on the alcohol rehabilitation team, the clinical psychologist in the Navy is in a unique position to make an extremely important contribution. This may be done by conducting studies of treatment effectiveness or keeping our medical and nonmedical colleagues aware of new research findings.

For the clinical psychologist interested in making alcohol rehabilitation a subspecialty, the Navy plans at this writing to recommend the establishment of a subspecialty designator for alcohol and drug abuse and permit such individuals to have back-to-back duty tours in this area. This is another example of the broadening horizons developing for the clinical psychologist in Navy uniform.

Navy Attitude Toward Drug Abuse

Because of the different legal and social attitudes toward drug abuse compared with alcoholism, this program is given a lower priority than alcohol treatment. Most drug-involved persons are summarily discharged, and distributors are usually court-martialed. Between 1974 and 1987, about 30,000 members of the Navy and Marine Corps had been discharged for drug abuse. Currently there is a single drug rehabilitation program, located at Miramar Naval Air Station, California, which processes about 100 cases a year. Most of these persons are eventually administratively discharged, but those who appear to be properly motivated and have responded well to treatment are given an opportunity to remain on active duty. In one study, about 31% were returned to duty, of which 68% met a 6-month criterion of acceptable job performance, resulting in a success rate for the entire treatment population of about 21% (Kolb & Gunderson, 1978). The installation of random urine testing by the Navy and a strict no-nonsense attitude toward drug use has apparently resulted in a dramatic decline in drug use in recent years.

Crisis and Postdisaster Intervention

The reader will recall that one of the most important mental health concepts utilized by the military has been that of early short-term treatment of combat fatigue close to the line. This work has been described under the rubric of proximity, immediacy, and expectancy. However, since the 1960s, there has been a growing awareness that these same principles apply to the victims of non-combat-related trauma, such as ship collisions, aircraft accidents, fires, explosions, tornadoes, floods, and the collapse of occupied structures. These have included such newsworthy disasters as the sinking of the Italian passenger liner *Andrea Doria* (Friedman & Linn, 1957); the collapse of the Hyatt Regency Hotel skywalks, containing hundreds of spectators (Wilkinson, 1983); the mass murder of 14 members of the same family in a small town in Arkansas (Landers, 1988); the near-tragedy at the nuclear plant at Three-Mile Island; numerous crashes of large jetliners, with huge losses of life; and the bombing of the Marine Corps barracks in Lebanon in October of 1983 (Smith, 1983). As described elsewhere, the sinking of the submarine *Thresher* in 1962 also falls into this category.

In the case of military personnel, the survivors, their families and friends, their coworkers, and, in some cases, their superior officers may all suffer post-trauma effects. In varying degrees, disasters appear to cause long-term emotional problems that can result in an increased incidence of medical board hearings (which convene to determine if a person is medically fit to remain on active duty), early discharges from the service, psychiatric hospitalizations, poor work performance, marital discord, and so forth. Also, it was discovered that these symptoms and problems usually do not respond to traditional psychiatric treatment (McCaughey, 1985).

The Collision of the *Belknap* and the *Kennedy*

On the night of November 22, 1975, the U.S. Navy cruiser *Belknap* was on maneuvers in the Mediterranean Sea and, because of navigational errors, collided with an aircraft carrier, the USS *Kennedy*. One man on the USS *Kennedy* was killed, but the ship remained intact and under way. However, the overhanging flight deck of the carrier tore away most of the superstructure of the USS *Belknap*, destroyed the air intakes to the boilers, electrical and communication lines, and fuel lines. As a result, fire broke out everywhere. During the next two and a half hours, fires continued to burn and the ship was in danger of sinking. Of the 336 men aboard the *Belknap*, 6 died of burns that night and another within 2 weeks. In addition, 46 crewmen suffered injuries, burns, or smoke inhalation and had to be evacuated by air. Of these, 5 were expected to have permanent disabilities (Hoiberg & McCaughey, 1981). Eventually, the ship was towed back to the United States, and most of the crew returned to Norfolk, Virginia, the home port of the *Belknap*.

It soon came to the attention of clinicians at the naval hospitals in Philadelphia and Portsmouth (Virginia) who saw the men of the *Belknap* that these sailors were having considerable difficulty during the posttraumatic phase of the accident. Most of the crew members seen by the clinicians realized that they were in distress and that somehow it was related to the collision. These crew members found it difficult to function at work, were uncertain about the cause of their distress, and were usually referred by an observant authority. Their families were also affected, showing various signs of dysfunction, but these signs were not always understandable to them (McCaughey, 1984).

In response to this problem, the psychiatric staff applied its own version of proximity, immediacy, and expectancy, described as brevity, centrality, and simplicity. Brevity meant that initial treatment should last for a short period of time—perhaps only 3 days. Centrality meant that the victims should be treated in one location that should be away from a medical facility in order to prevent identification of the victims as patients. Simplicity meant that the treatment plan should not involve intensive analysis but should rather be supportive and strengthen otherwise healthy defenses.

The Establishment of SPRINT Teams

On the assumption that early and aggressive intervention would result in lower morbidity, a team of mental health professionals trained in these techniques was established in 1976, known as the Special Psychiatric Rapid Intervention Team (SPRINT). The goal was to have in place a team capable of immediate deployment to anywhere in the world in order to lessen the adverse psychological consequences resulting from a catastrophe and enhance the recovery rate of the affected military unit.

The first SPRINT teams, located at three naval hospitals, were staffed by two psychiatrists, a clinical psychologist, a chaplain, a psychiatric nurse, and four corpsmen. An attempt was made to select personnel with operational experience. In addition the use of members having diverse training, age, and occupations was designed to facilitate rapid rapport with the victims. A variety of techniques was used. The psychiatrists would prescribe medication when needed, and all personnel would engage in various forms of group therapy.

How the SPRINT Team Functions

The procedure has been described as follows (McCaughey, 1985):

> Upon arriving at the scene, the team leader and others met with the commanding officer and other senior military personnel. Good liaison was of great importance since command approval allowed others to participate. Explaining the team's purposes, goals, and methods, distinguishing themselves from investigators, requesting confidentiality, and providing for support (telephone, billeting, transportation) were important

issues for the initial meeting. Key personnel at the command such as department heads, and others if they were assigned to the unit such as medical personnel, chaplain, or social worker, were given the same information and their support was requested. Personnel at high risk, such as survivors, those who recovered bodies or traded duty with one of the deceased, or family members of the deceased were identified at these meetings. SPRINT attempted to coordinate and facilitate the use of support groups already in place but not to supplant them. The presence of these groups varied considerably but usually included wives' clubs, local mental health and medical facilities, religious organizations, and casualty care assistance officers. Various means were used to communicate to the community the identity of SPRINT members and their mission. This included articles in the plan of the day and local newspapers or having announcements on television stations.

SPRINT's therapeutic goals were to deal with the immediate crisis and arrange for follow-up where necessary. A variety of techniques were used. Lectures describing what they might expect to experience were given to groups of varying sizes and composition. This teaching approach included such topics as what symptoms and feelings often occur following a tragedy and what would promote (e.g., expression of feelings) or retard (e.g., taking drugs or alcohol or suppressing feelings) resolution. In these deployments group therapy was used extensively; much more frequently than individual therapy. It was very desirable to meet with naturally occurring groups and do it in their natural environment. Examples of these groups are survivors, aircrews, personnel in various maintenance shops, and families. SPRINT members found that actively seeking these meetings was preferable to waiting for people to come to them. This was especially true of high-risk personnel including wives of the deceased, and survivors. While the number of meetings with each group varied from deployment to deployment, three or four times with each group was common. A group that was often unsuspected by themselves of needing help were the commanding and executive officers who by virtue of their positions as leaders might have been viewed as "strong" and unlikely to be affected by the tragedy. They often felt overwhelmed and unable to have support for their emotional needs. The phase involving therapy generally lasted less than two weeks and in several cases involved a memorial service at the end of the intervention. The memorial service symbolically acknowledged past and future shared risks and, in many cases, resolution of the tragedy.

Debriefings with senior officers occurred at the end of the deployment. The goals for these meetings were to critique the intervention and arrange for follow-up psychological care. These debriefings often closely followed a memorial service. At this time SPRINT often perceived that they were no longer needed, which was seen as an indication that resolution was progressing favorably. Upon returning to the hospital SPRINT members met amongst themselves to critique the intervention and suggest improved response techniques.

To date, SPRINT interventions have involved different team leaders working in a variety of extremely different situations, making it difficult to generalize their experiences. The outline presented above was based on what took place during many of the deployments. The following were recurring observations. It was very important to start the intervention as soon as possible because there seemed to be a period of receptivity lasting about 24 to 72 hours after the beginning of the tragedy. Arrival within 12 hours and before bodies were recovered was considered ideal. Following a tragedy, anger was commonly expressed and realistic or not, it was directed at all causes, including lack of training, inanimate objects (a civilian ship in one case), adverse weather, and personnel up and down the chain of command. Another observation was that the loss of the survivors' ship had a special meaning. In two instances where the ship sank, the crew was observed to be affected by the loss of not only shipmates but their places of work, personal belongings, and abode. Their identity, in part fostered over time by the powerful trappings of military life, [was] dramatically and traumatically gone. Salvaging part of the ship as a memorial was found to benefit the survivors.

SPRINT members spent considerable time dealing with survivor guilt, bereavement, and issues about death. As would be expected, survivor guilt also occurred among those who traded duty with one of the deceased or those who had made the watch list or duty rotation [e.g., those who were off duty at the time of the disaster or who worked in an area of the ship that was not affected by it]. A similar problem occurred among some of the wives. These wives felt guilty that their husbands had survived and were concerned about how to deal with the wives of the deceased. This was of considerable consequence since military families typically lived in a close community setting and were used for frequent social contacts. Another observation was the persistent denial by a spouse of her husband's death when the body was not recovered or recognizable. This denial of death occurred several times in spite of convincing evidence that the serviceman had not survived. All of these death-related issues forced many of the people involved in the tragedy to see their own vulnerability to death. A question commonly asked by service members was whether or not they should continue on active duty.

It was apparent that one of the most helpful functions of SPRINT was promoting accurate communication. In the midst of these crises it was observed that speculation, misunderstanding, and rumors tended to make a situation already filled with distress much worse. In one of the deployments it was not clear whether a murder or suicide had taken place, and in others the causes of the ship collisions or aircraft accidents were not understood. Disseminating accurate information about the cause(s) of the tragedy was often one of the beginning steps for resolution. (McCaughey, 1985, pp. 6–7)

Since the SPRINT teams were organized, they have responded to a variety of disasters. As might be expected in a military setting, the turnover of personnel has been routine, which frequently leaves openings for those interested in participating. This offers an opportunity for clinical psychologists (and others) stationed at or near one of these hospitals to participate in a rather unusual application of their mental health skills. This is another example of the varied and exciting role a Navy clinical psychologist can play.

Interestingly enough, the services of the early SPRINT teams were utilized primarily by the U.S. Coast Guard; no formal requests for assistance were received from the Navy. As so often happens in the military, the originators of the SPRINT concept, most of whom were stationed at the Portsmouth Naval Hospital, were eventually transferred to other duty stations, and the original interest and enthusiasm generated by this group waned. By early 1987, SPRINT teams existed primarily as organizations on paper.

The *Stark* and *Iowa* Disasters

In the wake of the *Stark* and *Iowa* disasters, however, the SPRINT concept was revived. On May 19, 1987, the frigate USS *Stark*, on duty in the Persian Gulf, was struck by two Exocet missiles, and 37 men were killed. Within 10 hours, a SPRINT team from the U.S. Naval Hospital at Portsmouth contacted and offered their help to the authorities at the Mayport (Florida) Naval Base, the home port of the *Stark*. They served as consultants to the local Casualty Assistance Calls Officers (CACOs) in helping them assist the families and dependents of the men from the *Stark* and in identifying workers who were having problems coping with the disaster themselves.

As a result of this experience, the Family Service Center and the CACOs at Mayport have intensified their efforts to be ready for a similar mishap. As the director of the center stated, "The lesson we learned from the *Stark* is that a system is in place to provide the support and training needed, and the system in fact works" (Adde, 1989a).

When an explosion aboard the battleship USS *Iowa* on April 19, 1989, took the lives of 47 sailors, a SPRINT team from Portsmouth Naval Hospital was aboard within 24 hours. At Norfolk Naval Base, *Iowa*'s home port, other team members made their services available almost immediately to the base's medical staff, chaplains, family service center counselors, and casualty assistance coordinators who, in turn, were providing assistance to friends and families of the ship's crew (Adde, 1989b).

Therefore, as of this writing (1988) it appears that the concept of SPRINT is firmly established in the Navy. Unfortunately, it has yet to be as well recognized in the other branches of the military, but the outlook is encouraging. For example, the U.S. Army suffered a disaster on December 12, 1985, when 248 soldiers of the 101st Airborne Division were killed when their transport plane crashed at Gander, Newfoundland. In December 1987, the Walter Reed Research Institute reportedly published a study of how the Army responded to the consequences of the disaster and made a number of specific recommendations very similar to those now in effect in the Navy's SPRINT program. However, it has also been reported that nothing from that study has to date (1989) found its way into the Army's regulation manuals (Adde, 1989b).

Another positive note is that a group on the staff of the Uniformed Services

University for the Health Sciences has made field observations of the responses to the Gander and *Iowa* incidents. Presumably, they will provide a resource for training our future military physicians in this important area.

As the idea of postdisaster intervention continues to gain recognition in the civilian sector and among the other services, Navy psychologists can once again point to the fact that they were among the pioneers of an important concept.

Duty With the Operating Forces–Not Just in *the Navy,* But of *the Navy*

The U.S. Naval Academy

The muscle and sinew of the United States Navy might be found at sea. And the nation's naval brains on the Potomac's right bank. . . . But a search for the soul of the Navy must begin by the River Severn, on Chesapeake Bay, in the town of Annapolis.

So wrote one historian of the role of the U.S. Naval Academy at Annapolis (DeCamp, 1974, p. 4). That it should be described with such reverence reflects the central role the Academy plays in shaping the character and conduct of the officers of the Navy. It deserves mention that psychologists have played a part in the development of the institution, at least in modern times.

The Founding and History of the Academy

The U.S. Military Academy at West Point, NY, the first of the four service academies to be founded, served as the model for the others: the U.S. Naval Academy, the U.S. Coast Guard Academy at New London, Connecticut, and the U.S. Air Force Academy at Colorado Springs, Colorado. In 1797 George Washington strongly advocated establishing a military academy, and Congress finally approved the idea in 1802. The idea of a naval academy, however, did not meet with similar approval. It was defeated by several sessions of Congress because of disagreement between the pronaval members from seaboard states and members of the inland states (Lovell, 1979, p. 28).

However, the Naval Academy was established in 1845 by a form of political sleight of hand. In that year George Bancroft, the celebrated historian after whom the famous Bancroft Hall at Annapolis was later named, was appointed Secretary of the Navy. When Congress was out of session, he arranged with Secretary of War William L. Marcy for Fort Severn at Annapolis to be used as a naval school. President Polk approved, and in October the Naval School was opened—to be renamed the United States Naval Academy in 1850. Prior to this, midshipmen had been trained at sea by apprenticeship. Recognizing the fait accompli, Congress voted money for its first years, but the fledgling school remained vulnerable to its critics.

Two events motivated support and assured its permanence. First, in 1842, before the Academy was founded, acting midshipman Philip Spencer, son of the Secretary of War, had been hanged for mutiny aboard the USS *Somers*, along with two enlisted men. This led to highly publicized pressures on Congress to change the conditions that could have allowed such an incident, especially the practice of permitting political influence to force upon the Navy unqualified and "unprincipled young rascals," as indeed was the case with young Spencer (Banning, 1963, pp. 81-83). Second, the industrial revolution was making sailing ships obsolete. In 1837 the Navy had launched its first steam-driven vessel, the *Fulton*, and funds had been appropriated for three additional steamships (Lovell, 1979, p. 28). Bancroft's argument for a school that would produce officers who had good technical knowledge and who were of high character quickly became very persuasive, and financial support continued for a national institution that Congress had played no formal part in creating.

Throughout this volume there have been frequent references to the Navy tradition of "getting the job done with whatever is at hand." Judging from the circumstances under which the Academy was founded, this tradition seems to have started early indeed.

The Naval Academy continued to grow and develop along traditional lines in the following decades. Many criticized the fact that it was more of a trade school than an academic institution, and that instead of educating, its primary goal was to develop character, patriotism, and above all loyalty to the Navy and to each other. Because the majority of the Academy's faculty was drawn from its own graduates after tours with the fleet, it also tended to create a form of intellectual inbreeding, which produced a rather insular, closed-club mentality that resisted change, either internally or from without. Even in World War II, all of the best commands were reserved for Academy graduates, especially on battleships, which were then seen as a favored route to flag rank (i.e., Admiral). These "ring-knockers,"[10] as they were called by their critics, looked down on reservists, whom they referred to as the "feather merchant[11] Navy," and with hostility and suspicion on members of the other services.

The Naval Academy's Curriculum

Prior to World War II, the Naval Academy was not held in high regard in academic circles, especially when compared with the standards used by prestigious civilian colleges. As described by one historian (Spector, 1985):

[10]So-called because of the way they were said to flaunt their graduation rings by rapping them on a desk or table as a way of drawing attention and currying favor with each other.

[11]A slang term for loafers or slackers—those who avoid positions requiring responsibility or effort.

The naval academy . . . was parochial, spartan, intellectually sterile, and pedagogically backward. In 1923 the Board of Visitors to the Naval Academy had observed that a "sound symmetrical general education is lacking." The academy's curriculum was "incapable of supplying even the fundamental training in the physical sciences," while the humanities were thrown together in a single academic department which the midshipmen eloquently referred to as "bull." Another Board of Visitors' report called attention to the "unspoken willingness" of the academy's staff "to use subjects of instruction as a means of discipline."

It seems unlikely that the leaders of the naval academy were greatly troubled by this type of criticism. The academy was intended not so much to stimulate the intellect as to mold character. "Character is the big thing," declared Admiral Thomas C. Hart; "it is presence and personality and looks, it is qualities of mind, but particularly . . . guts, all of that is in it." Successful midshipmen were expected to develop qualities of reliability, leadership, integrity, good judgment, loyalty to the service and to each other. It was this last that was especially stressed. Midshipmen left Annapolis with a lively regard for the reputation and standing of their service—and even more concern for their own reputation *in* the service. (p. 18)

Prior to World War II, the curriculum was closely prescribed, limited primarily to engineering and other technical and military subjects directly related to shipboard life. In the postwar years, the Military Academy took the lead in introducing the behavioral sciences and modern techniques of leadership into the curriculum. In 1946, the Military Academy created an Office of Military Psychology and Leadership and courses in applied psychology. This new program was headed by an Army officer, but its associate director was a civilian PhD with 25 years of experience in the field (DeCamp, 1974, p. 49). Courses were added in English and foreign languages, and the faculty was gradually upgraded toward the normative level of the PhD. In spite of some early resistance to changing the trade school model, the Military Academy continued to expand in the social sciences and the humanities. Today it has a staff of approximately 30 PhD psychologists, a separate department of behavioral sciences, and a well-staffed counseling center modeled after the modern university center. In addition it has maintained a mental hygiene unit under the Medical Department.

The Naval Academy did not follow the Army example; it carried into the early postwar years the trade school emphasis on teaching practical, applied military skills. West Point defined its goal as that of laying an educational foundation upon which an officer could build throughout his entire career; it was preparing future generals, not just second lieutenants. In contrast, at Annapolis the mission was that of producing immediately available junior officers (De-Camp, 1974, p. 54).

Like the other services' institutions, the Naval Academy is caught in an apparent contradiction of purpose. It celebrates cultural achievement and the

Table 6

Comparison of Intelligence Test Scores with Year-End Academic Standing, Freshmen, US Naval Academy, 1922–1923

Test groupings		Number in group	Year-end standings	
Category	Score		Number failed	Percentage failed
A	95–100	132	3	2.3
B	90–95	159	14	8.8
C	85–90	162	20	12.3
D	80–85	124	17	13.7
E	75–80	78	14	17.9
F	Below 75	76	15	19.7

Note. Several minor errors were found in the percentages shown in the original table. The figures shown here (Column 5) have been corrected. Adapted from "The Value of Psychometric Tests in the Navy," 1924, *Naval Medical Bulletin, 20,* pp. 213–214.

civilized pursuit of knowledge, but it also trains its sons and daughters for war. Since World War II, it has made and continues to make efforts to overhaul its curriculum more in the image of the modern university, yet it still remains a bastion of military stringency and discipline, and the home of seemingly eternal traditions. This issue was nicely defined in 1970 by Academy Superintendent Vice Admiral James Calvert when he likened the Academy's task to striking a delicate but dynamic balance between culture and might, between intellect and finely honed brawn; between, as he put it, Athens and Sparta (DeCamp, 1974, p. 5). (Athens was the intellectual capital of ancient Greece, taking its name from Athena, Goddess of Wisdom, whereas Sparta, another ancient Greek city-state, was famed for its tradition of rigorous military training of its citizens.)

Screening Efforts at the Academy

Perhaps the earliest exposure of the Naval Academy to clinical psychology was in 1922. The reader will recall that prior to this date, a cadre of Navy medical officers had made efforts to adapt the Binet-Simon tests to the screening of naval recruits. One of them, A. W. Stearns, MC, USNR, had developed his own version and visited Annapolis to demonstrate its applicability to midshipmen. The test was administered to the fourth-year class (freshmen) during the academic year 1922-23, and the results were compared with class standing at the end of the academic year. Scores were grouped into six categories (an arbitrary measure based on face validity was used rather than units under the normal curve), as shown in Table 6 ("The Value," 1924):

Note that the scores followed a regular progression and that a significant number of students fell into every category, including the lowest. Today it is doubtful if midshipmen are admitted who fall into any but the higher categories on an IQ test. However, these results were not considered strong enough at the time to justify use of the IQ as a requirement for admission. The Academy did experiment with the Otis Self-Administering (IQ) Test in the early 1930s (Rooks, 1935), but its use was abandoned because the tests based on academic performance in specific subjects such as Mathematics, Science, English, and Foreign Languages were thought to be better predictors of success with the Academy's rather specialized curriculum than IQ tests were. It was also thought that tests in specific subjects measured many of the abilities measured by the standard IQ test. While these conclusions were based on judgment rather than objective data, subsequent research has justified this approach. Civilian colleges today use IQ scores to identify students' academic ability, and, for those who have good potential despite poor performance or inadequate secondary school preparation, a flexible schedule of remedial courses is possible. However, in view of its rigid, lockstep curriculum and the fact that it cannot provide remedial courses, the Naval Academy continues to rely on tests in specific subjects to predict performance.

The Stearns-Eisenhower Report

Numerous studies have been made of the four academies since World War II, one of which was the Stearns-Eisenhower Committee Report of 1950. Robert Stearns was then president of the University of Colorado, and former general Dwight Eisenhower was president of Columbia University. This Committee was divided into a series of panels, each of which made a separate report; these were then combined in the final report. The committee made several recommendations designed to reduce the isolation of academies from the civilian academic community, one of which states (Stearns et al., 1950):

> There should be appointed to each Academy a psychiatrist familiar with the problems of young men, and a clinical psychologist, both of whom may have some teaching duties but whose principal efforts should be in the field of study and counseling of individual cases. If these are apt men, it will shortly be apparent that more staff of this type is needed. The importance of the attitudes and thinking of the individual, especially when he is being trained to lead others, cannot be overemphasized. . . . As a corollary to the above, courses in basic psychology should be given. In later years these could well turn out to be among the most important courses of the curriculum in view of the professional careers to be followed in the Services. It is recommended that the Department of Psychology should be organized on a par with other academic divisions. (p. 71)

The Stearns-Eisenhower group also recommended that:

> The time allotted to Psychology, Humanities, and Social Studies at all service academies be gradually increased to about one-quarter to one-

third of the total semester hours in the four year academy curriculum. (p. 58)

The First Mental Health Team

Since the Navy Medical Department at that time controlled the assignment of its own personnel, it apparently seized upon the opportunity offered by the Stearns-Eisenhower report and quickly assigned two men to the Academy.

The first mental health team consisted of Dr. George D. Wright, a psychiatrist from the Chicago area, and a psychologist, Dr. John J. Conger, then an Assistant Professor at the University of Indiana. Conger, who later became Dean of the School of Medicine and Vice President for Medical Affairs at the University of Colorado, and also served a term as president of the American Psychological Association, was an object of the previously described "great recall" of the Korean War. Like others, he was offered a stateside billet if he "volunteered" or an overseas billet if he were recalled involuntarily. It was related to the author that Conger replied, "I hear you loud and clear—I hereby volunteer."

Arriving at the Naval Academy in 1950, Conger and Wright were greeted by the Superintendent with surprise—he had not been informed they were coming. He expressed the opinion that mental health professionals were not needed at the Academy—an attitude that at varying levels of intensity still exists today. Nevertheless, the two men soon found themselves very much in demand, not only by the Medical Department but also by the midshipmen, who in gradually increasing numbers took advantage of the opportunity to discuss in confidence the many problems of adjusting not only to the school and the Navy, but also the usual travails commonly associated with their age group. After a few episodes of helping the administration resolve particularly awkward behavior problems, Conger and Wright also found their services much in demand by the Commandant of Midshipmen and the Superintendent, so much so that the latter two attempted to have Conger transferred from the medical to the executive department. This led to a tug-of-war with BuMed that was finally resolved by having Conger assigned to both groups. Conger eventually sat on the Midshipman Aptitude Board and participated in the teaching of the Second Class course in Leadership.

Conger's lectures on leadership did not follow the official manual for the course. As befitting a college professor, he based his presentations upon data from current textbooks and research findings in the fields of social and clinical psychology, including the large amount of research emanating from World War II. This frequently led to some confusion among his less flexible students, who found it difficult to reconcile his lectures with the official manual. In an attempt to learn the official position on teaching leadership, Conger traveled to Washington, but he discovered that no one person existed as an authority on the subject. In discussing the problem with a vice admiral who had an interest in the subject, he was told, "Why don't you just keep on doing what you're doing?"

Conger reports that the next thing he knew, people were coming from the Navy Department to learn from *him* the official policy on leadership! As one visitor said to him, "You must know—you're teaching it at Mecca!" As discussed below, this small beginning of inserting the behavioral sciences into the curriculum continued and today is still in progress.

Curriculum Recommendations

One of the Stearns-Eisenhower panels summarized its overview of the curriculum in the following (Stearns et al., 1950):

> In conclusion, your panel wishes to state its strong impression that in many ways the Service Academies as educational institutions are clearly superior to most civilian colleges. The reasons for the superiority lie primarily in the fact that the Service Academies know what they want to do—they have clearly defined their mission—something that most liberal arts colleges have failed to do. The result is obvious in the product. We have talked, both at West Point and Annapolis, with a considerable number of students and have invariably found them courteous and frank. Furthermore a difference is to be noted between upper and lower classmen that is by no means entirely the result of age and experience. The upper classmen bear themselves with dignity, appear to be well informed and are extremely proud of their profession and loyal to their institutions. The Service Academies have left their stamp on these men and it is a good stamp.
>
> At the same time, your panel cannot escape the conviction that the mission of the Service Academies has been somewhat too narrowly defined. On the intellectual side this mission appears to be to impart to each cadet or midshipman a minimum amount of information as efficiently as possible. Assignments are short, frequent and tend to be uniform among students. While a critical approach is not wholly avoided, the accent is on the positive. Teaching methods and the selection of teachers is often not such as to stimulate original inquiry either among teachers or students.
>
> Up to a point this is probably necessary and desirable. Skepticism frequently breeds indecision and to turn out a man beset by doubts is hardly the proper objective of Service Academy training. On the other hand it seems pretty clear that, while intellectual interest is stimulated and encouraged in academy classes, little opportunity is provided for developing such interest outside the classroom. There is simply no time for the intensive cultivation of special studies in which students have demonstrated their competence at either academy and the requirements of the academies do not encourage such activity. This condition seems to the panel to be wrong. (p. 61)

The Psychologists' Role Continues

In 1952 Conger was relieved by Allen E. McMichael, who carried on the schedule of counseling, teaching in the leadership course, and assisting the executive branch with specific case problems. He experienced the low acceptance level the line usually directed toward most Medical Department officers; in his

153

case, however, it was tempered by his World War II combat record and his recent experience in the combat zones of Korea, the latter being of especial importance to the Marine officers on campus. Becoming a member of the Regular Navy also spared him from the distance usually shown to Reserve Officers. McMichael was followed by a two-man team, John Laudenslager (now Captain, MSC, USNR, Retired) and Michael Connery (now Captain, MSC, USN, Retired), both World War II Navy veterans.

During this period the creation of a counseling center was recommended, but it was rejected on the grounds that it would weaken the leadership role of the Company Officers, who traditionally bore the responsibility of the welfare of individual midshipmen. (However, judging from a quasi-documentary novel written by a former Secretary of the Navy, James Webb [Webb, 1981], these same company officers were more often the source of rather than the solution to a student's problems). Participation in the leadership course was expanded, and the cumulative contributions of these psychologists were reflected in a rewriting of the leadership manual. Prior to this, the course had been designed to assist in providing leadership under shipboard conditions and the text was entitled *A Division Officer's Guide*. The new manual, entitled simply *Leadership*, barely acknowledged that it drew heavily on the behavioral sciences, and no author was noted—thus effectively precluding official recognition of the contributions to the curriculum made by these clinical psychologists.

Although they had firmly placed a foot in the door, psychologists at the Academy remained for many years restricted to their role as members of the Medical Department, with additional duties to the Executive Department.

A civilian academic dean was appointed in 1963, but change from the model of Sparta toward the image of Athens came slowly and in small increments. A succession of secretaries of the Navy, Congressional committees, representative groups of the civilian university community, and influential individuals exerted great pressure on the Naval Academy to make numerous changes: more civilian faculty, preferably at the PhD level; more academic freedom for the faculty; limiting the emphasis on naval professionalism to the summer sea cruises; less emphasis upon plebe hazing, athletics, and other traditional activities that detracted from academic pursuits; and a curriculum that included more electives, liberal arts, and the humanities. In addition to graduating a professional naval officer, the push was to grant a liberal arts degree comparable or superior to that of any civilian college.

In spite of these efforts, in the 1960s a move was made to again shift toward the Sparta model. Then-Superintendent Rear Admiral Draper Kauffman felt that the pendulum had swung too far toward the role of academics and maintained that the time had come ''for a re-emphasis on the production of a very good, immediately employable junior officer'' (Lovell, 1979, p. 173). Under his tenure the number of civilian faculty was reduced significantly.

The Present Situation of the Naval Academy

Although the rate of change is slow when compared with that at the Military Academy and the Air Force Academy, change has taken place at the Naval Academy. Until 1986, all of the psychologists assigned to the Academy were collectively responsible for mental health work, teaching, counseling the midshipmen and battalion officers, and serving the Superintendent and the Commandant in various ad hoc assignments. Now the different functions of the psychologists have been separated into appropriate groups. A mental hygiene group still functions under the Medical Department, but there is also a separate counseling center with three full-time PhDs assigned. The remaining psychologists are assigned to an academic department.

The latter two groups are nonmedical billets and represent a significant expansion of the role of psychologists beyond the traditional one of "assistant psychiatrist.'' Of interest is the fact that individual psychologists may transfer among these three groups if it is mutually agreeable, thus providing an opportunity for a broader experience while at Annapolis. Unlike the past, upper classmen may now leave the campus regularly, and many of them go to local drinking establishments. As might be expected, when this age group is first exposed to alcohol, a number of problems occur—some of them episodic, some more chronic and serious. One clinical psychologist is assigned full time to alcohol treatment, serving the local naval population as well as the midshipmen.

The Naval Academy may now be said to be comparable to a civilian 4-year college. There are 18 majors and a number of minors, most of them in engineering, mathematics, and other "hard'' sciences, but they also include majors in English, history, political science, economics, physics, chemistry, and foreign languages.

However, courses in leadership are considered the most important teaching responsibility of the psychologists, and in the absence of a separate academic department, the psychology faculty is assigned to the less prestigious Department of Leadership and Law. There are single courses in general psychology, social psychology, and personality theory, but in 1988 these were only electives. There are no courses in abnormal psychology, sociology, or anthropology, and in 1988 it was still possible for a midshipman to graduate without a single psychology course that a civilian university would accept for credit as a required course. However, now that the different functions have been formally identified—teaching, counseling, alcohol abuse, and mental hygiene—it would appear that the stage is set for psychologists to further demonstrate what they can do to ensure a growing role in the future of the Naval Academy—be it Athens or Sparta.

The Fleet Marine Forces

World War I—Treatment Near the Front

During World War I, the incidence of psychoses in the military was about equal to that of the civilian population, but the number of cases of so-called psychoneuroses among the troops was extremely high. The popular term used for these cases was "shell shock" or "war neuroses." Both the French and the Germans quickly realized that psychiatric casualties were best treated near the front instead of being sent back to base hospitals. By early 1915, both sides had established special treatment centers near the front. Only those who did not respond to treatment within a week or two were sent further to the rear to field hospitals; those of this group who did not respond or were obviously psychotic were sent to a base hospital (Miller, 1943, pp. 164–165).

Early in their involvement in World War I, the Americans also recognized the need for early treatment near the front and followed the French example (Bailey et al., 1929, p. 283). Prior to this time, the British evacuated all of their neurotic patients to England, but by the end of 1916 they realized that the results were very disappointing. The tendency of patients to fixate their symptoms into a pattern of chronicity became obvious, and many of them were discharged and pensioned, the latter being of such magnitude as to become an item of considerable fiscal concern. The British then followed the example of the Germans and the French. At that time, cases were sorted into five classifications:

1. A direct anxiety or fear state characterized by generalized shaking, nervousness, jumpiness, and sometimes dizziness and headache.
2. A type in which mental confusion or stuporous phenomena formed the central feature. These conditions were generally of short duration and were looked upon as more intense and severe instances of the first type.
3. Cases in which conversion symptoms, such as mutism and paralysis, were the most important elements. These were similar to the hysterical manifestations found in civilians.
4. Conditions in which amnesia or a fugue state constituted the main phenomenon.
5. Combined types of cases in which a war neurosis developed in conjunction with an organic disorder or with a previous neurosis (Miller, 1943, p. 120).

By far the largest group was Type 1, which composed about 70% of the total. Type 3 made up 20% of the total, with the other three groups accounting for the remaining 10%. Today the group with the highest potential for rapid return to combat is usually placed under the single label of "combat fatigue" or "battle fatigue" (BF).

The primary dynamic operating in a majority of cases was a man's need to handle his feeling of guilt for letting down his comrades, as well as his pride and identification with his unit. To evacuate all of these people to the rear also had a demoralizing effect on those still fighting, who often viewed a psychological casualty as a coward or slacker. To justify his evacuation and removal from the war zone, a man was motivated to retain his symptoms—sometimes for months and years until they evolved into a state of chronicity that was highly resistant to treatment.

Basically, these men fell into three groups: (a) those who were essentially in good mental health but developed transient symptoms under the stress of combat or simply became physically and mentally exhausted, (b) those who were in a relatively fragile state of adjustment prior to combat but who had made an adequate or even a highly successful adjustment to precombat life, and (c) those who possessed a preexisting condition that was exacerbated by combat. Early treatment near the front was of greatest benefit to the first group and, to a lesser extent, some of those in the second group. It is doubtful if very many of the third group ever returned to combat.

By the end of the war, both the Germans and the Allies were in agreement on the general principle of early treatment, preferably "within the sound of artillery," but there were interesting differences. At each treatment unit, whether at the front, at a field hospital several miles to the rear, or a base hospital still in the theater of war, the exact form of treatment depended upon the personality and training of the medical officer in charge. In some locations the treatment was "kind but firm," and in others it was more firm than kind.

World War I—The French Method of Treatment

The latter description was more often true of the front line units of the French Army. As Salmon, an American Army psychiatrist, described it (Bailey et al., 1929):

> The method of treatment and management varies with the class of cases. The true commotionne [suffering from a concussion or shell shock] is treated with all sympathy and kindness. He is kept in bed until he feels able to get up, which is generally within a week, and is then treated as a convalescent until he leaves, which is ordinarily within two or three weeks. Quite a different course is taken toward the emotionne [neurotic], or toward the commotionne who shows signs of developing neurotic symptoms. Such a patient is given to understand at once that such symptoms as trembling, failure to move a limb or portion thereof, deaf mutism, etc., are not symptoms of disease but rather failure in will, a defect in character, that persistence in the demonstration will cause the man to be regarded as a malingerer, which will eventuate in his punishment, perhaps by court-martial. Two forms of punishment are available to the neurologist at the center itself. One of these is the threat that the "permission" or leave, to which every French soldier is entitled after discharge from the hospital, will be taken away from him if he persists in functional symptoms. He will not be allowed to go home, he is told, but will be

returned directly to the front. The other form of punishment is solitary confinement. The soldier presenting hysterical symptoms is put in a room by himself, locked in, and is not permitted to read, write, or smoke. He is told that the trouble with him is in his will and that the best way to recover the will is by silently reflecting in the dark. In addition to these means of combating the outbreak of hysterical symptoms, electricity with persuasion is used or the rougher quick method of suddenly turning on strong electric currents in the region of the part showing signs of defaulting function. By these various measures the French maintain that it is not necessary to send many functional cases back to the interior. Certain cases of true commotionne who do not recover in the army centers are sent to the interior for further treatment or convalescence. All organic cases are evacuated to the interior as rapidly as possible. (p. 295)

There was no prescribed method of treatment for these cases, and methods varied among physicians, including the use of punishment in the form of electric shock therapy (known as the Faradic Brush), solitary confinement, or modified psychoanalysis. However, the modal method of treatment appeared to be the initial use of hypnotics and sedatives if required, rest and quiet, a good diet, an accepting and encouraging attitude on the part of the treatment staff without any suggestion that the man would not return to duty, and sometimes an educational program in which the symptoms were explained and assurance given that they would recover. In the majority of cases, the symptoms disappeared with this type of treatment (Miller, 1943, p. 29).

Psychological casualties varied from 20% to 50% of those in combat, depending upon the intensity and length of engagement with the enemy. However, before the British reversed their policy of evacuating all psychiatric casualties to England, the vast majority of them never returned to any form of duty and most of them became pensioners. Of those treated at advanced posts, about 65% of the British and Americans returned to combat and, perhaps because of their stricter attitude, about 90% of the French returned to the front line. (It is not known if the French had a higher recidivism rate.) From the treatment centers further removed from the front line, about 75% of the British returned to duty and about 55% of the Americans. However, not all of these latter cases returned to actual combat (Miller, 1943, p. 31).

Elements of the U.S. Second Marine Division served in France, supported by naval medical personnel who manned aid stations near the front line, sometimes coming under enemy fire. They operated primarily as first aid stations and as a means of processing patients to the rear to army field hospitals (Strott, 1947). Therefore, the history of treating psychiatric casualties in the U.S. Army overseas presumably applies also to members of the Marine Corps. There appears to be no record of Navy psychiatrists' serving with the Marines in France.

During the early days of World War I, psychiatric treatment of the British and French forces was minimal but gradually took on increasing importance as it was found that more and more men could be quickly returned to combat. Treatment routines varied widely but were generally based on the common-sense routine of "rest 'em, reassure 'em, and return 'em." Late in the war, a group of physicians trained in psychodynamic psychiatry appeared on the scene who believed that war neuroses were invariably related to repressed emotions that must be exposed and explored, either by abreaction or under hypnosis (it must be remembered that the influence of Freud had only begun to manifest itself about this time). However, the pressure of time did not allow for extended analyses, and many symptoms were dissipated with minimal environmental treatment, sometimes in two or three counseling sessions. Contrary to psychoanalytic theory, the symptoms did not return, nor did the men show undue psychic distress in spite of their "unresolved conflicts" (Miller, 1943, pp. 27–30).

In spite of this experience during World War I, psychoanalytic theory was to embrace the theory of symptom substitution until well into the 1960s, when work in the field of behavior modification finally demonstrated empirically that simple removal of phobic or hysterical symptoms does not inevitably lead to the appearance of a substitute symptom or produce negative psychological effects.

World War II—The Army's Failure to Treat Casualties Early

The experience of the French, British, and American armies in successfully treating men at the front was well documented in 1929 by the U.S. Army Medical Department (Bailey et al., 1929). However, the truth of the time-worn adage that "those who do not know history are doomed to repeat it" was again revealed in World War II around the issue of early treatment of psychological casualties in combat.

Army authorities at that time, both lay and medical, believed that psychiatric disorders occurred only in predisposed individuals and weaklings. This led to the reliance on the screening by psychiatric interview—usually only a few minutes. Men with any indication of a "psychoneurosis" were routinely hospitalized and discharged. The results were disastrous (Glass, 1966). By September 1943, the stateside rate of Army enlisted men discharged for psychiatric reasons peaked to a rate of 35.6 per 1,000 men. If this rate had been maintained, 225,000 men per year would have been discharged. It was not until November 1943 that the Army ordered that each soldier be considered on a case-by-case basis. During the war 398,000 persons were discharged from the Army for neuropsychiatric reasons—a black mark against American psychiatry and a personal handicap for those individuals unnecessarily labeled as being inadequate or inferior.

The situation overseas was not much better. Although the psychiatric discharge rate was a bit lower than stateside, an inordinate number of men were being lost by discharge for psychiatric reasons. It was not until June 1946 that the Army recognized the field of preventive psychiatry and that the psychiatric discharge rate could be heavily influenced not only by length and intensity of combat, but also by unit morale, leadership, opportunities for rest and recreation, and a variety of management policies. The use of psychiatrists to advise field units of these procedures did not begin to materialize to any significant degree until the end of the war approached.

In spite of the experiences of World War I, during World War II very little effort was made to apply the principles of proximity, immediacy, and expectancy. A few psychiatrists in hospitals near the front line did establish Exhaustion Centers where combat-weary soldiers could recover and return to duty. However, these centers were not systematically installed and depended upon the individual initiative and sophistication of each psychiatrist (Glass, 1966, p. 411). It is not surprising that the rate of psychoneurotic discharges in the U.S. Army during World War II was 4.8 times higher than in World War I (Glass, 1966, p. 772).

World War II—The Navy's Lower Incidence of Psychiatric Casualties

During most of World War II, the Navy and Marine Corps filled their personnel requirements with volunteers, not having to utilize the draft until the latter stages of the war. As a result, in addition to having more highly motivated personnel, the Navy was able to set higher physical and mental standards and, because they were volunteers, to separate unsuitables administratively without regard to Selective Service regulations. As discussed earlier, the Navy also had psychologists in place at Naval Training Centers before the war started, and this produced a more sophisticated and effective screening program. The Army consisted mostly of draftees, it had lower mental and physical standards, and it had to follow more extensive bureaucratic and legal procedures. The result was that the psychiatric discharge rate for the Navy and Marine Corps before and after recruit training was lower and administered more quickly, thus placing a lesser demand upon hospital facilities.

There appears to be no evidence that the treatment philosophy of the Navy was any more enlightened than that of the Army. Psychiatric casualties aboard ship and ashore were routinely shipped to base hospitals and discharged. However, this process did not pose the same threat to the personnel pool of the Navy as it did to the Army and therefore seemed to be an issue of small concern, even at the end of the war. In addition, the rate of battle fatigue casualties in the Navy was far lower than that of the Army (Chermol, 1985). Interestingly, even though formal recognition of the efficacy of early treatment was apparently lacking, this issue was mentioned in a number of communiques from the battlefield. For example, during the fighting on Guadalcanal, the following was written: "Of alleged mental cases, 50% should have been diagnosed as battle fatigue, another 20% as borderline battle fatigue. When given relief and rest, 75–80% returned to duty" (Fourteenth Corps, 1943). However, such reports from the combat zone appear to have had little or no effect upon official policy.

The Korean War—Early Effective Treatment

During the Korean War, the valuable lessons learned in World War I and relearned in World War II were applied much earlier. Nevertheless, the war began so abruptly and men were thrown into combat so quickly that the buildup of supporting units lagged behind. For several months psychiatric casualties were evacuated directly to Japan or the United States, and few of them returned to combat. At one point these casualties were siphoning off as much as a third of some front line units. Fortunately, the "corporate memory" of World War II still existed in such men as Colonel Albert J. Glass of the U.S. Army and the Chief of Neuropsychiatry of the Navy, Captain George N. Raines. Glass for the Army and Commander Sam Mullin for the Navy were sent to Korea to establish front line treatment programs and to educate other medical personnel in the management of psychological casualties.

Unlike the situation in World War II, the Navy's treatment routine, though simple in design, was deliberately planned. The primary prescription was rest, hot food, mild sedation, and encouragement. At the peak of action, the psychiatric aid stations returned about 70% of the men to combat within 10 days. About 25% were moved to rear area hospitals but were suited for noncombatant work in Korea or Japan, and about 5% were finally evacuated to the United States (Drury, 1952). The recidivism rate for the Marine Corps was only about 6% (the U.S. Army reported about 80% were returned to duty, but their recidivism rate was almost 33%).

As in previous wars, the Navy made liberal use of paraprofessional personnel, usually recruited from among hospital corpsmen and, even more frequently, other patients. This resulted in a great deal of peer counseling, which was the most effective method with certain patients. In addition, Commander Mullin made frequent trips to other medical units in order to indoctrinate their personnel in the management of psychological casualties. As a result, fewer men were actually sent to the aid station. Although a knowledge of psychodynamics was essential for diagnosis, no attempts were made at long-term psychotherapy. Even at stateside naval hospitals, long-term therapy was used only with a few patients in order to satisfy the requirements of a few residency training programs, such as those at Philadelphia and Bethesda. Usually within 90 days, patients were either returned to duty, discharged as outpatients with a referral to the VA, or discharged and transferred to a VA hospital.

With the First Marine Division in Korea, the complement eventually included two clinical psychologists and two psychiatrists. As of 1988, each Marine division had at least one billet attached for a clinical psychologist.

Coping With Crisis

An interesting anecdote illustrates how useful was the previous military experience of these psychologists. While stationed with the medical battalion behind the front lines, Ensign Allen McMichael (now Captain, MSC, USN, Retired) found himself to be the lone mental health professional present as the unit was given orders to move to the rear because of the advancing enemy. Some hospital patients were evacuated by air and others transported by truck. Available transportation soon became exhausted, and about 40 psychiatric patients were left behind until vehicles could be summoned from the division. At 1600 hours (4 p.m.), a group of tanks rolled in to defend the area vacated by the dismantled field hospital, including the setting of explosive charges on a nearby bridge. Forced to move south, McMichael organized his men, who, as part of the treatment philosophy, had remained in full uniform and were not treated as hospital patients. Drawing upon his long service in the Marine Corps during World War II, McMichael described the ensuing activity as follows:

> I had about 40 patients, 2 corpsmen, to trek about 10-15 miles. I organized them into teams of 4 (retaining as much of each team that had already been working together as possible). I told them what our situation was as I knew it, that we were going to straddle the road to the next hospital, marching in lines of fireteams [i.e., 4 infantrymen], 5 paces between members of each fireteam, 5-10 paces between fireteams, and that I expected them to follow me as well as maintain strict march discipline. This meant no talking, no lights, no cigarettes, and a 10-minute break every hour until we met our transportation that was probably underway right now to get us. I gave each fireteam a number, assigned odd numbers to the left side of the road and the even numbers to the other side. I put one corpsman at each end, and one in the middle of the road, with the unnecessary instruction to get out of the way of any trucks by jumping into the nearest ditch. I led off the march on the road, but moved back to the middle after the start to get the proper distances between men and fireteams in conformance with the terrain. We started out just before 1700 [5 p.m.] and everything went well into dark. We stopped for our breaks, I visited each team of 4 at each break, reassuring them that we were going to make it without difficulty. At dark some trucks rumbled by us heavily loaded with ammunition, but it heightened the spirit in the fireteams which enabled us to pick up the pace and, as I recall, we had a good moon by which to see. Fortunately, there were no sounds of incoming/outgoing artillery and no mines along this stretch of well-traveled road. We walked into the hospital area at about 2230 [10:30 p.m.] to find my corpsman just getting field ambulances ready to pick us up. We had marched nearly ten miles. The hospital found us spare cots, food,

and I started sending most of these patients back to duty the next day.
(A. E. McMichael, personal communication, May 24, 1987)

The Concept of Crisis Intervention

Another interesting feature of learning to treat psychiatric cases during combat was that it firmly established the concept of crisis intervention. For many traditionally trained clinicians, it was remarkable to see so many kinds of cases respond to a protective and supportive environment and a few reality-oriented counseling sessions. In the 1960s, civilian psychiatric institutions "discovered" the efficacy of quick and short intervention, not by learning from the military experience, but largely from the extensive work in the field of suicidology done under the auspices of the National Institutes of Health (Shneidman, 1967). Originally, phone-in and walk-in suicide centers were established around the nation. Later their role was widened: Most of them were called crisis intervention centers and their telephone services were called hotlines. Clinicians familiar with the military experience no doubt looked upon this civilian "innovation" with interest.

The Vietnam War—A Different Pattern of Casualties

During the Vietnam War, the principles of proximity, immediacy, and expectancy were not overlooked, but the situation was quite different from that in World War II and Korea. Not only were the physical conditions and the psychological climate different, but also the pattern of psychiatric casualties was unlike that of previous conflicts. For all the services, cases of combat fatigue accounted for less than 6% of all psychiatric hospitalizations in Vietnam, and virtually all of these individuals were returned to duty. Even when these cases were treated at the second or third echelon of treatment of a hospital ship, depending where it was steaming at the time, 78% were returned to combat (Strange & Arthur, 1967). In World War II, there were 101 psychiatric casualties per 1,000 troops per year; in Vietnam this dropped to 12 psychiatric casualties per 1,000. The evacuation rate of psychiatric patients showed a similar decline. In World War II, 23% of all patients medically evacuated from the war zone were psychiatric patients; in Korea this dropped to 6% and in Vietnam it dropped to less than 3% (Renner, 1973).

Combat in Vietnam involved small units in scattered encounters with the enemy, with periods of relative calm and safety interspersed, during which times the men enjoyed good food and recreational facilities, including access to bars and brothels (Bourne, 1970). Also, there were many more support personnel than combat troops—sometimes in a ratio as high as 10 to 1. A unique feature of this war was the fact that all tours of duty lasted only for 12 months, thus giving each man a goal and a higher expectation of survival. In addition, medical treatment was always close at hand, including swift evacuation by helicopter to field or base hospitals. As a result, the number of medically treated Marines who died was only 1.4%, compared with 2.95% during World War II, a decline of more than 50% (Palinkas & Coben, 1985b).

However, the lower rates of psychiatric disorders in Vietnam were based on the studies conducted during 1965 and 1966. As the war heated up and the fighting became more intense between 1967 and 1972, there is some evidence that the earlier rate of 12 per 1,000 men increased to about 34.3 per 1,000 men—close to the rate of 37 per 1,000 men reached in Korea (Palinkas & Coben, 1985a).

But Vietnam produced its own pattern of psychiatric disorders: a sharp increase in the number of character and behavior disorders, usually associated with alcohol or drug abuse. Many of these cases were not given psychiatric diagnoses but were handled administratively. As a result, Navy and Marine Corps brigs in Vietnam were seriously overcrowded, and dishonorable discharges increased 53% in the year 1969 (Renner, 1973).

The Vietnam War—Psychologists on Duty

Psychologists were attached to each of the two Marine Corps divisions stationed in-country. In addition, they were stationed at the primary receiving hospitals in Japan, Okinawa, and Guam. As discussed elsewhere, the United States did not mobilize quickly for this war—it just slowly escalated. Even though the number of clinical psychologists in the Navy increased steadily during this period, the reason for it was the gradually expanding role of clinical psychologists in the total naval establishment rather than a function of mobilization.

The psychologists serving in-country in Vietnam operated as part of a mental health team, including a psychiatrist and two to four hospital corpsmen. While generally new to the military, they had been schooled in the philosophy of proximity, immediacy, and expectancy. Unlike the situation in World War II and Korea, the most frequent referrals were character disorders. The men were counseled and their commanding officer was advised about the situation. If they continued to pose problems, they were processed and sent to a hospital in-country, one of the Navy hospital ships, or to a base hospital, such as Subic Bay in the Philippines. A number of fragile individuals displayed psychotic symptoms under the stress of combat, but there were relatively few cases of battle fatigue.

A type of case peculiar to Vietnam was the not-infrequent instance of a reaction to a toxic drink the men would obtain out in the bush. Those affected were grossly paranoid, suffered delusions, and were extremely agitated. They were given large doses of Thorazine (chlorpromazine), an antipsychotic tranquilizer; after sleeping for several hours, the men returned to normal.

Most of the men who were unable to adjust to combat had preservice histories of marginal adjustment. Vietnam also produced the much publicized phenomenon of "delayed stress syndrome," in which a person would develop severe symptoms weeks or months after combat and after having returned to civilian life. When such symptoms appeared in career military personnel after they had returned to the United States, the symptoms were usually short-lived and recovery was complete. Those who displayed these symptoms in civilian life very often had a marginal preservice history and lacked a good social support system, such as an intact family life and rewarding employment.

As in most billets, the psychologists in Vietnam had to function in several roles. As one expressed it: "I would be a clinician during the day and a paramedic and neurologist at night."

On the average, initially the men in Vietnam were better educated and better trained than those in World War II and the Korean War. However, one factor that may have contributed to the spectrum of disorders seen in Vietnam is that clusters of men were from the less educated and the lower occupational categories. The mental ability of men in 1965 when the Marines entered Vietnam was considerably higher than it was in the late 1960s, when draftees entered under lowered mental standards, whereas the better educated and better employed were often motivated to avoid the draft and did so by staying in school or seeking exemptions. Not only did the younger draftees of the late 1960s come from a drug-oriented culture in the United States, but also a disproportionate number were from inner-city populations, where asocial behavior was more the norm than the exception.

The Submarine Service

The submarine service is one of the elite branches of the Navy. Its personnel are among the brightest and most highly motivated, especially in this nuclear age. Traditionally, they have always been volunteers and received extra pay for hazardous duty. Today's nuclear submarine is quite habitable, and cruises of 60 to 70 days while the boat is submerged are not uncommon, but this has not always been the case.

Conditions Aboard Submarines

The early boats (submarines are called boats, not ships) used during and after World War I were cramped and poorly ventilated. On the surface, the men were subjected to the fumes of oil vapor from the engines, and when submerged, to the gases from the storage batteries, fumes of cooking, odors of perspiration, bad teeth, flatus, and so on (Brown, 1920). (In a take-off on the old Army barracks song, "Old Soldiers Never Die—They Just Fade Away," it was said that "Old Submariners Never Die—They Just Smell That Way.") Noise levels were very high, especially in the engine spaces, and regular sleep patterns were difficult to establish. Bunks were squeezed into small spaces, including atop the stored torpedoes.

When the boat was submerged, the relative humidity was high, with considerable condensation forming on the bulkheads and a tendency toward dampness. Variations in atmospheric pressure were common, and when the boat surfaced the sudden change in pressure would cause discomfort or even damage to one's hearing. When the boat was on patrol, the practice was to remain submerged during the day and to recharge the batteries at night while on the surface. Only a few of the crew saw daylight or breathed fresh air during the 6- to 8-day patrols. The lack of physical exercise, the artificial light, the monotony, and the crowded conditions tended to lead to a lowering of resistance or even exhaustion, especially under the added stress of wartime conditions. During the years prior to and during World War II, the submarine became larger and more habitable, but the problems, while of lesser magnitude, remained very similar. From the crew's point of view, the one notable exception was the advent of modern refrigeration, and serving the best food in the Navy soon became a tradition.

Conditions under combat were extremely stressful. World War II logs of surviving boats describe the mental strain not only of hearing depth charges explode nearby but also of leaky bulkheads, loss of lighting and power, and working under temperatures ranging as high as 130 degrees (Shilling & Kohl, 1947, pp. 117-128). The dramatic and extreme conditions depicted in numerous war movies were not exaggerated. Compared with other branches of the Navy, losses were high; about 18% of all the boats that saw combat were lost (U.S. Naval History Division, 1963, p. 1). However, the losses to the enemy were tremendous, allowing the United States to eventually sweep the Pacific of the Japanese fleet. In addition to the loss of nearly its entire merchant fleet, Japan lost more than 30% of its submarines.

The diesel boats used during World War II were about 300 feet long and carried a crew of about 75 men. Today fleet ballistic missile submarines (FBMs), nicknamed "boomers" in Navy slang, are the largest of the nuclear boats. They are 560 feet long and carry a crew of about 165. The nuclear submarines contain two to four decks; the crew's quarters are divided into compartments containing four to six bunks with spaces between them of two to three feet. Onboard movies are shown regularly, and there is enough open space for lounges and for the off-duty crew to utilize the ship's library or stereo equipment. There is an automatic clothes washer and dryer and also hobby facilities, such as a machine shop and photographic darkroom. A massive air conditioning system keeps the temperature between 68 and 72 degrees the year round, and under all conditions the humidity is at about 50%. Carbon dioxide "scrubbers" provide a sealed atmosphere for more than 60 days at a time, and there are facilities for changing the air completely within 20 minutes by means of snorkeling equipment (Polmar, 1963, pp. 80–84).

A tongue-in-cheek observation made early in the history of nuclear submarines was that "they need to surface only once every 4 years in order for the men to reenlist.'' Originally each man was permitted a short look at a landfall, thus giving him a reassuring ''reality fix'' on the outside world. Today this is accomplished by use of a TV monitor connected to the periscope, displayed regularly in the crew's quarters.

Screening for Submarine Duty

As previously noted, some psychological testing of applicants for the submarine force took place in the 1920s. During World War II, these men were subjected to the usual screening that took place during recruit training, and when they applied for the submarines, they were given a short interview by a psychiatrist. This usually consisted of interviewing 10 men at once in a group and openly asking each man such questions as, ''Did you ever have sexual intercourse?'' There appeared to be an expected distribution of ''yes'' and ''no'' answers, neither of which, to the author, seemed to influence the outcome of the screening.

Further screening took place during the training process, especially when recruits were using the Escape Training Tank, a 100-foot high cylinder of water. Within it, each man had to learn to ascend to the surface and to simulate an exit from a sunken submarine in a regulated and disciplined manner in order to avoid deadly air embolisms in the bloodstream. Any evidence of either physical or social claustrophobia was especially noted. (The former is a fear of being in enclosed spaces, while the latter is a condition in which a person is unable to adjust to the close living quarters and lack of privacy aboard submarines.) These landmark water towers are now obsolete because the working depths of submarines are measured more in miles than in feet, and rescue work is focused more on the use of the Deep Emergency Rescue Vehicle, which can operate at tremendous depths.

Submariners have always had the reputation of having a high degree of esprit de corps of the type usually seen among groups of elite, highly trained persons who must exercise a high degree of interdependency in order to be effective and to survive. While this has resulted in sometimes spectacular confrontations with other branches of the Armed Forces, in the Submarine Service only a minimal number of men have been expelled for infractions of discipline or incompatibility with their shipmates. Traditionally, the frequency of psychiatric casualties in the Submarine Service has been extremely low in both wartime (Duff & Shilling, 1947) and peacetime (Ninow, 1963).

The first psychologists to work systematically in support of the Submarine Service were experimentalists, most of them stationed at the Submarine Base at New London, Connecticut, during and following World War II. They first worked on problems of audition, such as measuring the aptitude of sonar operators by means of the Seashore Measures of Musical Talents, and color and night vision, the latter focusing on the night vision of lookouts at sea and techniques of dark adaptation. To these two research divisions, a program of personnel selection was added in 1942, screening for those auditory and visual skills most important to the operation of submarines at sea. This three-faceted program at first functioned as part of the Medical Department of the Submarine Base but became part of the Medical Research Laboratory (MRL) when it was officially established in June 1946 (Weybrew, 1979).

The Personnel Selection Branch soon focused on the psychosocial variables associated with submarines. In 1951 Ensign Dennis Briggs, MSC, USN, the first uniformed clinical psychologist stationed at the laboratory, initiated a series of studies on small-group dynamics. In 1958 H. Barry Molish (now Commander, MSC, USNR, Retired) joined the clinical staff, and for the next 8 years he was the primary uniformed clinical psychologist associated with the Submarine Service. At any one time one or two uniformed psychiatrists were also stationed at the laboratory.

Psychology's Role in the Nuclear Submarine Era

The advent of nuclear power ushered in the modern submarine Navy, and the activity of the laboratory focused on psychological screening and the psychological, auditory, and visual correlates of performance and habitability in the new boats.

The first atomic submarine, the *Nautilus*, was commissioned on September 30, 1954. Prior to this, many questions remained unanswered, such as how long a crew could remain submerged without undue psychological and physiological consequences, and whether new personnel standards and selection techniques were needed. In order to explore these questions, in January 1953 a diesel boat was moored dockside; 23 volunteers were sealed inside and studied for a period of 2 months. They were given a variety of psychological and physiological tests before, during, and after this period. Essentially, the findings showed that such prolonged confinement was not necessarily detrimental to their well-being or job performance (Faucett & Newman, 1953). Subsequent experience with the nuclear boats under real conditions supported these conclusions. Psychologically, the concern of the psychologists moved from a clinical frame of reference, in which they dealt with an abnormal population, to the study of normal persons in special environments (Faucett & Newman, 1953).

The clinical psychologists and psychiatrists established an intensive screening program for the first nuclear sailors, including psychological test batteries and one-on-one clinical interviews. However, as was later shown in numerous studies of recruit screening by Plag and his colleagues, the interview was soon found to be of minimal usefulness, so it was abandoned, and psychological testing was minimal. Rather, the group concentrated on reacting to individual cases for counseling or crisis intervention. In addition, attention was given to the families and dependents of the crews. Each submarine was manned by alternate crews, known as the "blue" and the "gold." The families of both crews were given base housing, and while one crew was at sea, the other crew and their families would form a support group and extended family for the other. In addition, the clinical psychologist and the psychiatrist would offer their services as needed, including counseling the adults, extending their services to crisis intervention visits to crew members' homes, and consulting with local school authorities whenever a dependent child needed support and guidance. In essence, Dr. Molish and his colleagues operated a full-service counseling and guidance center in support of the developing nuclear age in the Navy. This not only gave valuable insights into many factors affecting the morale and performance of the "nukie" sailors, but so eased the family burden of the husband's being absent for long cruises that it had an extremely positive effect on the reenlistment rate.

While stationed at the Submarine Base, Molish also served a term as president of the Southeastern Connecticut Mental Health Association—another example of how many Navy clinical psychologists have been involved in their local civilian communities.

The psychologists assigned to the submarine force were also called on to assist families in the face of great tragedy. On April 9, 1962, the newly commissioned atomic submarine USS *Thresher* sank with 129 persons while undergoing sea trials off the Atlantic coast (Whitestone, 1973). The effect on their families was, naturally, catastrophic. Many observers have since claimed the loss was due to faulty construction design and slipshod workmanship (Gray, 1986, pp. 208–213), which made the loss all the more heart-rending. The resulting effort to provide mental health services was predictive of those programs that have since been developed in civilian life to help the survivors of disasters—another example of pioneering efforts on the part of psychologists in the military (see section on Postdisaster Intervention).

The clinicians at New London not only studied and screened the submariners but also frequently followed them aboard the boats to observe their adjustment and performance. This tended to produce a closeness between the crews and those they good-naturedly referred to as "our shrinks." This situation also gave rise to an anecdote that is still recounted at social gatherings of old-timers. In August 1958, the largest submarine ever built to date was launched—the USS *Triton*. In order to test its advanced capabilities and to demonstrate further the long-term submersibility of the atomic submarine, President Eisenhower ordered it on a top-secret mission to circumnavigate the globe.[12]

Under the command of Captain Edward L. Beach, a renowned World War II submariner and well-known author, preparations were made without revealing to the crew the nature of the cruise. In the strictest confidence, Captain Beach

---

[12]It was coded "Cosmic"—a classification that then limited disclosure to only the president of the United States and the commander leading the mission.

invited Benjamin Weybrew, civilian psychologist then directing the Personnel Selection Branch of the Medical Research Laboratory, to accompany him as an observer "on a top-secret trip that would take them all over the world." Weybrew assumed that President Eisenhower had in mind a series of public relations visits at a number of South American and European ports. In anticipation he purchased two new suits, including a white Palm Beach, a lightweight suit appropriate for tropical climates or summer wear. However, as the boat submerged outside of New London, the captain announced that their next port of call would be New London!

Once they recovered from their own surprise, the crew soon learned of Weybrew's expectations of an exotic pleasure cruise and often kidded him. Also, knowing that Weybrew was observing the effects of prolonged submersion on their behavior, one sailor feigned distress by pulling a pack of matches on a string, calling it "Fido" and talking to it as if it were alive. (The author, however, was never made privy to the disposition of the sailor or to whether the new suits were subsequently put to good use.)

In addition to gathering important scientific and engineering data, Captain Beach had hoped to complete the trip around the world in 80 days, perhaps in tribute to the well-known movie popular at the time. However, because of minor delays the trip was completed in 84 days, on May 10, 1960. The giant A-boat had traveled submerged for 36,335 nautical miles on its "shakedown" (i.e., initial) cruise.

The Medical Research Laboratory

As described, the Medical Research Laboratory at the Submarine Base at New London was the scene of considerable clinical research—primarily in the screening and selection of submariners. They were also involved in a number of habitability studies, especially with the advent of nuclear power in 1954. This interest was broadened to include the habitability of other small-group environments, such as the station at the geographic South Pole, radiation fallout shelters (an interest motivated by the tense threat of nuclear warfare with the Soviet Union), and space stations. While stationed at New London, Commander Molish not only assisted in the psychological screening of men volunteering for wintering over in the Antarctic but also made a visit to the South Pole in order to gather data on their adjustment. Dr. Molish was an authority on the use of Rorschach's Inkblot Test, having received his doctorate at the University of Chicago under Samuel Beck, who introduced the test into the United States in 1932. While still on active duty, Molish subsequently coauthored the third edition of Beck's famous text on the subject. When he visited the South Pole, therefore, Molish took pleasure in administering the first Rorschach ever given at "the bottom of the earth"!

During the late 1960s, the activity of the clinical psychologists at New London decreased markedly, and traditional hospital billets replaced them at the Naval Hospital at the Submarine Base—now listed as Groton, Connecticut. (The base was built in the small rural town of Groton in 1898 and originally used the Post Office address of New London; it became a submarine base in 1916. Today Groton is larger than New London, and for many years it was a sore point with Groton natives to have the base "located" in New London. It took many years of political maneuvering to persuade the Navy to officially change the address in 1960.)

As of 1987, there were no uniformed clinical psychologists stationed at the Naval Medical Submarine Research Laboratory, and the excitement and glamor of being a researcher-clinician during the birth and development of this phase of the nuclear age has faded. However, the Submarine Service is today one of the most important components of global strategy, not only using its intercontinental ballistic capability as one of the primary deterrents of nuclear war but also playing a constant game of "cat and mouse" with the Soviet Navy, engaging in a wide variety of secret missions, and continuing to research the fathomless depths of our "inner world." If a uniformed clinical psychologist were to be associated again with this activity, it would still offer the prospect of personal excitement and professional growth.

The Naval Air Service

In 1907, less than 4 years after the Wright brothers made the first flight in a powered aircraft, the U.S. Army formed an aeronautical division and purchased its first heavier-than-air machine from the Wrights in 1909. The U.S. Navy followed suit in 1910 and was soon making landings and take-offs from platforms superimposed on existing ships. By 1913, nine officers of the Navy and Marine Corps had qualified as pilots. A seaplane tender, the *Wright*, was commissioned in 1921, followed a year later by the Navy's first aircraft carrier, the *Langley*. Naval aviation remained much in the experimental stages until the carriers *Saratoga* and *Lexington* were commissioned in 1927 and the *Ranger* in 1928. By then all battleships and cruisers were fitted with planes launched from catapults and hoisted aboard after a flight. The U.S. Navy also developed the technique of dive-bombing, an invention often wrongly attributed to the German Luftwaffe (Turnbull & Lord, 1949).

The Necessity of Screening Pilots

The advent of World War I made clear the need for a strong air force, and the Navy was soon recruiting and training pilots in increasing numbers. The first psychological tests used to study and screen pilots were limited to tests of psychophysical skills, such as vision, audition, balance and reaction time. Research was also conducted on the effect of altitude (i.e., anoxia) on performance

(Dunlap, 1918, 1919). However, it was also recognized that it would be desirable to be able to test for "judgment and emotional control" (Bachman, 1918).

As in the treatment of the insane and the screening of recruits, the first uniformed men to practice clinical psychology in the Naval Air Service (NAS) were medical officers. In 1919 (and earlier) it was argued that "the ear specialists and the eye specialists have long established themselves in aviation and, it is believed, have swung the pendulum too far to the side of the eye and ear being the all-important organs in the profession of flying. It is time that a reaction [was] brought about and that the neurologist [the term then used for psychiatrist] occupied as strong a foothold as do the eye and ear specialists" (Pillmore, 1919). In the same article, the author referred to the fact that "the doctor [i.e., physician] often has to work as a psychologist" and argued for the establishment of a separate medical subspecialty in aviation—which, of course, is today a reality.

It was recognized that an aviator did not require extraordinary abilities and that a person of average or slightly above average physical and mental skills could still become a good pilot. Also, since most men had been carefully screened or performed well on active duty before being allowed to volunteer, nearly all of them were found to be physically qualified for flight training. It was long suspected that the extremely strict physical requirements, which exceeded those set for officers in general, were not related to success in aviation. It was not until 1929 that it was demonstrated empirically that once a person qualified even minimally on a variety of measures of vision, hearing, and balance, these tests bore no relationship to subsequent flying performance. The author concluded that "aeronautical adaptability must be determined through neuropsychiatric examinations" (Ickstadt, 1929). On this basis, a search was begun for non-physical variables that correlated with success as a pilot.

Early Testing Efforts

One of the first efforts to study this problem (Parsons, 1918) was a survey of naval flight instructors, who were asked to state what they considered were the essential qualities of a successful aviator. The following list resulted:

1. Coolness under strain.
2. Dependability to always do the correct thing at a critical moment.
3. Mental and physical alertness.
4. Persistence and perseverance in . . . [one's] ambition to become a successful aviator.
5. Intelligence.
6. Athletic ability and good muscular coordination.
7. A keen sense of equilibrium.
8. A good [ability to] judge . . . velocity and distances.

A variety of laboratory instruments was used for measuring some of these factors, many of them designed by two psychologists from Harvard University, L. E. Troland and H. E. Burtt.

These tests included having a subject do rapid addition of numbers under stress while hooked to a machine for measuring changes in pulse and respiration in order to measure "coolness," or presence of mind; measures of vision and audition; tactual reaction times; depth perception; and maintaining equilibrium while rotating in a swivel chair. One of the more interesting tests was an adaptation of the Word Association Test first introduced by Galton in 1897. Designed to detect fear of flying, a subject was exposed verbally to 100 words, 50 of which referred to flying and 50 which were unrelated. The person was required to respond to each word with the first word that came to mind, and the response time and content were recorded. It is interesting that in a follow-up comparison of scores with the training records of 47 pilots, this single test suggested that if selection had been based on these reaction times, the "poor or fail" rate would have decreased from 15% to 7% (Parsons, 1918).

Some of these tests obviously correlated significantly with success in pilot training while others did not, but unfortunately the statistical tools in common use today were not routinely available, such as tests of significance and multiple correlation (these techniques were developed around the turn of the century, but in the United States they were not commonly available in textbook form until the late 1920s and early 1930s). An examination of the data from this study strongly suggests that with modern methods of data analysis, the researcher had available the raw data from which to devise a highly valid tool for pilot selection. Unfortunately, the author was unable to find evidence of any continuation of this work at the time.

The Flight Surgeon's Role

The systematic application of psychological methods in the selection and training of naval aviators apparently was not instituted until the advent of World War II. However, by 1928 or before, the billet of Flight Surgeon had been created, and both physical and psychological screening of fledgling aviators became primarily that person's responsibility. In addition, during the training he was expected to assume a supportive role. One flight surgeon described it as follows (Rhoades, 1928):

> They (students) become, more or less, his wards; he watches their progress throughout the course, talks to and advises them professionally, treats minor ailments, and tries at all times to keep himself informed as to their progress in flight training, and of their general mental and physical condition. (p. 503)

During the rather extensive physical examination, the flight surgeon was expected to form additional clues as to each pilot's "temperament, intelligence, and volition." Time permitting (a factor that must have reduced its reliability), a formal psychological examination was conducted. This consisted of an interview that focused on "the candidate's family history, personal history, his social life, education, habits, hobbies and occupations, his worries, phobias, complexes, athletic ability, and finally the effect of the wear and tear of the world on his nervous system, his mentality, and his make-up" (Rhodes, 1928). (This was obviously an ambitious expectation; today's clinical psychologist will recognize the inherent risk of very low validity and reliability resulting from this process.)

The literature describing the kind of examination conducted in 1928 (Rhoades, 1928) was, unfortunately, only a recommendation. As in the case of recruit screening, the medical officer of that day was allowed a great deal of personal discretion in selecting the elements of the examination, especially the psychological part. This undoubtedly produced less than maximum reliability among examiners and different geographical locations.

However, the medical officer in question, Lt. Comdr. Rhoades, attempted to reduce the results of his psychological examination to a rating system that was concise and more useful. He created a checklist of eight descriptive adjectives and rated each man in each category as "above average," "average," or "below average." He also created anchor points for two-extreme categories as follows: cheerful-depressed; aggressive-submissive; intelligent-stupid; precise-vague; quick-slow; retentive-not retentive; controlled-restless; attentive-inattentive. Each man was then given an overall rating according to the sum of these ratings.

Based on the physical and mental examinations, the flight surgeon then made a judgment as to whether the man would succeed in flight training. Presumably, as he gained experience by following a number of classes through training, the medical officer refined his examination and his predictions became more accurate.

While Dr. Rhoades probably did not realize it, he had used a technique that decades later was to become known as the Adjective Checklist (ACL). One version of this technique, developed at the well-known Institute for Personality Assessment and Research at the University of California, has become one of the most widely used personality tests (Gough, 1960). Dr. Rhoades's work appears to be another example of the ingenuity of the Lone Rangers of the Navy Medical Department.

The Testing Program at Pensacola

By 1928, the Naval Air Service was finding that, while a suitable number of men were volunteering for flight training the number successfully completing the course was declining, whereas the demand for pilots was increasing. Recognition was also building that physical standards above a certain minimum were not adequate predictors and that psychological measures were needed. It was also recognized that such measures were not being appropriately used and that they lacked standardization as well. Therefore, in 1928 the Bureau of Medicine and Surgery directed that the situation be studied at the naval installation in Pensacola, Florida; data were to be collected on psychological predictors of successful completion of pilot training. This work was initiated and first reported on in 1930 by Captain Dallas G. Sutton (1930), who later became Chief of Psychiatry for the Bureau of Medicine and Surgery. As recounted earlier, Sutton was also responsible for recruiting the first uniformed clinical psychologists immediately prior to World War II. It is perhaps of historical note that the U.S. Army had conducted psychological research on predictors of pilot success as early as 1918 (Henmon, 1919) and had been routinely screening its applicants since 1921. The Navy, however, chose to rely upon the initiative of its individual medical officers, as in many other situations.

In initiating the study, Sutton (1930) discussed the role of the person gathering the data as follows:

> The psychologists [i.e., Flight Surgeons] should have a background of practical psychiatry in addition to a knowledge of laboratory methods. Medical officers having a superficial knowledge of psychology are a liability rather than an asset and for that reason, if the service is going to stress the mental element in aviation medicine, physicians of the proper type should be trained in sufficient numbers to handle the problem. Otherwise opinions expressed will carry very little force and confidence will not be maintained. (p. 11)

It is of interest that Sutton, as did his colleagues throughout the Medical Department, viewed the practice of psychology as within the province of the medical officer, usually a psychiatrist, thus promoting the practice of clinical psychology in the Navy without calling it that. (Should the modern reader perceive this as a lack of deference to the profession of psychology, it should be recalled that two of the psychological instruments most identified with the profession of clinical psychology were developed by physicians—the Inkblot Test by Hermann Rorschach in 1921 and the Thematic Apperception Test by Henry Murray and his colleagues in 1938.)

Sutton's study involved the psychological examination of 628 candidates for flight training at Pensacola. A psychological examination form was designed to bring out indications of "instability" in candidates—that term being the overall rubric used for those qualities considered unsuitable for pilot status. While the data were to be based upon "a carefully conducted psychological examination," they were derived entirely from an interview of the type previously described. The interviewer would then subjectively evaluate each subject on those qualities hypothesized to be relevant to flight training and rate them on the traditional four-point scale. These qualities were courage, stability, aggression, concentration, intelligence, and reaction time. The latter was found to be unrelated to success as a pilot, but it was a useful tool for the examiner in personally relating to each man while examining him and thus helping him judge the other traits. In Sutton's study (1930), 212 officers and men were rated as "good" aviation material and 416 rated as "poor." The ratings were not used in the selection of the candidates but were compared with their performance ratings at the end of training.

Of the 212 selected as good material, 148 qualified (70%) and 64 (30%) either failed or required additional training in order to qualify—usually marginally. Of the 416 rated as poor material, 345 (83%) failed or needed additional training. The overall rate of successful prediction was 78.5%. Furthermore, the accident rate of the poor group during training was twice that of all the pilots in the Navy during the fiscal year of 1928 1929 and more than four times that of the Pensacola group rated good (De Foney, 1931). This study was replicated two years later in subsequent classes at Pensacola, and the findings were essentially the same (De Foney, 1933).

Given the extremely poor reliability and validity of the psychiatric interview as the basis of personnel selection, as shown by the work of Plag et al., previously described, these findings appear to be remarkable. However, this level of success is most likely to be accounted for by the fact that the applicant population was not well screened prior to training and represented a very wide range of talent, including a significant number that were obviously unfit.

In those early years of naval aviation, nearly all physically fit volunteers were accepted into flight training, including enlisted men as well as officers. In the sample studied, 53% were enlisted, of which 22% were unrated (i.e., were below Petty Officer rank) seamen. Most of the officers were college-educated and had successfully completed the basic training course for all line officers, which probably accounted for the fact that while more than 60% of the officers were successful, only 19% of the unrated seamen graduated. It is generally easier to judge when a person is obviously unfit for pilot training than when fit, which was reflected in the fact that the investigators were correct 83% of the time in labeling subjects as poor material but correct only 70% of the time when they judged subjects as good material. In other words, these interviewers had the luxury of evaluating an applicant pool that was wide-ranging in aptitude for flight training. Today this pool consists of individuals who have all been subjected to higher educational and aptitude standards for application. In statistical terms, this is known as a problem in restriction of range, and it is not likely that these early results could be duplicated on modern Navy populations.

Regardless of what by today's standards would be judged primitive research methodology, these pioneering efforts to apply the techniques of clinical psychology clearly demonstrated not only that psychological factors were extremely important in aviation but that they could be measured and applied in a very cost-effective manner—thus assuring clinical psychologists of another important role to play in the future of the Navy.

The Evolution of the Psychologist's Role

When the first clinical psychologists entered the Navy in 1941, the original intent was to use them for recruit screening, but a certain number were also assigned to air stations, where they served on selection boards and, as described earlier, soon worked themselves into a variety of other jobs, such as counseling and serving on aptitude boards. They also were stationed at recruiting and induction centers, where they screened applicants for the Air Service. The group also included a number of nonclinical psychologists whose primary function was to develop a comprehensive program of pilot selection, but they were all commissioned in the category of Hospital Volunteer Reserves (Special Service) [H-V(S)], and no formal distinction was made between clinical psychologists and aviation psychologists. However, they did operate under the medical section of the Bureau of Aeronautics and had their own director—John G. Jenkins, PhD, a former faculty member at the University of Maryland.

As they demonstrated their skills, this group became involved in a wide variety· of tasks. The late Irving R. Stone (Commander, MSC, USNR, Retired) even became involved in the sub-specialty of night vision training and established the program at North Island, California, Naval Air Station—no doubt a testimony to his broad education in general psychology.

When the Medical Service Corps was established in 1947, a separate section on Aviation Psychology was created with Allen D. Grinstead (now Captain, MSC, USN, Retired) as its first Head. Its primary task, as it is today, was to continue to improve on techniques of pilot selection and to conduct research in a wide variety of projects on physiological and human engineering problems in aviation and aerospace. On an individual basis, some clinical psychologists have worked with the Aviation Psychology group, and there have been cases of individual cross-transfer. Today the Navy clinical psychologist associated with the aviation community does so through assignment to Medical Department facilities at or near naval air stations.

The first uniformed clinical psychologist assigned to the NAS at Pensacola after World War II was the late Jesse Harris (Captain, MSC, USNR, Retired) in 1955. He was officially assigned to the Naval Air Station but functioned primarily with the School of Aviation Medicine. Dr. Harris was involved in the diagnostic evaluation of pilots and provided psychotherapy to many dependents. He participated in starting a volunteer clinic in the city of Pensacola—one of the very first mental health clinics in that part of Florida. He also sat on the Aptitude Board, which was responsible for making decisions concerning the retention of pilots in training. Having completed his PhD in 1955 at Duke University, Dr. Harris also published several research papers while at Pensacola on such subjects as visual conflict, motion sickness, and the effects of 100% oxygen inhalation on human performance. After his tour ended in 1958, he remained in the Active Reserve and completed several 2-week tours at his former duty station. For many years afterward, Dr. Harris served as Professor and Chairman of the Department of Psychology at the University of Kentucky.

At this writing (1988), billets for Navy clinical psychologists exist at Naval Air Station (NAS) Miramar, San Diego, California; NAS Jacksonville, Florida; U.S. Marine Corps Air Facility, Cherry Point, North Carolina; NAS Yuma, Arizona; NAS Lemore, California; and at the Naval Aerospace Medical Institute, Pensacola, Florida.

Each of these billets can be especially exciting. For example, before his current assignment to the Security Battalion at Quantico, Virginia, Lt. Comdr. Forrest Sherman was assigned to the medical clinic at NAS Yuma, Arizona. In that position, he served in the traditional Lone Ranger type of billet. He was the first clinical psychologist to be assigned there and was essentially a one-man mental health unit. There was a military population of about 4,000 and their dependents, plus a large number of retired military personnel, a group that increased in numbers each winter season as the usual "snowbirds" migrated south. There existed very few mental health facilities in either the military or civilian community, and Dr. Sherman was actively involved in both. In addition to serving the military and their dependents, he also participated in the establishment of a civilian mental health center for the city of Yuma, including consultative support to the local school system. During this tour he also learned to fly a Huey helicopter and became an honorary member of the flight squadron.

Another interesting assignment is at the Naval Aerospace Medical Institute at Pensacola, Florida, formerly known as the School of Aviation Medicine. At this writing (1987), the billet is staffed by Lt. Comdr. Laszlo Navradszky, MSC, USN. The mission of his unit is to train flight surgeons and aerospace medical residents, evaluate aviators and flight students for fitness for duty, respond to consultation requests, and sit on the pilot Review Board. He lectures to the flight surgeons and supervises them during their clinical practicum. Prior to college, Dr. Navradszky was drafted into the U.S. Army in 1969; he served with the 82nd Airborne Division and accumulated 15 parachute jumps before his discharge. He completed college under the GI Bill, graduate school under a Navy scholarship, and internship at Bethesda Naval Hospital. Since he has been on active duty, Dr. Navradszky requested and completed training at the Navy Scuba Diving School at Coronado, California, and flies his own private plane, which he maintains nearby. He has been selected for outservice training in neuropsychology at a major university. Dr. Navradszky is an excellent example of how Navy psychologists are afforded the opportunity to influence the nature of their individual careers—quite contrary to the opinion held by some civilians that a

Navy career exists in a format that is rigid and fully under the capricious control of others.

Early in the history of naval aviation it was recognized that its personnel had many special needs, both psychological and medical. The position of Flight Surgeon was created and, as previously described, this person was expected to create a close working relationship with the aviators—especially the pilots and air crews. Today's flight surgeons, usually recruited from the ranks of general physicians, must complete a 6-month course that includes land and water survival training, operational medicine, and 7 weeks of primary flight training. They are also expected to maintain minimum flight time as "special crew" (i.e., in addition to the regular crew). However, very few psychiatrists qualify as flight surgeons, and even fewer clinical psychologists acquire the background in order to provide for the special mental health needs of air personnel. Today aerospace physiologists and experimental psychologists are expected to complete a course very similar to that of the flight surgeons and to maintain minimum flight time, but there is no similar program for clinical psychologists. In advocating such a program, Parker (1987) has argued that:

> . . . while graduates of the flight . . . curriculum are in no way aviators, they are perceived among the aviation community as having a better appreciation of the aviator's and aircrew's difficulties than nonaviation . . . personnel. The factors of perception and credibility are especially crucial in addressing psychological problems. . . . For this reason, training of ACPs [aviation clinical psychologists] would be invaluable to the Navy. (pp. 349–350)

The SERE (Survival, Evasion, Resistance, and Escape) Program

As the Vietnam War progressed, an increasing number of American service personnel—most of them downed fliers—were being captured by the enemy. Between 1960 and 1973, over 455 Navy and Marine personnel were reported captured or missing in action, of whom 291 were eventually returned (McCubbin et al., 1974). It soon became evident that U.S. troops could benefit from specialized training that would allow them to cope with the threat of capture by the Viet Cong. Designed primarily with the downed flier in mind, a then-highly secret program was initiated in 1960, designated by the acronym SERE (Survival, Evasion, Resistance, and Escape).

Once afoot in enemy territory, the subject's first objective to practice techniques of survival, such as how to find water and food and improvise shelter in a variety of environments, such as the desert, mountains, or jungle. The subject focuses on how to avoid capture, including the use of camouflage, how to use local brush and other materials behind which to hide, and how to get to a location to be picked up by friendly forces—usually by helicopter. A variety of techniques are taught on how to resist giving information to the enemy and how to give misinformation, how to resist propaganda, how to deal with the stresses of captivity, and how to make plans to escape if one is captured.

Because the Vietnam War was socially and politically sensitive, it was thought that the establishment of such a training program was likely to be attacked by those vehemently opposed to the U.S. presence in Vietnam and thus threaten the conduct of a program designed to save American lives. The first program, therefore, was located in the Southern California desert under the strictest security. (A second program was subsequently operated in rural New England.) In effect, it was a base that "did not exist." The concern was constant that Viet Cong agents would infiltrate the program and, by learning the techniques being taught, would be able to establish their own countertechniques among those already in captivity. The author does not know to what extent the enemy extracted such information from sources within the United States, but it has been reported by former POWs (prisoners of war) that the Viet Cong knew of the base and interrogated them about the content of the curriculum.

The program has expanded to include all personnel "at the greater risk of capture" and now trains a certain number of Marines and SEALs. However, because the program is voluntary, only a limited number of personnel in the high-risk categories are processed.

The SERE Program's Content

The course is 5 to 7 days long. Participants are given 2 days of classroom instruction, followed by 3 days of field training in the use of equipment approximating the type they are likely to have available under real circumstances, such as a parachute, knife, and so on. They are taken to the beach and shown how to catch crabs and fish and how to dig for fresh water alongside the ocean. They spend time in both desert and mountain environments, learning how to navigate by day and night, and engage in "sneak and peek" exercises, which include the use of camouflage, evasion tactics, and so forth. They are then released into the countryside and attempt to avoid capture by "hostile forces." Nearly all of them are "captured" by the next day and then given 2 hours of "captivity training" in the classroom; for the next 24 to 28 hours, they are placed in the Resistance Training Laboratory (i.e., prison compound). Here they are subjected to a program of harassment and physical punishment—the latter being carefully programmed and monitored in order to avoid injury or abuse. These techniques are designed more to intimidate than to inflict pain, such as a judo throw that takes place over plowed sand, or a shove against a wall that is carefully padded. Confinement boxes are used, such as the Viet Cong used in Vietnam, but unlike those in Asia, these have air holes, they are monitored for air and temperature, and they are used only for periods of no more than 20 minutes. All physical techniques of harassment have been approved by the Chief of Naval Operations, and to guard against abuse an officer is present when these techniques are used.

The instructors are senior enlisted personnel selected for their teaching and theatrical talents. They dress in simulated enemy uniforms, imitate foreign accents, and subject their "victims" to loud commands, verbal threats, and propaganda speeches, including the demand that they sign confessions and renounce their American citizenship.

During the last day, the trainees are debriefed and given a critique of their performance, emphasizing their mistakes as a positive learning experience. They are also given an opportunity to express their own reactions, both in groups and in a one-on-one format. Nearly all of the students mention the realism of the training and how they "got caught up in it."

The Psychologist's Role in SERE

The program has been in existence for about 30 years, and a uniformed psychologist has been a member of the staff most of that time. Among the psychologist's duties is to screen all new instructors and, if necessary, reevaluate them approximately every 6 months. The psychologist also counsels the instructors for any short-term problems and monitors their behavior with the students, making sure they do not themselves "get caught up in it" and unnecessarily abuse a student or get personally involved with their role as the enemy.

The psychologist is also a member of the curriculum committee, which regularly evaluates the curriculum and, when necessary, recommends changes. The psychologist conducts seminars in techniques of resistance, such as the use of imagery, how to appear confused (and thus uncooperative), and how to use best one's own talents for exaggerating injury or giving misinformation. The psychologist's individual clinical skills are used to counsel not only staff members but also those students who become so involved in the training that they exhibit panic attacks, physiological reactions, claustrophobia, and sometimes the conviction that they are actually imprisoned and not likely to be released.

A recent addition to the curriculum is material in the field of terrorism, a problem that has become an international issue since the 1960s. Because being a POW has much in common with being held as a hostage in a foreign country, many of the lessons learned in SERE are applicable. In addition to teaching the psychological aspects of coping with captivity, the program provides information on how to avoid being kidnapped, bombed, or ambushed and how to elude pursuit in an urban environment.

In many ways the clinical psychologist must operate as an organizational or social psychologist, studying and influencing the program as a system, thus putting to use broad training in the field of general psychology—another example of the diverse and exciting world of the Navy psychologist.

The psychologist's position at SERE is currently (1987) held by John L. Sexton, Lieutenant, MSC, USN. He is a 1972 graduate of the Naval Academy and served nearly 8 years in the Marine Corps as an artillery officer. During that time, he realized he was responsible for a great amount of counseling among his men and became interested in advancing his skills in that area. He earned a master's degree in counseling while on active duty and then left the Corps in order to study full time for his doctorate in clinical psychology, returning to active duty in the MSC upon its completion. As is true of a number of Navy psychologists, Dr. Sexton brings to his position a breadth of experience and knowledge far beyond that gained in graduate school.

The SEALs (Sea–Air–Land Teams)

The SEALs are the Navy's commando force. However, SEALs are no ordinary commandos. Expert scuba divers, they are hit-and-run raiders trained for infiltration, demolition, sabotage, and reconnaissance. The reconnaissance of invasion beaches is one of their basic missions, but they also blow up ships, harbors, dams, bridges, and power stations and cut rail and supply lines. They also engage in combat, and as trained parachutists they may be called upon for such tasks as dropping into a hostile jungle in order to complete a variety of specific missions.

Training is intensive to the point of being almost abusive. The basic course, which is only the first of many in a continuous stream throughout the SEALs' careers, consists of six months of round-the-clock training and drilling, including 5-mile ocean swims, 14-mile overland runs, and mountain climbing exercises in full combat gear weighing between 50 and 90 pounds. Each amphibious warrior is proficient with at least 11 different combat weapons and is an expert at detonating a wide range of explosives, including Bangalore torpedoes, limpet mines, and cratering charges. On underwater missions, they use sophisticated breathing systems that enable them to stay submerged for up to 6 hours without leaving telltale bubble trails in their wake. In a typical year, only about 30 percent of those who start training are graduated and assigned to active duty as SEALs.

In addition to playing a significant role in Vietnam, SEALs were used in the Cuban missile crisis in 1962 and in the Dominican Republic in 1965. They were very active during the Grenada invasion in 1983, as well as in the Beirut area when the U.S. Marines were present in 1963. It can be assumed that they were very involved in the 1987 crisis in the Persian Gulf. They have been called by many the most accomplished and ferocious fighting men in the world (White, 1987).

The Evolution of the SEALs

The modern-day SEALs have evolved from the early days of World War II, when the Italians formed a group of underwater swimmers equipped with rubber suits and an oxygen-breathing apparatus who blew up two British warships in Alexandria harbor. The Italian Tenth Light Flotilla, as they were known, rode astride a torpedo-shaped craft that carried a warhead of 300 pounds of explosives. It was driven by storage batteries and could navigate submerged at about 3 miles per hour. In response to this unique threat, the British organized the Frogmen and the American Navy produced the Naval Combat Demolition Unit (NCDU). The NCDU had its first trial under fire during the Allied invasion of Normandy in 1944. Each 13-man NCDU team, reinforced by members of the Army Engineers, was among the first to land, and under fierce enemy fire attached demolition charges to the many concrete, steel, and timber obstacles the Nazis had embedded into the shoreline. The casualty list was about 50 percent, but the NCDU members established themselves as effective warriors. This group evolved into the Underwater Demolition Teams (UDT), and they continued to distinguish themselves throughout the Pacific campaign against Japan until the end of the war (Best, 1962).

The present-day SEAL force was created in 1962 by President Kennedy, and since then it has gradually expanded into the exceptional fighting force it is today. After the U.S. forces encountered difficulty in the attempted rescue of hostages in Iran, the Reagan administration revitalized the Special Operations Forces (SOF) in all of the Armed Forces in 1982, including the Army's Delta Force, which is composed of men screened from already highly qualified Army Rangers and Green Berets. As of this writing, the most recent focus of the SOF has been on combating the spread of terrorist attacks around the world. At a moment's notice, one or more of these groups is capable of responding to emergency assignments anywhere in the world (Manning et al., 1986). For the SEALs, this has meant doubling the number of personnel in the program, with a goal of 2,000 enlisted men and officers by 1990. It is apparent that this elite force will occupy an increasingly important role in the Navy's future (Jenkins et al., 1987, p. 39).

The Role of the Psychologist in SEAL Team 6

One of the best groups of this select force is SEAL Team 6, located at Little Creek, Virginia (Jenkins et al., 1987); the first Navy clinical psychologist to work with the SEALs was assigned to this unit. At this writing (1988), the billet was held by Thomas C. Mountz, Lt. Comdr., MSC, USN. Dr. Mountz is a regular member of the team and has undergone enough of the SEAL training program to allow him to accompany them on their assigned missions throughout the world. The psychologist routinely screens all applicants for Team 6 and is a permanent member of a board charged with making a variety of personnel decisions. Clinical skills are especially important for monitoring and alleviating, when possible, the extremely high stress level under which these men operate. Team members are on constant alert; they can be shipped out without advance notice and be gone for a few days or for a month or more without their families' knowing their whereabouts or the nature of their mission. The team is deployed considerably more than 50% of the time.

Team 6 has become especially proficient in antiterrorist maneuvers throughout the world. It has also participated in such diverse assignments as being involved in the security arrangements for the 1984 Olympic Games in Los Angeles, the 1988 Olympic Games in Seoul, South Korea, and the Statue of Liberty's Centennial in New York in 1986. They have also trained security forces in a number of foreign countries, several of which have thwarted attempts to terrorize American citizens and installations abroad.

The psychologist serves as the primary mental health professional available to the families, and Mountz has established a communications network so that when he is away he can receive and return phone calls to distressed dependents from virtually anywhere in the world. If he does not intervene directly, he is able to refer them to a variety of support systems in the Norfolk area, such as the naval hospital, Navy chaplains, or one of the petty officers he has trained as lay mental health workers. In addition, he acts as chairman of an ombudsman group consisting of five wives of team members.

Dr. Mountz also coordinates the alcohol and drug abuse program for his command and informally and formally counsels his charges regularly on alcohol, family, and other personal problems common to this age group. His work also includes a variety of mission-oriented tasks, and he also serves as command casualty and assistance officer and as liaison to other military medical resources.

Mountz is currently the only mental health professional assigned to a Special Warfare Team, and his assignment epitomizes the Lone Ranger type of billet occupied by numerous Navy clinical psychologists. His work also illustrates the kind of assignment that allows one to be "*of* the Navy as well as *in* the Navy," providing for an almost limitless exercise of one's psychological expertise, as well as the satisfaction of contributing so directly to the mission of the Navy and the nation.

Forensic Psychology

The experienced Navy psychologist is likely to find the interesting field of forensic psychology on his or her list of skills eventually. In the past, psychologists have been assigned to naval prisons and brigs, although none are at present. However, when such an installation is located within the service area of psychologists stationed, for example, at a naval hospital or a recruit training command, they are frequently asked to examine and advise on the disposition of personnel charged with any of the full array of offenses, ranging from AWOL to rape or murder. This may also include charges of child or spouse abuse if the act was committed on a federal reservation; the work involves not only counseling military families in which such abuse has occurred but also diagnosing the family situation and making recommendations to the authorities.

Psychologists may also be asked to testify at a court-martial as expert witnesses or, in their capacity as officers, to serve as members of the court. Their opinion may be asked about such issues as the role of insanity in the committing of a crime, the mental state of the defendant or the accused, and the role of alcohol and drugs in producing illegal behavior as well as use of intoxication as a legal defense.

When insanity is an issue in a court-martial, a formal Sanity Board may be convened. Membership on this board has in the past been limited to medical officers, but since 1987 clinical psychologists have been officially allowed to serve as full members. Historically, this is of interest because for many years physicians and psychiatrists bitterly opposed allowing a psychologist to testify in civilian courts on matters of insanity or feeblemindedness. However, as the various states began to license psychologists after World War II, this gradually changed. That this status is now formally recognized in the Uniform Code of Military Justice (UCMJ) finally updates in the Armed Forces what was a long and arduous battle between the fields of psychiatry and psychology in the civilian sector.

On a large residential base, such as exist in the Marine Corps, there is ample opportunity for the Navy clinical psychologist stationed there to provide support consultation to the local Provost Marshal, whose organization is charged with responsibilities not unlike those of a police department in a small city.

The Psychologist's Role in the NSIC

In recognition of the fact that clinical psychologists possess skills that can be applied to the forensic area, a billet was created with the Naval Security and Investigative Command (NSIC). This service is charged with investigating all crimes committed within naval jurisdiction or by naval personnel, such as theft, murder, and espionage. In the years following World War II, this group was best known for its work in discovering homosexuals in uniform (homosexuality was then a court-martial offense) and seeking out suspected communists, especially during the Joseph McCarthy era of "Red bashing." Today the NSIC is a much more sophisticated organization and its mission greatly enlarged. In recent years a series of espionage cases received considerable publicity, such as the Walker-Whitworth case, in which naval personnel sold communication secrets to the Soviets; the Pollard case, in which a Navy civilian employee sold secrets to Israel; and the Marine Corps guards stationed at the U.S. Embassy in Moscow, who were accused of illegally associating with Soviet agents and compromising security.

As of 1987, the psychologist assigned to this work, Lt. Comdr. David N. Hiland, MSC, USN, operates primarily as a forensic psychologist, but he is also trained as and holds the title of Special Agent. This additional training is patterned after the FBI Academy program at Quantico, Virginia. Hiland qualifies quarterly with revolver and shotgun, and he has received instruction in unarmed self-defense, techniques of investigation, counterintelligence operations, and the application of the Uniform Code of Military Justice—the legal framework within which the military must function. Dr. Hiland teaches courses in hostage negotiation and stress management and serves as liaison with behavioral scientists in other federal agencies. He also participates in the investigation of crimes, including the creation and use of psychological profiles of suspected criminals, and develops actuarial (statistical) tables for the "most probable" offender in specific cases. He also uses hypnosis as an investigative aid. While he is not in a health-care billet, Dr. Hiland is viewed as the staff psychologist and responds to local crises, such as evaluating a Special Agent, working with the victim of a serious crime, and offering short-term counseling to those staff members who request it.

The Marine Security Battalion

The Marine Security Battalion is a free-standing battalion that reports directly to the Commandant of the Marine Corps. It is presently located at the Marine Corps Combat Development Command at Quantico, Virginia. The battalion is responsible for selecting and training noncommissioned officers for duty at the 140 American embassies and consulates around the world. Their task is to guard the physical integrity of each installation, control access to the premises, and protect classified documents. These officers became the object of public attention in April 1987 when several of those stationed at the Moscow Embassy were accused of illegally associating with female Soviet agents and allowing them access to restricted areas, which presumably compromised our national security. Most of the charges were subsequently reduced or dropped, but the resulting publicity created a scandal, including *Time* magazine's picture of a Marine with a painted-in black eye. This incident raised the issue of how these officers were selected and the nature of their character and psychological stability (Wilentz, 1987).

Two years before, in October of 1985, the commanding officer of the battalion, (now) Brig. Gen. Walter Boomer, had recognized the need for better screening of the students and preparations were under way to improve the program. At Boomer's invitation, Forrest A. Sherman, Lt. Comdr., MSC, USN, then stationed at the medical clinic at Quantico, studied the problem; with the assistance of Dr. Peter Finley, a reservist clinical psychologist (now Colonel, USMCR, Retired), he submitted suggestions. As a result a new billet was created, and Dr. Sherman became the battalion's first psychologist in July 1987 (Jones, 1987).

Sherman has initiated efforts to: (a) design, validate, and implement a program for the psychological screening of all applicants to the school; (b) establish a program of education and intervention to reduce alcohol abuse; and (c) improve the mental health environment of the school and to establish a support system for improving it for the officers in the field, including courses in the impact of culture shock, the management of stress, and how to access mental health facilities. The senior officers are given additional training as lay mental health workers. Sherman is also creating a worldwide telephone network between himself and the guard units overseas in order to provide support and advice.

The tours of duty are currently for 3 years, during which time a person may rotate among two or three different countries. However, because of the sensitivity of the location, those being rotated into Moscow or Leningrad are returned to Quantico for additional screening by Sherman before they go to Russia. Unfortunately, this program was not operating in time to prevent the problems at the U.S. Embassy in Moscow.

As the only officer of the Navy Medical Department assigned directly to the battalion, Sherman is also attempting to centralize a system for ministering to the general health needs of the widely scattered guards. This will include a central location to monitor their health records and to document the need for and completion of routine procedures such as annual physicals, inoculations, and treatments. It is also planned to inventory all medical facilities available to each of the far-flung installations so that quick response is possible for both routine and acute medical needs, including referral or evacuation to the nearest appropriate source of treatment. Some readers will recognize this effort as a systems analysis in public health, a subject not likely to be included in the average graduate school curriculum in psychology. This provides another illustration of the diverse and interesting ways in which Navy psychologists are able to apply their broad training. It also reflects the previously described definition of clinical psychology as "that which clinical psychologists do."

For many years, Marine guards at embassies and consulates were considered "window dressing," and most men were accepted simply on the basis of volunteering and looking "sharp." However, in recent years the attacks upon U.S. installations by terrorists and the increasingly sophisticated attempts by enemy agents to infiltrate the system have recast the role of these officers. They are now expected to display an increased amount of responsibility and psychological stability and to be expert in the use of antiterrorist skills, including the carrying of fully loaded weapons at all times, facility in the use of "quickdraw" techniques with small arms and shotguns, urban riot control, and bomb disposal ("Low-tech threat," 1987). Most recently the Department of Defense has announced plans to admit women into the Security Battalion (Ford, 1988). The contribution of Navy psychologists to this program promises to be substantial, and they are likely to find this assignment exciting and rewarding.

CHAPTER 23

Research

As is true in the civilian sector, most clinical psychologists in the Navy do not have a high publication rate. Their primary role is to provide psychological services—a task that can more than occupy a normal work day. However, while research is not required in the Navy, it is encouraged, and there are many unique opportunities for research. For example, the Navy and Marine Corps represent a huge pool of subjects about whom one can not only gather extensive data but also execute the follow-up studies needed in many kinds of research. In addition to psychiatric patients, there is also a wide range of medical patients and normal persons, including dependents.

The career track of a clinician does not usually provide for full-time research assignments, and promotion to senior rank is not based on such billets. However, single tours of duty at one of the Navy's research installations do take place—especially if the person has a special interest or talent in the field. Sometimes these tours include administration as well as the conduct of hands-on investigations. A significant number of clinical psychologists in uniform have published substantially, not only adding to their military record but enhancing their reputations in the field at large. In many cases this has allowed them to qualify for a higher level of employment following their military service.

It is in the area of research that the distinction between clinical psychology and general psychology becomes most obscured. As one catalogues the research to which Navy clinical psychologists have contributed, the range and variety of subject matter is amazing. Not only have they worked in the traditional areas of mental health and psychopathology, but they have also accomplished much in such areas as psychophysics, psychophysiology, human engineering , sociology, personnel selection, epidemiology, statistics, psychometrics, safety, and industrial psychology. This is a testimony not only to the broad training possessed by this group but also to their creativity and versatility.

In other sections of this book, some of the research activity by these psychologists has been described—at the Submarine Base at Groton, Connecticut, in the field of aviation at such places as the Naval Air Station at Pensacola, Florida, and at the various recruit training centers. Two other installations have a history of providing an opportunity for clinicians to engage in research—the Naval Medical Field Research Laboratory at the Marine base at Camp Lejeune, North Carolina, and the Naval Medical Research Institute at Bethesda, Maryland (NMRI).

Naval Medical Field Research Laboratory

Because of his civilian background in research, the author, Frederick L. McGuire, was assigned in 1952 to the research laboratory at Camp Lejeune. This base was home to the Second Marine Division and contained more than 25,000 personnel and their dependents. As the only psychologist at the laboratory, the person occupying this billet was permitted free rein to propose and conduct research in areas of his or her choice. For example, McGuire's predecessor, a civilian nonclinician, had researched and instituted a highly successful program in re-medial and speed reading for base personnel that became a model for the Marine Corps.

In addition to a number of studies designed to explore a wide variety of hypotheses, McGuire launched a program in the study of psychological factors associated with private motor vehicle accidents. (At that time more Marines were being killed and wounded on U.S. highways than in combat in Korea.) Because such work requires a huge population for study, the Marine base location offered an opportunity not available elsewhere. This research resulted in publication of the first empirical study on the subject completed in this country—and the second in the world. McGuire continued to work in this field throughout his military and civilian career, and he received an award for research from the National Safety Council in 1968.

Because of the pioneering nature of this work and its importance to both the civilian and military communities, it attracted a great deal of attention. BuMed constructed an elaborate and colorful 35' x 8' display and presented it at numerous medical and scientific meetings around the country. Reprints were requested from U.S. and European centers, and McGuire was asked to make presentations at numerous national and international meetings. These events represent another instance in which the importance of work pioneered by the Navy was equal to or greater than that in the civilian sector.

Two other clinical psychologists followed McGuire at the Camp Lejeune laboratory—James A. Spingarn, now a practicing psychotherapist in New York City, and Robert R. Knapp, currently the founder and owner of EdITS, a pub-lisher of psychological tests in San Diego, California.

Spingarn describes his role as being, among other things, a troubleshooter for problems arising on the base. Two such episodes illustrate nicely the fascinating variety of problems that often characterize the work of a clinical psychologist in uniform. Spingarn writes:

> I was called upon to investigate an outbreak of hysteria among female personnel in a machine records room. My survey revealed a high noise level in the work area of a particular frequency of sound which could produce sudden breaks from concentrative ability in some of the more vulnerable workers. Hysteria, being contagious in a group setting, would then spread to the more pent-up and histrionically inclined until a mass reaction occurred. Work broke down temporarily until calm once again supervened. The remedy was new sound insulation in the barracks housing these particular machines.
>
> On another occasion I was requested to look into what seemed an unusually frequent occurrence of alopecia areata (baldness suddenly appearing in half-dollar sized patches) among enlisted men and for which there was no explanation. Extensive interviewing revealed two significant factors: they had either been re-called to active duty involuntarily (during the Korean War) and/or had recently received "Dear John" letters from wives or sweethearts left behind. (J. A. Spingarn, personal communication, November 1987).

Spingarn also participated in double-blind studies of seasickness remedies, experimented with hypnosis as a technique for enhancing human performance in the field, and saw patients in psychotherapy. Before his discharge in 1957, he was also sent to Johns Hopkins Hospital to study electroencephalography. In summing up his tour, he writes: "The military, in granting young people large responsibilities, helps in their growth and supports their enthusiasm for contributing as much as they can to the needs of the service. I, for one, appreciated the system."

Robert Knapp, who succeeded Spingarn, was able to pursue his interest in psychometrics, which subsequently became the focus of his civilian career. He studied personality correlates associated with helicopter pilot performance in the Marine Corps and psychometric predictors of sick bay visits.

Among the laboratory's accomplishments was the pioneering development of life-saving body armor used by the Marine Corps as well as civilian police departments. Unfortunately, however, the laboratory has since been decommissioned.

Naval Medical Research Institute

Founded in 1942, the Naval Medical Research Institute (NMRI), located in Bethesda, Maryland, was initially involved in the development and testing of devices for use by the fleet. Early studies focused on protective clothing, desalination of sea water, aviation oxygen equipment, insect repellents and insect control, and the effects of tropical environments and immersion in cold water. During this period vaccines and body armor were tested and night vision, nutrition, oral hygiene, and tropical and parasitic diseases were investigated. Following World War II, the institute expanded dramatically to embrace many disciplines of medical research. The world's first tissue bank was organized here in 1949; America's first astronauts received part of their training at NMRI; early versions of the heart-lung machine were perfected; the freezing techniques that make sperm banks possible were developed; and one of the world's most sophisticated complexes for hyperbaric studies exists here—for the study of problems encountered by man in an underwater environment.

Today, with a staff of 450, NMRI is engaged in such project areas as combat medicine and the treating and healing of wounds, advanced surgical techniques, infectious diseases, tissue transplantation, tropical diseases (a unit is maintained in Lima, Peru), and reaction to and protection from environmental stresses, such as hot and cold temperatures, radiation, and toxic substances.

Several clinical psychologists have contributed to the output at NMRI. Following several tours at BuMed, John E. Rasmussen (now Captain, MSC, USN, Retired) participated in studies in habitability environments. This research involved the question of how people could exist, perform, and survive in such locations as nuclear submarines, the South Pole, space stations, and fallout shelters. Several studies were conducted in which volunteers were confined for 2 weeks in a shelter that was 48 feet long, 25 feet wide, and 5 feet underground, simulating an attempt to survive the radiation fallout from a nuclear attack. All supplies and equipment for survival were prestored and self-contained, and all air intake was carefully filtered. During this period physiological, nutritional, bacteriological, dental, and psychological studies were conducted on the inhabitants. From these studies, several important guidelines emerged for survival under such conditions (Rasmussen, 1963; Ross et al., 1966).

In 1987, now-retired Commander John F. House, MSC, USN, completed his tour as Specialty Advisor to NavMedCom for Clinical Psychology, accepted a research billet at NMRI, and engaged in studying the responses of normal persons to a variety of physiological and psychological stressors. As a clinician who has a subspecialty designator in research, Dr. House also served a previous tour at the Naval Health Research Center at San Diego (see below), where he studied relaxation techniques and biofeedback as applied to psychiatric patients for insomnia and anxiety reduction. He also participated in a number of studies of sleep and circadian rhythms.

Naval Health Research Center

The focal point for research in areas related to psychiatry and clinical psychology in the Navy has for many years been the Naval Health Research Center at San Diego, California. Originally designated as the Navy Medical Neuropsychiatric Research Unit, the center was organized in large measure by the efforts of John E. Rasmussen, who was then serving as Chief of the Clinical Psychology

Section. The popular legend is that the idea of a separate research unit was born during a refreshment break at the Grant Hotel in San Diego when Rasmussen was challenged by then-Chief of Psychiatry George N. Raines to stop complaining about the lack of research relevant to the mission of the Navy and "do something about it." With the help of Raines and his successor, the late John E. Nardini, the unit was commissioned in 1959.

The first uniformed clinical psychologists assigned to the research unit were Allen E. McMichael and the author, Frederick L. McGuire. The other "plank owners," as the original crew of a ship is known, included civilians Eric K. Gunderson, Laverne C. Johnson, John A. Plag, and the first Scientific Director, Walter L. Wilkins, then a Professor of Psychology at St. Louis University. All were originally trained as clinical psychologists. Wilkins had also been one of the first clinical psychologists to join the HV(S) group during World War II. Prior to Pearl Harbor, Dr. Wilkins was stationed at the Marine Corps Recruit Depot in San Diego and participated in the hectic days of the mass screening of recruits when hostilities broke out. He remained in the Reserves and eventually retired as Captain, MSC, USNR. Dr. Wilkins retired from civil service in 1977 after a distinguished career as one of the most talented research administrators in the country. In that same year, Dr. Plag also retired. Dr. Johnson was appointed Chief Scientist, a position he held until his retirement in 1987, when he was succeeded by Dr. Gunderson, who, in turn, retired in 1989.

In an address given in 1981 by Captain Paul Nelson, then Chief of the Medical Service Corps, the creation of the unit was described as follows:

> It became evident that the Navy Medical Department needed to develop an in-house psychiatric research capability, staffed with professionals of the many disciplines required and devoted full-time to research. This capability should not be an integral part of any operational, training, or therapeutic community, but it should be geographically and organizationally accessible, and by mission related to those activities. . . . From many angles, the Navy Medical Neuropsychiatric Research Unit [is] unique—not only in the defense research establishment of this nation, but among psychological and psychiatric units of any sort worldwide. It was practical, yet theoretical in substantiation of Kurt Lewin's dictum that "there is nothing so practical as a good theory"! It was scholarly, yet responsible to everyday problems. It was discerning, yet inclusive. It was "dust bowl empiricism," yet clinically intuitive. It was modest, yet great. It was learned, yet learning. (P. D. Nelson, personal communication, 1987)

The unit's three major areas of research were, and have continued to be: (a) to evaluate the efficacy of recruit psychiatric screening and assessment procedures in practice since the 1940s, and also of alternative approaches; (b) to determine the special problems of psychiatric adjustment in unusual naval environments and develop methods for mitigating them; and (c) to assess the role of cortical and psychophysiological activity in perceptual, motor, and cognitive performance.

In the more than 30 years of its existence, the center has produced some outstanding work in these and other areas. Perhaps its best known work was in recruit screening. As described in the previous section of this book, this research not only placed recruit screening on an empirical basis and carried it to the cutting edge of scientific knowledge, but it also clearly demonstrated tremendous cost-effectiveness and cost-benefits to the Navy.

Operation Deep Freeze

One of the research center's active projects is Operation Deep Freeze. In cooperation with the International Geophysical Year, during which scientists gathered data about the Antarctic as well as the rest of the earth, in 1955–56 the Navy established stations on the Ross Sea and one at the geographic South Pole, both of which are still maintained. The latter is named the Amundsen-Scott Station, after the only two explorers ever to have led successful expeditions to the South Pole. Numbering about 20 Navy personnel and civilian scientists, this group is completely isolated from the rest of the world for nearly 12 months. Once the Antarctic night sets in, they cannot get to the outside world, and help cannot reach them even in the event of extreme emergency. That region is larger than the United States and Europe combined, but it contains no vegetation or wildlife except along its coasts. The coldest temperature in the world was recorded here—minus 109.6° Fahrenheit. Temperatures rarely go above freezing, the winds are almost constant, including 200 mile-per-hour blizzards, and the ice cap in some places is 10,000 feet thick.

The group exists entirely on its own supplies. However, they are relatively comfortable: They live in heated buildings, they have plenty of good food, they have specially designed clothing, and they have a small library and a few recreational devices such as a Ping-Pong table and record players. The commanding officer of the station is usually a Navy medical officer who is also responsible for medical and health care. Nevertheless, they have to work extremely hard not only to collect scientific data but to maintain the station. A small mistake could be fatal—if the station burned down, they would certainly perish from exposure. They have to limit their working time outdoors because of the danger of frostbite, and especially during the long night, they have to be careful not to wander far from the station and risk getting lost in the white wilderness. Once the 6-month-long night sets in, they are, for all practical purposes, confined to the limits of the indoor working spaces.

This situation made for an ideal real-life laboratory. In 1958 the group was headed by Lt. Sidney Tolchin, MC, USN. According to a preset protocol, he administered a variety of psychometric devices to the men throughout their tour. This not only resulted in some of the first empirical data on psychological adjustment at the South Pole but also in one of the first publications of the new unit (McGuire & Tolchin, 1961).

Over the years a number of psychological, biological, and geographic studies have been conducted in the Antarctic, and in addition to participating in research projects, Navy clinical psychologists have been especially active in the screening of volunteers sent to winter-over. This work has continued uninterrupted to this date (e.g., Gunderson, 1966; Palinkas, 1985).

In the early years, the psychological screening for Antarctica took place at the Seabee supply base at Davisville, Rhode Island, and from this location all of the supplies for the Antarctic were gathered and shipped. This also gave rise to several oft-repeated anecdotes. One of these included the time a supply officer who later was found to be psychotic ordered thousands of Ping-Pong balls instead of the small quantity appropriate for recreational use, apparently under the delusion that in an emergency they could be used as flotation devices. The seriousness of this mistake was the fact that the Ping-Pong balls would have replaced a shipment of vitally needed heating oil! Fortunately, the switch was caught just prior to loading.

Center for Prisoner of War Studies

One of the most interesting programs initiated at NHRC was the Center for Prisoner of War Studies (CPWS), directed by civilian clinical psychologist John Plag and partially supported by the U.S. Army. The establishment of the center in 1972 was motivated by humanitarian concern for the welfare of our prisoners of war (POWs) in Vietnam during the late 1960s, as well as concern for the immediate and long-term welfare of their families and the families of those men declared missing in action. Data were collected upon such phenomena as the effects of stress upon human performance and the adjustments of families— particularly on children who endured long periods with the father absent. There was also an effort to understand further the etiology and pathogenesis of the morbidity and mortality of World War II and Korea, which, by comparison with Vietnam, was excessively high (Plag et al., 1979).

Over a period of years, a variety of researchers and disciplines contributed to studies at the POW Center, including, of course, a number of uniformed and civilian clinical psychologists. Studies were conducted under the rubrics of Medical, Captivity, and Family, and a large library and archival center was also established.

In comparison with POWs from World War II and Korea, it was found that the Vietnam returnees came back in better health and continued to show less disease. Also, when compared with their fellow aviators (as most of them were) who had a similar military background but had not been held captive, Vietnam POWs appeared to show no basic differences in any of the major biological systems.

The physical, environmental, psychological, and social stresses experienced by the POWs were also studied. One of the main findings was that each prisoner perceived the captivity experience in his own particular manner. Differences were a function of personality, previous experience with stress, and the particular prison environment. The supportive effects of command structure were evident, with the senior officers contributing much to the coping ability of the younger men. The type and effectiveness of each person's coping mechanisms depended on his age and rank and whether he had to endure solitary confinement. The high intelligence, maturity, and strong sense of mission of this group were also of paramount importance in tolerating captivity stresses.

It also became evident that SERE training had definite survival value, and it was recommended that the program be continued and expanded. The research program also produced a number of suggestions for updating the curriculum—another example of how psychological research in the Navy can have a direct payoff for the operational forces.

A 5-year longitudinal study of the families of the POWs compared their physical and social health with the families of naval aviators who flew in Vietnam at about the same time but who were not captured. A remarkable finding was that most wives and children were able to survive their ordeal with little effect from the stress. In fact, for some men and their families, captivity and separation served to strengthen their bonds and build new resources. These research findings also produced a number of suggestions on how to help Navy families cope with the routine deployment of husbands and fathers.

Research on POW families at the center produced several tangible long-term benefits for the Navy at large. In 1973, the center published an assessment of the needs of wives of POWs/MIAs (missing in action). It proposed that the Navy and Army establish a formal Family Assistance Program that would put into practice what had been learned from research (Hunter & Plag, 1973).

Since that time several tri-service conferences have been held in order to highlight the need for services by all military families. The catalyst for establishing these programs was the immediate need for service to the POW/MIA families, as demonstrated by the work at the POW Center, but it was soon enlarged to include the general military population. As a result, there exists today a service-wide program of family assistance funded by the Department of Defense. At bases in each of the branches, Family Service Centers have been established, staffed by civilian and uniformed personnel from a variety of disciplines, including clinical psychology, social work, medicine, and the clergy. These centers played a central role in assisting the families of those personnel involved in the disasters aboard the USS *Stark* and the USS *Iowa*. Another result has been the creation of billets for commissioned social workers in the Navy, a duty assignment that did not exist in the Navy until it was encouraged by the work initiated at CPWS, though the U.S. Army has employed social workers for a long time.

Traditionally, large segments of the military have been composed of unmarried men, and the old cliche was, "If the military had wanted you to have a wife, they would have issued you one." Today family members outnumber active duty personnel, and it is evident that if military men and women are able to perform effectively, the needs of their families will have to receive high priority, especially among the younger enlisted personnel. This indicates that family services is one more area in which there will be an increasing need for the services of clinical psychologists.

In 1979, the POW Center was for all practical purposes disbanded. However, since that time all ex-POWs have been given annual medical examinations at the Naval Air Station in Pensacola, Florida, and longitudinal studies on their well-being continue.

While it was in existence, the POW Center provided a unique opportunity for Navy clinical psychologists to integrate their clinical and research talents with those of physicians, biochemists, psychiatrists, sociologists, epidemiologists, legal officers, and physiologists and to benefit from an association with a talented and patriotic group of men and their equally dedicated families.

In 1988, the Naval Health Research Center had a staff of about 85 military and civilian personnel. In addition to the civilian clinical psychologists, there is usually at least one uniformed psychologist attached. A number of the latter have rotated through while completing their PhD dissertations, and others have served in the role of Executive Officer (the Commanding Officer is usually a medical officer). Today the mission of the Center is more simply defined but much broader in scope: "To support fleet operational readiness through research, development, tests, and evaluation on the biomedical and psychological aspects of Navy and Marine Corps personnel health and performance, and to perform such other functions or tasks as may be directed."

The research programs are currently carried out by four departments: Environmental Medicine, Health Psychology, Behavioral Psychopharmacology, and Environmental Physiology. Research into the many aspects of the physical and psychological stresses of naval environments has produced significant work in preventive and clinical psychiatry, neurology, psychopharmacology, biochemistry, infectious disease, psychophysiology, physical fitness, social psychology, sleep, sleep loss, sustained performance, epidemiology, occupational health, health psychology, and computerized medical information systems—a feast of opportunities for the research-minded psychologist.

The pattern of irregular assignments of clinical psychologists to full-time research billets is very likely to continue in the future, but when they do occur they offer a fascinating and enriching opportunity.

Epilogue

CHAPTER 24

The Personal World of a Navy Clinical Psychologist

Most people derive a sense of identity from the nature of their work. In addition, society affixes a certain amount of prestige and social status to various occupations. In numerous surveys over the years, for example, such occupations as physician or judge have usually ranked near the top, as has Army/Navy officer (e.g., Cattell, 1942). Also ranked highly by the general population are the titles of professor and psychologist. It follows that Navy psychologists can expect to be accorded similar status in any list of occupational titles. However, they will find that they are members of more than one group; they will derive certain benefits and responsibilities from each of three rather disparate communities— Psychology at large, the Navy at large, and Navy psychology—and will have the luxury of some control over the extent to which they participate in each of them.

Junior clinical psychologists entering the Navy usually give priority to establishing themselves in the general field of psychology. There is often the need to finish the doctoral dissertation, achieve state licensure, focus on one or more subspecialties, and polish clinical skills. If the individual does not plan to make a career of naval service, time is also spent in planning the details of a career in civilian life.

Benefits of Navy Life

The early years in the Navy can also be financially comfortable. Students attending a university on a Navy scholarship are extremely well paid compared with the average graduate student, and this is equally so when they are completing the predoctoral internship. This favorable state of affairs remains during the first few years of active duty, Navy pay and benefits being very comparable to civilian employment at that level. Depending upon one's aspirations, the financial rewards remain more than adequate compared with, say, the salary of a college professor or a hospital staff psychologist. The opportunity for early retirement and pursuit of a second career also translates into a substantial cash benefit.

Unfortunately, as one becomes more senior in the Navy, the comparison with civilian income is much less favorable.

While personal motives vary, most naval officers experience a sense of pride in performing both a patriotic and a public service. Episodes during the Vietnam War notwithstanding, there is a feeling of satisfaction in knowing that, if only in some small measure, one has served one's country and can identify with that class of Americans known as veterans. A sense of group identification is not uncommon. Even if it is only secretly, it is a rare American who does not experience deep emotion when witnessing or participating in a formal military parade or the playing of the national anthem at a public ceremony. The candid officer/psychologist would also have to admit to a certain amount of pride in wearing a uniform that so publicly identifies him or her as a person of above-average social standing and intellectual and occupational achievement.

Family life can also be pleasant in the Navy. Moving to a new location every few years is seen by some as a handicap, but others enjoy the change and the broadening and educational benefits of travel. Unlike their colleagues in other branches of the Navy, psychologists are seldom assigned a duty station to which dependents cannot accompany them. In fact, most clinical psychologists have completed their entire careers without prolonged family separation. In addition, unlike the Army and Air Force, most Navy stations are located in desirable seaports or metropolitan areas.

An active social life is also available to the family. At those stations in more remote areas, such as at some Marine Corps bases, there is a close sense of community among the families, and recreational and educational facilities are usually superb. In those urban areas where military personnel are dispersed throughout the civilian community, the lack of cohesion is usually compensated for by the cosmopolitan nature of the location (e.g., Washington, DC, or Philadelphia). The existence of job security for a member of the Regular Navy is also viewed as a plus by many families.

Opportunity also exists for psychologists interested in enhancing their careers in the general field of psychology. While research and publication are not required, they are encouraged. If one is so motivated, it is possible to engage in a wide variety of research projects. As in civilian life, this may involve working beyond the traditional 8-hour day, but one can be assured of access to a wide variety of populations for psychological study as well as use of facilities. Presentation of one's work at professional meetings is also encouraged; while the availability of travel funds may vary, release-time is almost always permitted. If they are so motivated, there is no reason that Navy clinical psychologists cannot publish regularly—as many of them have.

Enhancement of one's clinical skills is possible not only by working with a variety of military populations but also through attendance at meetings and short courses. Release-time and frequently financial support are available for this. At this writing, increased use is being made of the ACDUINST (active duty under instruction) program, in which psychologists are assigned to postdoctoral study at an appropriate university.

Disadvantages of Navy Life

One possible disadvantage of Navy life compared with civilian life is that because of changing duty stations one cannot always establish roots in a local community of psychologists and participate in long-term activities, such as serving as an officer of professional societies or building long-term programs. However, identification with the field is usually established through membership in the American Psychological Association and other national and international groups.

Perhaps the most important distinction to be made between the professional life of Navy clinical psychologists and that of many of their civilian counterparts is the element of freedom and responsibility. As has been highlighted throughout this volume, contrary to the perceptions of many civilians, the Navy offers clinical psychologists almost an inordinate amount of responsibility early in their careers and combines it with an extraordinary amount of freedom in which to fulfill it. As previously described, clinical psychologists are often the only mental health workers of any type in a given location. Not only must they be self-sufficient and able to improvise, but also they are often responsible for a large community of active duty personnel, their dependents, and sometimes a civilian population.

To some this translates into a sense of loneliness and lack of structure; to others it represents an opportunity to express their individuality and to broaden their professional horizons. For the latter group this has resulted in a job that many describe as "fun rather than work"; for the former it often results in a shorter tour of duty. However, this twofold characterization does not preclude the fact that while many ex-Navy psychologists felt that the Navy did not fill their personal requirements for a career, nearly all of them have expressed satisfaction with the experience and agreed that it contributed to their professional growth and preparation for a career in the civilian sector. A significant number remain in the Active Naval Reserve: they join a local unit, drill regularly, perform 2 weeks' active duty once a year, and receive retirement pay when they reach the age of 60. Many have found that these funds, when combined with other resources, have either permitted early retirement in civilian life or made retirement more comfortable.

This is not to say that all clinical psychologists in uniform have an entirely positive experience. For some families, moving between assignments is neither feasible nor acceptable. There is no guarantee that one is going to have competent or amenable superiors or colleagues. (However, there is always the prospect that the next assignment will be more pleasant or that certain individuals will be transferred.)

In times of national emergency, those in uniform are subject to sudden assignment to places where one is separated from one's family and, possibly, placed in harm's way—although to date no clinical psychologist has suffered injury or death because of hostile action. As one progresses through the ranks, increasing effort is made to assign one to a station that is acceptable, but there is always the risk that during a naval career some assignments will be incompatible with an officer's wishes. However, psychologists in the Regular Navy are usually consulted about upcoming transfer and have strong input prior to each reassignment.

Some Navy families expect to receive high-level medical and dental care for the officer, spouse, and children. While U.S. military medical departments are generally able to provide the best care in the world under combat conditions, they are sometimes below pay-for-care civilian standards. The average naval officer can expect that on occasion he or she will have to provide supplemental or alternative medical and dental care for his or her dependents.

For some individuals, psychologists included, the mere idea that an authority has excessive power over one's daily life, even in the abstract, is unacceptable. In the author's opinion, this is more myth than fact in the Navy Medical Department, which is no more restrictive than civilian life with its various constraints.

Other Issues

Other issues are sometimes raised by the civilian psychologist contemplating entry into the Armed Forces. Some individuals who are morally opposed to war may question whether they should so actively support the military. The answer to this is clearly one of personal choice, but it must be remembered that as a member of the Navy Medical Department, the clinical psychologist is a noncombatant. The psychologist's role is to provide psychological services to individuals, many of whom may be just as opposed to war and are not in uniform by choice. Regardless of the personal beliefs of the psychologist, these persons are entitled to psychological services as fellow human beings.

The question has been raised as to whether the clinical psychologist has divided loyalties when a patient or client shares confidences that may be in direct conflict with what the Navy perceives as its best interests, and whether the psychologist should reveal these confidences to higher authorities. In practice this has proven to be a nonissue. In the author's experience, when senior Navy psychologists are asked this question, their unanimous opinion has been that in fact this has never been a problem. For example, agents of a hostile foreign power have never been known to seek psychotherapy from a psychologist in uniform or have never shared this type of secret with the therapist. Other information, such as hating one's commanding officer or harboring thoughts of desertion, are not considered appropriate grounds for breaching a client's right to confidentiality. In practice, such individuals sooner or later solve such problems by finding ways to separate themselves legally from the service. The Navy does not view members of its Medical Department as informants or depend upon them to be directly responsible for maintaining military discipline in the ranks. However, if patients indicate they plan to harm themselves or others, a situation not unique to the military, psychologists deal with the issue just as they would in civilian life.

There is another important but often overlooked contribution the noncareer military officer makes—that of helping retain civilian control over the military establishment. The American form of democracy was established with the idea that ultimate control of the nation is in the hands of the people. In many countries, this is impossible because a strong military force rules the nation unilaterally or is able to dictate who is in office. Corruption of officials and imprisonment of dissenters are usually present in such situations.

At any one time, the majority of officers in the U.S. Armed Forces are products of civilian schools and do not view the military as a permanent career. As civilian-soldiers, either on active duty or as members of the Active Reserves, their point of view and influence on the day-by-day conduct of the uniformed services is a vital counterbalance. It is often taken for granted, but history shows clearly that without this constant flow of civilian input, a democratic nation risks being unduly influenced by a militaristic minority. Whether as a psychologist or as a member of the line, every member of the officer corps of the U.S. Armed Forces who serves only briefly contributes to this important influence.

The Future of Clinical Psychology in the U.S. Navy

T his section was prepared with the assistance of a committee of senior and retired Navy psychologists located in the Washington, DC, area. On February 17, 1988, this group met at Bethesda, Maryland, and brainstormed their ideas about the issues and directions that would characterize Navy clinical psychology in the years ahead. In addition, each of them has given continued help throughout the writing of this book. With the thanks of the author, they are identified as follows: Bruce Becker, Captain, MSC, USNR-R; Patricia W. Crigler, Captain, MSC, USN; William G. Cumming, Jr., Captain, MSC, USN, Retired; John F. House, Commander, MSC, USN, Retired; Robert D. McCullah, Captain, MSC, USN; Frank A. Mullins, Captain, MSC, USN; and Paul D. Nelson, Captain, MSC, USN, Retired.

The Problem of Variable Budget Support

The committee unanimously agreed that some circumstances in the Navy would never change, such as the variable level of budget support ranging from feast to famine and all points between. In spite of this, the number of authorized billets for clinical psychologists has not decreased thus far, and there is every indication that they will continue to increase. As of February 1988, there were about 115 authorized billets, as opposed to the two psychologists on active duty in 1948. Just as the civilian population had to learn about the benefits of psychology over the years, the Navy had to be educated about what clinical psychology can offer and how it can meet various needs identified in the service. This was not only true in the early years of the MSC, it was also the reason for the gradual buildup that began in the 1960s as psychologists began to offer services in such areas as alcohol rehabilitation, counseling (at Annapolis), and a number of operational billets such as those at SERE and SEAL units. As discussed below, there are still many places in which service could be provided, but the Navy has recognized that it would be counterproductive to promise services if the personnel were not available and the new billets not continually filled. This has dictated a policy of requesting new billets while simultaneously requesting the additional personnel—a process that is continuous but that necessarily takes place in small yearly increments.

The Problem of Continuity

The issue of continuity in any one billet will probably remain a problem. Since many assignments are of the Lone Ranger type and transferees do not always overlap, a particular job may be redefined each time a new psychologist arrives. In some billets, this may not be a problem because there is so much to do that any one person can attack only a small portion. In other billets, where the needs are rather well defined and circumscribed, continuity is a problem because a newly assigned uniformed psychologist must use valuable lead time in order to make the position fully operational. In some commands, especially those staffed primarily by civilians, the continuity problem may be unacceptable to the local managers, and it has sometimes caused them to consider replacing a uniformed psychologist with a civilian. Because the employment of civilians (these are Civil Service positions) is under the control of local commands, NavMedCom has minimal influence, and the issue of uniformed versus civilian personnel will probably remain unresolved in the foreseeable future. The same is true of the problem of the lower efficiency created by the rotation among uniformed psychologists.

The Need for Suitable Personnel

What type of person should the Navy recruit for its clinical psychology services in the future? To date the practice has been merely to accept the best applicants available as measured by the usual graduate school standards. The route of entry usually has been through the internship program; as discussed below, it will probably be more so in the future. Fortunately, Navy internships are financially very competitive, and the applicant pool is not only larger than needed but continues to attract well-qualified people. However, entering psychologists seldom have a working knowledge of the Navy, and their image of clinical practice is often limited to that of the so-called 50-minute-hour, together with some exposure to hospital inpatients, and they expect to receive training compatible with that image. At present, that type of internship training is being offered at Bethesda, but it appears that it should also include exposure to the "real" Navy, such as the fleet, the Marine Corps, and other operational billets.

One solution is to recruit personnel with active duty experience. To date, the arrival of such people has been fortuitous, but perhaps in the future it should be planned. Perhaps scholarships should be offered to young line officers who either desire a change in their naval careers or who are serving as Reservists. As recounted earlier, Lt. John L. Sexton, MSC, USN, currently serving with the SERE program in California, is an Annapolis graduate, who, after serving 8 years in the Marine Corps, left the service on his own initiative to become a clinical psychologist and reentered the Navy after receiving his doctorate. Active recruiting of such individuals could well be part of the Navy's future.

Graduate students with prior enlisted experience have also proven to be an asset to Navy psychology. A number of enlisted individuals currently on active duty possess a bachelor's degree. Perhaps they could be encouraged to apply to a graduate program in clinical psychology and, if accepted, be awarded scholarships.

It is generally agreed that recruitment of licensed practicing psychologists will never become a good source of personnel. These people are generally established in a community or work situation, and joining a mobile society does not usually appeal to them or their families. However, there are individuals in special situations to whom this type of career change is attractive, and they are, of course, encouraged to apply for a commission. One drawback is that these people are usually older than 35, the age limit currently in place for first-time commissions. There seems to be no reason that this age limit could not be raised to, say, age 42, which would still allow one to complete a full 20-year tour. Such a waiver now exists for physicians, nurses, and psychologists in the U.S. Army and Air Force. This appears to be not only feasible but also cost-effective and apparently awaits only administrative initiative.

Revitalizing the Recruitment Process

Research for this book highlighted one glaring deficiency in the recruiting process. It was discovered that the Medical Service Corps and, of course, the clinical psychology program, is generally unknown to the average Navy recruiting station. Not only are these programs unknown to recruiting officers, but also there is no literature about them on hand to refer to in answering queries. Numerous instances have been found in which interested psychologists or graduate students have called the local Navy recruiter, only to be turned away by a lack of information or because the recruiter attempted to recruit them for a line commission. Giving every recruiting station a small supply of brochures describing the Navy clinical psychology program appears to be a simple and cost-effective response to this problem. Psychology departments in universities should also be supplied with similar information. Furthermore, this should not be an ad hoc procedure; routines should be established in the Navy whereby these locations are regularly resupplied. As described below, this would be an excellent use of psychologists in the Active Reserve.

It seems apparent that the process of recruiting clinical psychologists into the Navy needs to be revitalized. The Specialty Advisor for Clinical Psychology to the Commander of the Naval Medical Command (i.e., Chief Clinical Psychologist) has currently a long list of assignments. These include being Head of the Psychology Department at Bethesda Naval Hospital and monitoring the assignment and performance of all clinical psychology billets throughout the Navy, including the internship program. In the absence of personnel assistance for that particular task, very little time can be given to the recruitment of new psychologists. In the future this must change—as is noted below, a very cost-effective solution is available.

The MSLO Program

For many years, the Navy Medical Department maintained among its Active Reserves a program known as the Medical Student Liaison Officers (MSLO). These members of the Active Reserve were faculty members at most of the medical schools in the United States. They acted as liaison persons for those medical students who had received Navy scholarships in their school, and they recruited new applicants. Through their personal contacts in the local naval district and the (then) Bureau of Medicine and Surgery in Washington, DC, they answered questions, obtained and passed on information relevant to the students' careers, arranged the details of their summer tours of duty, and facilitated a desirable first tour of active duty after graduation. In many cases, MSLOs took their own two weeks of ACDUTRA (active duty for training) at a location where most of their medical students had been assigned and cooperated with the local commander in helping them receive the maximum benefit from the experience. Generally, this resulted in a productive and pleasant liaison among the local command, the medical students, and the faculty of the medical school involved. When these tours were reported to the incoming freshman class of the school, they proved to be a powerful recruiting tool for the naval scholarship program. Many MSLOs took students on weekend tours of naval hospitals, ships, and bases. Social events were also held at local officer's clubs.

Appended to the program, albeit informally, was the authority of the (then) Chief of Clinical Psychology to appoint in each naval district a Commandant's Representative for Psychology. In addition to serving with a local unit of the Active Reserves, these representatives recruited psychologists for the Navy, including experimentalists as well as clinicians. For each episode of contact, such as speaking to graduate students or staffing the Navy booth at a psychological convention, representatives were awarded an appropriate number of retirement points—one of their primary motives for being in the Reserves. Much to the Navy's detriment, both programs were the victim of a general reorganization of the Reserves in the early 1970s.

There is apparently no reason that the recruiting of psychologists cannot be enhanced by the revitalization of a program that uses the services of former uniformed psychologists, clinical and experimental, now in the Active Reserve. Existing regulations stipulate that members of the Reserve can receive retirement points by any activity considered to enhance their professional careers and thereby increasing their usefulness to the Navy in the event of a recall to active duty.

This may include attendance at professional meetings, consultation with active duty naval personnel, publication of articles relevant to issues of concern to the Navy, or any special activity that is approved in advance as being supportive of the interests of Navy psychology.

It is therefore recommended that a senior member of the psychologists now in the Active Reserves be given the additional duty of coordinating the recruitment of psychologists. This person would create a network of other former Navy psychologists around the nation who would receive retirement points by contacting psychologists and graduate students in their geographical area. This person would, of course, act in concert with the recruiting activities of the Specialty Advisors for Clinical, Aviation, and Research Psychology. Because of the significant number of retirement points this activity could generate, it would be seen as a highly desirable billet for a Reservist.

Internship and Licensing

There are those who argue that a 2-year internship is needed in order to prepare one for the independent practice of clinical psychology. For example, physicians spend the last 2 years of medical school on clinical rotations plus a 1-year internship before they can qualify for state licensure, and a 3 or 4-year residency is not unusual before independent practice is begun, even for those in general practice (i.e., family medicine). If a 2-year program becomes the national norm, the Navy will, of course, be required to follow suit. In view of the many one-person assignments now held by Navy psychologists, it may be well to consider taking the lead in such a program. This would not only produce junior psychologists with superior training, but it would also add to the number of payback years required and thereby lengthen the average tour of active duty.

As of 1988, all health-care persons in the Armed Forces were required to be licensed in some state or in Washington, DC. When psychology interns graduate, they are given a year to become licensed; if they fail the examination, they are given a second chance. If they fail a second time, however, they have to be released from active duty. This means that those interns without PhDs have to complete the dissertation very soon after beginning active duty. As described elsewhere, this will place a burden on the Navy to facilitate psychologists' completion of their degrees or risk losing their services. In previous years, one could remain on active duty and even enter the Regular Navy without the doctorate or a license.

It is this writer's opinion that the Navy has not been suitably aggressive in helping interns complete their dissertations. This point of view, understandably, is not shared by all those individuals who in the past have had this responsibility—some argue that if students are suitably motivated they will complete the work, and that at the very least the Navy has always given them passive cooperation. The counterargument to this position is that not only will the Navy risk losing a number of individuals trained at its expense, but also that because senior Navy psychologists are, by definition, professional leaders and motivators, they should regard this as just one more challenge to their ability as officers and experts in human behavior. (Needless to say, this issue produced rather spirited discussion in the February 1988 committee meeting.)

State licensure is usually designed to certify a minimal level of competence in order to protect the public from charlatans. As in medicine, the ultimate certification of competence is examination by a board of one's peers. In psychology this function is performed by the American Board of Professional Psychology (ABPP), an affiliate of the American Psychological Association. In addition to giving evidence of ethical practice and active participation in local or national affairs, one must have 5 years of experience before being allowed to take the full-day examination. Several state and national agencies, including the Veterans Administration, have lobbied for many years that board-certified psychologists, like physicians, should be given bonus pay. As Navy psychology grows and absorbs the increasing trend toward a higher level of competence, board certification of its senior clinical psychologists should at least become an important credential for promotion. (In 1989, legislation authored by Senator Inouye was enacted (PL 101-189) that gives special pay to military psychologists who are board-certified.)

The Problem of Parity With the Other Services

As of 1988, the Navy did not have parity with the Army and the Air Force in the number of psychiatrists or clinical psychologists on active duty. For example, the Navy (including the Marine Corps) has one psychologist per 9,000 active-duty personnel (in round numbers), whereas the Army has one per 6,700 and the Air Force has one per 4,300 persons on active duty. In 1988, the Army had 16 clinical psychology interns in training and the Air Force had 23, whereas the Navy had only 8; this in spite of the fact that the active-duty strength of the Army and Navy are approximately equal and the Air Force has approximately 20 percent fewer members than either of the other two branches.

This means that in comparison to other service personnel, the mental health needs of the men and women of the Navy and their dependents are underserved and that operational commanders are not receiving the kind of psychological assistance needed. It seems unlikely that this unequal state of affairs is the intent of either Congress or the Department of Defense. It therefore appears that this represents another task ahead for Navy psychology. As of June 1988, a proposal has been reissued to increase the number of clinical psychology internships from 8 to 16 and, in addition to USNH Bethesda, to place them in Portsmouth and San Diego. Assignment to the latter locations may expose entering psychologists to the "real" Navy, responding to a problem mentioned earlier. However, in order to achieve parity with the Air Force, this number needs to be increased to about 30 entering interns per year.

The Emergence of Psychologists as Independent Practitioners

Nationwide, the profession of clinical psychology is assuming a primary as well as a supportive role. Before and during World War II, clinical psychologists were perceived as primarily psychometric technicians in support of psychiatry and education. After the war this began to change. By the 1980s, clinical psychologists were licensed independent practitioners, performing diagnosis and therapy that is officially recognized not only by other professions, state and federal agencies, and legislatures, but also, perhaps most importantly, by those who pay for psychologists' services, such as insurance companies and individual clients. In most states they do not have to work under supervision of a psychiatrist or other physician or have patients referred by physicians in order to receive reimbursement. There is now a strong movement to allow clinical psychologists to have hospital privileges and to admit and treat patients independently—a movement already successful in parts of the country.

Of importance to psychology is that the profession of psychiatry is changing from a psychoanalytic-psychosocial model to a medical-biological one. Psychiatrists are moving from the community and the consulting room back to the hospitals and affiliated clinics. Psychotherapy in its various forms and the many types of counseling and guidance are increasingly being performed not only by psychologists but also, as in California, by master's-degree-level personnel such as licensed marriage, family, and child counselors (MFCCs) and licensed clinical social workers (LCSWs). Not only have decades of research failed to show that these people are less competent or produce less effective results in those areas in which they offer competing services, but also, in this era of dwindling financial resources and skyrocketing medical costs, they are more cost-effective. Furthermore, nonpsychiatric physicians are proving themselves equally adept in the use of psychotropic medications and often develop an effective partnership with non-MDs in treating a patient. In addition, clinical psychologists are continually demonstrating their skill in working with nonpsychiatric patients and people who are generally considered to be within the normal range—an area not taught in the average psychiatric curriculum.

In 1988 these changes are very much in evidence in the Navy. While the number of psychiatrists is about equal to the number of clinical psychologists, only about 65% of their billets are filled, compared with about 80% for the psychologists. In addition, the number of psychiatrists has been showing a long-term but steady decline, whereas the opposite has been true for the psychologists. There has also been a disproportionate number of senior uniformed psychiatrists rotating into administrative and command billets, leaving by default more clinical and operational assignments to be filled by psychologists. For many years there has been a trend in the Navy Medical Department to fill billets with psychologists when a psychiatrist was not available. This entire pattern not only promises to continue but may accelerate. The Department of Defense has also recognized that it is far more cost-effective to fill a position with a PhD than with a physician. Economics rather than clinical or scientific evidence may prove to be the primary agent of change.

Clinical psychology is not only demonstrating an increasing level of independence from psychiatry, but also the nature of its supporting role is changing. Traditionally, clinical psychologists in medical institutions have been part of the department of psychiatry or, at the very most, a separate division of that department. However, for many years the Veterans Administration, the nation's largest employer of clinical psychologists, has had separate departments of psychology in their hospitals. The director of that department not only supervises the clinical and research services provided directly by the department but also negotiates with other departments for psychological services—usually in the form of assigning a psychologist to, say, the Department of Medicine or the Department of Physical Rehabilitation, including the Department of Psychiatry. Sometimes referred to as the ''Kelly Girl'' (i.e., temporary) model of providing services, it was established in 1987 at the Bethesda Naval Hospital on a trial basis, but promises to become permanent as it has at other military hospitals. This arrangement not only removes psychology from the administrative control of psychiatry, it also provides an easier route for giving services to nonpsychiatric patients.

The Field of Health Psychology

This type of separate organization also facilitates the growth of another area of services that is expanding throughout the nation as well as in the Navy— health psychology. Especially important to the mission of the U.S. Navy is the emphasis this specialty places on the prevention of disease and the promotion of health through behavior change. Because average psychiatric inpatients are poor candidates for a return to a full tour of duty, their treatment and rehabilitation is not given high priority. This move toward separating and better defining the roles of psychologists and psychiatrists in the Navy—the former emphasizing prevention and short-term outpatient care and the latter focusing on the medically ill inpatient—can only serve to encourage an increase in numbers and importance of the role for psychologists in the Navy.

Although clinical psychologists obviously play a key role in the field of health psychology, many types of behavioral scientists can, and do, make important contributions. As Lightner Witmer noted in 1907, clinical psychology is not the exclusive province of the psychologist, and it can also be said that health psychology is not the exclusive province of the clinical psychologist. This means that in the Navy as well as in the civilian sector, it can be expected that a variety of health professionals will be active in the field of health psychology, such as physicians, nurses, social workers, hospital corpsmen, and administrators in both health care and the line. However, it is clear that Navy psychologists will probably play the most important role—not only because so much of their training is specifically related to the field, but also because they are the largest group identified with this activity.

As practiced in its Division of Health Promotions, health psychology in the Navy (and, of course, in the Army and the Air Force) is one of the largest such programs in the nation. As such, it becomes not only a model for the civilian sector but also an excellent forum for experimenting with new areas of application and research in program evaluation. With the huge population of the military, it is possible not only to conduct outcome studies that are not feasible in civilian settings but also to perform studies in cost-effectiveness and cost-benefits. This should be a golden opportunity for the entire field, including an excellent source of dissertation research for psychology interns.

As optimistic as this sounds, one cannot overlook the fact that, like its civilian counterparts, the Navy Medical Department is not especially eager to submit its programs to the unyielding scrutiny of empirical research. However, the financial and professional careers of individuals in the military are not as vulnerable to the potentially negative results of having their programs evaluated as their civilian counterparts are—in fact, in many cases it might be career-enhancing. In the author's opinion, this could be a wonderful opportunity for not only psychologists interested in program evaluation research but also for cooperation between government agencies; for example, the National Institutes of Health could provide the funding and the Navy the population for a study. Providing leadership and expertise in this area would be a natural role for Navy psychologists of the future.

Toward a New Model for Human Services

These trends—the increasing administrative and professional independence of clinical psychology, the expansion and consolidation of health psychology, and the extension of the use of clinical psychologists to a wider variety of nonpsychiatric billets—point toward specific possibilities. One is that in addition to continuing their traditional role of working with hospital patients, clinical psychologists will be the most numerous providers of all outpatient services and the primary provider of psychological services to the operating forces of the Navy.

This suggests that in addition to traditional psychiatric-medical treatment, the Navy will move toward a new model for supplying human services. In large civilian corporations, this model exists under the rubric of Employee Assistance Programs. In one form, this might consist of a "one-stop" collection of services in one location where service personnel and their dependents can come or be referred for a wide variety of personal problems, including family stress; substance abuse; problems on the job; career guidance, including options in civilian life; sex education; and physical and mental health. While clinical psychologists would play a major role in such a model, it would obviously be staffed by multidisciplinary personnel. This would allow not only for the contribution of the different helping professions, but also, in times of shortages of any one discipline, it would allow the gap to be filled by those with the required skills regardless of designation. That is, for a given client, a psychiatrist may substitute for a psychologist, a social worker for a chaplain, a psychologist for a vocational guidance counselor, and so forth. As previously described, this would be another instance of the Navy tradition of "doing the job with what is available."

In its early days, clinical psychology was viewed by many as a subspecialty or a professionalization of the main field. In spite of the fact that it lacks clear definition, clinical psychology is spawning a variety of subspecialties, each with its own problems of definition. At the same time psychology at large is striving to remain united under a single banner. In order to accommodate its diverse membership of more than 68,000 and its 47 separate interest groups, the American Psychological Association has been reorganized into three separate subgroups—the Science, Practice, and Public Interest directorates. There is also increasing pressure to recognize the argument that a core content exists for all psychologists, regardless of their "specialty." As stated by Matarazzo (1987):

> I know of no university departments of psychology that today offer a predoctoral curriculum of graduate courses in psychology that is discernibly different, in terms of broad content, processes, and principles, for tomorrow's would-be teachers, scientists, and practitioners of clinical, experimental, social, industrial, or developmental psychology. (p. 893)

He also states: "The [academic] core that differentiates psychology from physics, economics, history, and other cognate disciplines has remained the same since psychology first became a university discipline 100 years ago." In Matarazzo's view, "There is only one psychology, no specialties, but many applications." Given the Navy's wide diversity of assigned tasks, this view fits very well the image of clinical psychology in the Navy.

The Question of Subspecialty Designators

However, some applications of psychology are more intensive and circumscribed than others, and they do border on qualifying as true specialties. While it is left up to the reader to decide which applications qualify for this list, it should be noted that a similar trend toward subspecialization is occurring in the Navy and may well be part of its future. At the present time, Navy psychologists are divided into three categories—aerospace experimental psychology, clinical psychology, and research psychology. The aerospace group is further specialized;

for example, these psychologists must complete a ground-school course and maintain a minimum amount of flight time as "special crew" in order to pursue their work while aloft. In recognition of this, they are awarded an insignia similar to that given to pilots and flight surgeons—a pair of wings joined by the symbol of the Medical Service Corps.

This has led to the belief that clinical psychologists in the Navy should have a similar designation after qualifying in the fields of aviation and submarines. It is argued, for example, that members of the military aviation community deal with a rigorous and hazardous life-style that is unique and stressful. While these personnel are generally healthy, they are still susceptible to the medical and psychological problems such a life-style can produce, including the presentation of ostensibly organic symptoms in reaction to an underlying psychological problem. As in civilian life, it can be assumed that a large percentage of otherwise normal persons presenting physical symptoms to a physician are reacting to an emotional problem. It can be further assumed that, as has been shown with nonmilitary patients, early psychological intervention can alleviate many physical symptoms and have a significant effect in reducing the utilization of medical services (Rosen & Wiens, 1979). Because aviators are not permitted to fly if there is the slightest suggestion that they are not in top physical and mental condition, such intervention may prevent costly interruptions or termination of many careers.

It is argued that clinical psychologists can best meet these mental health needs if they are directly knowledgeable about the nature of the stresses facing their clientele and that they will have greater credibility if they are perceived as members of the aviation community (Parker, 1987). A similar argument is made for the needs of submariners. As in the case of flight surgeons and physicians in submarine medicine, these clinical psychologists would be given appropriate training and experience and would be awarded the appropriate insignia. Both subspecialties, as well as those in neuropsychology, forensic psychology, and alcohol rehabilitation, may well be part of the future.

The Role of Women Psychologists

It is generally agreed that women could easily play a larger role in Navy psychology. As of February 1988, they constituted about 15 percent of clinical psychologists on active duty. As described elsewhere in this volume, women in the Navy are still not universally receiving equal status and treatment. However, this does not appear to be so among clinical psychologists or in the Medical Department at large. In fact, they are probably more often given equal treatment there than in the civilian sector. For example, a 1983 survey of PhD psychologists in the United States revealed that women were paid an average salary that was $5,700 less than men (Howard et al., 1986)—but this is not true in the military.

For the years 1987 and 1988, about 30 percent of the clinical psychology interns recruited were women, but apparently the attrition rate is higher than that of men when they complete their obligatory tour. It appears that in the future special policies will be needed in order to increase the recruitment and retention of women psychologists.

The Question of Structuring the Psychologist's Role

The 1988 committee gave considerable discussion to the question of whether clinical psychology in the Navy should be better defined and structured, as has been the case in the Army. Since 1948, chief psychologists in the Navy have actively resisted such attempts on the grounds that, unlike the other services, the command structure is much more decentralized and that the lack of detailed job descriptions has produced very desirable levels of flexibility and freedom to innovate. As one member of the panel observed, "Career psychologists have never met a duty station they couldn't change."

Another obstacle to the creation of a formal model for Navy psychology is that, more often than not, when psychologists arrive at new stations, they find that more needs to be done than one person can possibly accomplish, and they must have the freedom to match their individual skills and interests to appropriate segments of the job—an approach that usually operates to the benefit of everyone concerned.

It was finally pointed out by the committee that the field of clinical psychology at large has never successfully created a model for itself. The so-called Boulder Model of scientist-practitioner has proved to be useful for the purpose of planning on the part of universities, but it has never served as a good model for practitioners. Many individuals express a need for structure and definition in their work, and they are unhappy in an amorphous environment. In 1988, as it was in 1900, such individuals are not likely to be happy as clinical psychologists— especially if they are in the Navy.

The Issue of Creating a Separate Corps

Along with the other allied health professionals, psychologists in the U.S. Air Force have separated themselves from their Medical Service Corps and formed a Behavioral Sciences Corps. This raised the issue of whether the number of clinical psychologists on active duty in the Navy has reached the critical mass necessary for a separate corps. The current 115 clinical psychology billets are not enough to meet this requirement. This would mean that several other disciplines would have to be included in the new corps, such as social workers, podiatrists, pharmacists, and so forth, and probably all of the approximately 1,200 members of the Health Care and Sciences Section of the MSC. This would not serve to further the goals unique to clinical psychologists, particularly it would not address the kinds of problems that now exist in having a broad mixture of disciplines working under the same administrative umbrella. In addition, this corps would contain only half as many members as the present MSC, thus diminishing the influence and power base that comes with larger numbers. It was agreed that such a change would not be advantageous at this time, if ever.

The Need for Improved Communication

A future task for Navy clinical psychology is to improve communication within its own ranks. Geographically, personnel are spread rather thinly. Although they may enjoy being part of the local scene, most of them also have a need to identify actively with other Navy psychologists and with psychology at large. This requires the opportunity to attend regional and national meetings as well as to maintain a steady flow of verbal and written exchanges. It is often pointed out, however, that travel funds for professional meetings may be very limited or not available at all. However, this is often the result of the low priority given to such activity rather than a problem with the availability of money. A higher priority can be given to this use of funds only on the basis of administrative decisions made by senior officers; this will occur only if they change their view of what is important for Navy psychology.

Improvement in communication can only happen if the senior uniformed psychologists exert leadership in motivating or requiring all clinical psychologists to attend and participate in these meetings. Travel by military aircraft can often be arranged, as can low-cost housing when meetings are held near military establishments. Not only is it left to senior psychologists to "discover" the resources for such activity, but they must set an example by being as professionally active as they wish the junior officers to be. Unfortunately, this approach to increased communication has not been in evidence in recent years.

Historically, one part of the communication network among clinical psychologists in the Navy was the so-called Navy Party, which for many years took place annually at the meetings of the American Psychological Association. Under the leadership of the clinical psychology section in Washington, DC, this was a social event of considerable usefulness. It included not only active-duty personnel but also Reservists, former active-duty people, a variety of civilians with Navy research contracts, and colleagues from the other services. The group invariably included a significant number of distinguished clinical psychologists from around the United States, and relationships were established that remained active for years, including ones especially important to the junior officers. Financial support came from the largess of some of the senior psychologists, private firms, and the creative juggling of resources. It was the direct result of the efforts of a few administrators who recognized the event's importance, but, like so many activities that rely on the personal efforts of a few, the Navy Party died out in the late 1960s as these officers moved on to other positions. This event should obviously be reinstituted.

In summary, it may be said that the future of clinical psychology in the U.S. Navy is very bright. There is every indication that its numbers will continue to grow and that there will be more and more opportunities to serve in an increasingly varied array of fascinating work environments. The history of this group is admirable, but the years ahead give even greater promise.

References

Adde, N. (1989a, May 1). Surviving tragedy. *Navy Times*, pp. 1–53, 58.

Adde, N. (1989b, May 8). The hidden victims. *Navy Times*, p. 39, pp. 46–48.

Anastasi, A. (1976). *Psychological testing* (4th ed.) New York: Collier-Macmillan.

Angelo, L. E. (1985, July 15). Memorandum [from Director, Medical Service Corps] for MSC Officers, Career Update Information. Ser 093F/10/85.

Announcement. (1941). *Psychological Bulletin, 38*(4), 306–308.

Bachman, R. (1918). The examination of aviators. *Naval Medical Bulletin, 12*, 30–41.

Bailey, P., Williams, F. E., Komora, P. O., Salmon, T. W., & Fenton, N. (1929). *The medical department of the U.S. Army in the World War. Volume X. Neuropsychiatry*. Washington, DC: U.S. Government Printing Office.

Banning, K. (1963). *Annapolis today*. Annapolis: U.S. Naval Institute.

Bernreuter, R., Maxfield, F., Paterson, D., Reynert, M., & Fryer, D. (1937). The proposed American Association for Applied and Professional Psychologists. *Journal of Consulting Psychology, 1*, 14–18.

Best, H. (1962). *The webfoot warriors*. New York: John Day Co.

Bisch, L. E. (1919). A routine method of mental examinations for naval recruits. *Naval Medical Bulletin, 13*, 198–228.

Boring, E. G. (1929). *A history of experimental psychology*. New York: Appleton-Century-Crofts, Inc.

Boring, E. G. (1950). *A history of experimental psychology* (2nd ed.). New York: Appleton-Century-Crofts, Inc.

Bourne, P. G. (1970). Military psychiatry and the Viet Nam experience. *American Journal of Psychiatry, 127*, 481–488.

Bremner, M. K. (1943). Women psychologists in the WAVES, SPARS, and Marine Corps (W-R). *Psychological Bulletin, 40*, 377–378.

Brown, A. W. (1938). Reports of the AAAP: Organization of the clinical section. *Journal of Consulting Psychology, 2*, 77–82.

Brown, E. W. (1920). Medical and hygienic aspects of the Submarine Service. *Naval Medical Bulletin, 14*, 8–17.

Butts, H. (1910). Insanity in the Navy. *Naval Medical Bulletin, 4*, 459–575.

Butts, H. (1911a). The mental examination of candidates for enlistment in the Navy and Marine Corps. *Naval Medical Bulletin, 5*, 29–38.

Butts, H. (1911b). The mental examination of fifty recruits who became insane soon after enlistment. *Naval Medical Bulletin, 5*, 295–312.

Butts, H. (1912). Further observations on the insane of the Navy. *Naval Medical Bulletin, 6*, 193–212.

Carlson, E. H. (1989, Spring). The practice of Navy clinical psychology in remote sites. *Navy Clinical Psychology Newsletter*, pp. 42–47. Washington, DC: Bureau of Medicine and Surgery, Office of Comdr. James A. Scaramozzino, Clinical Specialty Advisor for the Navy.

Cattell, J. McK. (1890). Mental tests and measurements. *Mind, 15*, 373–381.

Cattell, R. B. (1942). The concept of social status. *Journal of Social Psychology, 15*, 293–308.

Chermol, B. H. (1985). Wounds without scars: Treatment of battle fatigue in the U.S. Armed Forces in the Second World War. *Military Affairs, 49*, 9–12.

Colbach, E. M. (1985). Ethical issues in combat psychiatry. *Military Medicine, 150*, 256–265.

Crowe, R. R., & Colbach, E. M. (1971, March). A psychiatric experience with Project 100,000. *Military Medicine, 136*, 271–273.

Dallenbach, K. M. (1946). The Emergency Committee in Psychology–NRC. *American Journal of Psychology, 59*, 496–482.

DeCamp, G. (1974). *The Blue and Gold, the Annapolis story.* New York: Arco.

DeFoney, C. G. (1931). A psychological study made on candidates for aviation training. *Naval Medical Bulletin, 29*(2), 191–204.

DeFoney, C. G. (1933). A second psychological study made on candidates for aviation training. *Naval Medical Bulletin, 31*(2), 103–111.

Deutsch, A. (1948). *The shame of the states.* New York: Harcourt Brace.

Diagnostic and Statistical Manual of Mental Disorders (DSM-I). (1952). Washington, DC: American Psychiatric Association.

Ditman, K. S., & Blinn, K. A. (1963). Sleep levels in enuresis. *American Journal of Psychiatry, 111*, 913–920.

Drury, M. (1952, November 1). "Treat 'em up front and treat 'em early." *Collier's*, pp. 20–23.

Duff, I. F., & Shilling, C. S. (1947). Psychiatric casualties in submarine warfare. *American Journal of Psychiatry, 103*, 607–613.

Dunlap, K. (1918). Medical studies in aviation IV: Psychological observations and methods. *Journal of American Medical Association, 71*, 1382–1400.

Dunlap, K. (1919). Psychological research in aviation. *Science, 49*, 94–97.

Erie, J. R. (1972). The Navy Medical Service Corps: Whence and whither? *U.S. Navy Medicine, 60*, 22–28.

Faucett, R. E., & Newman, P. P. (1953). *Operation Hideout* (Report No. 228, Vol. XII, No. 13). New London, CT: Medical Research Laboratory, U.S. Naval Submarine Base.

REFERENCES

Fernberger, S. W. (1932). The American Psychological Association—A historical summary, 1892–1930. *Psychological Bulletin, 29*(1), 1–89.

Fisher, J., Epstein, L. J., & Harris, M. R. (1967). Validity of the psychiatric interview. *Archives of General Psychiatry, 17*, 744–750.

Ford, A. (1988, February 6). A few good women want to travel. *Los Angeles Times* (Orange County Edition), Part II, p. 3.

Fourteenth Corps. (1943, October 31). HQ Office of the Surgeon, Medical Service, New Georgia Campaign.

Franz, S. I. (1908). Examination of the insane. In W. A. White (Ed.), *Outline of psychiatry* (Ch. 7, pp. 65–93). New York: Journal of Nervous and Mental Disease Publishing Co.

Franz, S. I. (1912). *Handbook of mental examination methods.* New York: Journal of Nervous and Mental Disease Publishing Co.

Freud, S. (1950). Heredity and the aetiology of the neuroses. In E. Jones (Ed.), *Sigmund Freud, Collected papers* (Vol. I, 6th ed., Ch. VIII). London: Hogarth Press. (Original work published in 1896).

Friedman, P., & Linn, L. (1957). Some psychiatric notes on the Andrea Doria disaster. *American Journal of Psychiatry, 114*, 426–432.

Gannon, J. H. (1979). *A history of the Medical Service Corps of the United States Navy.* Unpublished manuscript.

Garfield, S. L. (1965). Historical introduction. In B. B. Wolman (Ed.), *Handbook of clinical psychology* (Ch. 6). New York: McGraw-Hill.

Gerstle, M., Wagner, R. L., & Lodge, G. T. (1943). The inept naval recruit. *Naval Medical Bulletin, 41*, 480–491.

Glass, A. J. (1966). Army psychiatry before World War II. In A. J. Glass & R. J. Bernocci (Eds.), *Neuropsychiatry in World War II* (Vol. I, Ch. I). Department of the Army. Washington, DC: U.S. Government Printing Office.

Goddard, H. H. (1917). The place of intelligence in modern warfare. *Naval Medical Bulletin, 11*, 283–289.

Gough, H. G. (1960). The adjective checklist as a personality assessment research technique. *Psychological Reports, 6*, 107–122.

Gray, E. (1986). *Few survived: A comprehensive survey of submarine accidents and disasters.* London: Leo Cooper.

Gunderson, E. K. (1966). *Selection for Antarctic service* (Report No. 66-15). San Diego, CA: Naval Health Research Center.

Gunderson, E. K., & Kolb, D. (1980). *Causal factors in alcohol rehabilitation success or failure* (Report No. 80-10). San Diego, CA: Naval Health Research Center.

Harris, D., & Firestone, R. (1957). Are enuretics suitable for the armed services? *Journal of Clinical Psychology, 13*, 91–93.

Healy, M. (1987, December 22). Navy will put more women aboard ships. *Los Angeles Times* (Orange County Edition), Part I, p. 29.

Helgesson, O. (1943). Some current features of psychiatry in the United States Navy. *American Journal of Psychiatry, 97*, 633–650.

Henmon, V. A. (1919). Air service tests of aptitude for flying. *Journal of Applied Psychology, 3*, 103–109.

Hildreth, G. H. (1933). *A bibliography of mental tests and rating scales.* New York: Psychological Corporation.

Hoch, E. L., Ross, A. O., & Winder, C. L. (Eds.). (1966). *Professional preparation of clinical psychologists.* Washington, DC: American Psychological Association.

Hoiberg, A., & McCaughey, B. G. (1981). *Collision at sea: The traumatic aftereffects* (Report No. 81-39). San Diego, CA: Naval Health Research Center.

Holden, C. (1987, April 3). Is alcoholism treatment effective? *Science,* pp. 20–22.

Holtzman, W. H., & Sells, S. B. (1954). Prediction of flying success by clinical analysis of test protocols. *Journal of Abnormal and Social Psychology, 49*, 485–490.

Hopper, G. (1986, September). Go ahead and do it [editorial column, quoted]. *The Officer,* p. 14.

Howard, A., Pion, G. M., Gottredson, G. D., Flattau, P. E., Oskamp, S., Pfafflin, S. M., Bray, D. W., & Burstein, A. G. (1986). The changing face of American psychology: A report from the Committee on Employment and Human Resources. *American Psychologist, 41*, 1311–1327.

Hunt, W. A. (1945). Clinical psychology in the Navy. *Journal of Clinical Psychology, 1*, 99–104.

Hunt, W. A. (1956). *The clinical psychologist* (p. 58). Springfield, IL: Charles C Thomas.

Hunt, W. A. (1975). Clinical psychology in 1944–45. *Journal of Clinical Psychology, 31*, 173–178.

Hunt, W. A., & Stevenson, I. (1945). Psychological testing in military clinical psychology: I. Intelligence testing. *Psychological Review, 53*, 25–35.

Hunt, W. A., & Wittson, C. L. (1949). Some sources of error in the neuropsychiatric statistics of World War II. *Journal of Clinical Psychology, 5*, 350–358.

Hunt, W. A., Wittson, C. L., & Burton, H. W. (1950). A further validation of naval neuropsychiatric screening. *Journal of Consulting Psychology, 14*, 485–488.

Hunt, W. A., Wittson, C. L., & Hunt, E. B. (1952). Military performance of a group of marginal neuropsychiatric cases. *American Journal of Psychiatry, 109*, 168–171.

Hunt, W. A., Wittson, C. L., & Hunt, E. B. (1954). The serviceability of military personnel of low intelligence. *Journal of Clinical Psychology, 10*, 286–287.

Hunter, E. J., & Plag, J. A. (1973). *An assessment of the needs of POW/MIA wives residing in the San Diego metropolitan area: A proposal for the establishment of family services* (Report No. 73-39). San Diego, CA: Navy Medical Neuropsychiatric Research Unit.

Ickstadt, A. J. (1929). Physical qualifications and aeronautical adaptability. *Naval Medical Bulletin, 27*, 9–16.

Jacoby, A. L. (1919a). Disciplinary problems of the Navy. *Mental Hygiene, 3*, 603–608.

Jacoby, A. L. (1919b). Treatment of military offenders. *Naval Medical Bulletin, 13*, 229–236.

Jenkins, H. E. (1915). Mental defectives at naval disciplinary barracks, Port Royal, S.C. *Naval Medical Bulletin, 9*, 211–221.

Jenkins, J. G. (1942). Utilization of psychologists in the U.S. Navy. *Psychological Bulletin, 39*, 371–375.

Jenkins, J. G. (1945). Naval aviation psychology. (1). Field service organization. *Psychological Bulletin, 42*, 632.

Jenkins, J. G. (1947). Keynote address. In G. A. Kelly (Ed.), *New methods in applied psychology*. Proceedings of the Maryland Conference on Military Contributions to Methodology in Applied Psychology, November 27–28, 1945. University of Maryland, College Park, MD.

Jenkins, L., Mussi, C., McKinley, M., Masci, D., & Barnett, R. (1987, December). Navy SEALs, special warriors. *All Hands*, pp. 4–40.

Jones, M. (1987, December 7). Psychologist to profile embassy guards. *Navy Times*.

Jones, R. F. (1926). Selection of personnel for submarines. *Naval Medical Bulletin, 24*, 461–477.

Kilburg, R. R. (Ed.). (1984, October). Psychologists in management. [Special issue]. *Professional Psychology: Research and Practice, 15*(5).

Knox, H. A. (1914, March 7). A scale based on the work at Ellis Island estimating mental defects. *Journal of American Medical Association, 12*(19).

Kolb, D., & Gunderson, E. K. (1975). *Alcoholism in the United States Navy* (Report No. 75-79). San Diego, CA: Naval Health Research Center.

Kolb, D., & Gunderson, E. K. (1978). Post-treatment outcome for youthful Navy drug abusers. *Journal of Drug Education, 8*(1), 19–28.

Kolb, D., & Gunderson, E. K. (1985). Research on alcohol abuse and rehabilitation in the U.S. Navy. In M. Schuckitt (Ed.), *Alcohol patterns and problems: Series in psychosocial epidemiology, Vol. 5* (Ch. 5, pp. 157–177). New Brunswick, NJ: Rutgers University Press.

Korchin, I. J. (1976). *Modern clinical psychology* (pp. 41–47). New York: Basic Books.

Korman, M. (1976). *Levels and patterns of professional training in psychology*. Washington, DC: American Psychological Association.

Landers, S. (1987, January). Dix hand-picked St. E site. *APA Monitor*, p. 20.

Landers, S. (1988, March). Mass murder, A community responds. *APA Monitor*, p. 24.

Lewinski, R. J., & Pennington, L. A. (1943). Professional sources and training requirements of the psychologist in Class H-V (S) of the Navy. *Psychological Bulletin, 40*, 519–527.

Lincoln, P. S. (1936). Human engineering in the Navy. *U.S. Naval Institute Proceedings, 62*, 352–356.

Louttit, C. M. (1939). The nature of clinical psychology. *Psychological Bulletin, 36*, 361–389.

Louttit, C. M. (1941). Psychological work in the United States Navy. *Journal of Counseling Psychology, 5*, 225–227.

Louttit, C. M. (1942). Psychological examining in the United States Navy: An historical summary. *Psychological Bulletin, 39*, 227–239.

Louttit, C. M. (1943). Psychologists in the Navy. *Psychological Bulletin, 40*, 375–376.

Louttit, C. M. (1944). A study of 400 psychologists commissioned in the U.S. Naval Reserve. *Psychological Bulletin, 41*, 253–257.

Lovell, J. P. (1979). *Neither Athens nor Sparta? The American service academies in transition.* Bloomington, IN: Indiana University Press.

Lowndes, D. H. T. (1912). Recruiting in the Navy. *Military Surgeon, 30*, 560–564.

Low-tech threat to high-tech: Marine Corps forms anti-terrorist security forces. (1987, December). *The Officer*, pp. 23–26.

Malzberg, B. (1959). Important statistical data about mental illness. In S. Arieti (Ed.), *American handbook of psychiatry*, Vol. 1 (Ch. 7, p. 164). New York: Basic Books.

Manning, R. A., Emerson, S., & Kaylor, R. (1986, November 3). Special forces: Can they do the job? *U.S. News & World Report*.

Masson, J. (1984, February). Freud and the seduction theory. *Atlantic Monthly*, pp. 33–53.

Matarazzo, J. D. (1980). Behavioral health and behavioral medicine. Frontiers for a new health psychology. *American Psychologist, 35*, 807–817.

Matarazzo, J. D. (1987). There is only one psychology, no specialties, but many applications. *American Psychologist, 42*, 893–903.

McCaughey, B. G. (1984, January). *Naval disaster: The psychological symptomatology* (Report No. 84-2). San Diego, CA: Naval Health Research Center.

McCaughey, B. G. (1985, October). *U.S. Navy psychiatric rapid intervention team (SPRINT)* (Report No. 84-41). San Diego, CA: Naval Health Research Center.

McCubbin, H. I., Dahl, B. B., Metres, P. J., Jr., Hunter, E. J., & Plag, J. A. (1974). *Family separation and reunion: Families of prisoners of war and servicemen missing in action.* Washington, DC: U.S. Government Printing Office.

McDaniel, F. L. (1919). Report of the Psychiatric Division on recruits entering incoming detention camps. *Naval Medical Bulletin, 13*, 854–858.

McGuire, F. L. (1954, June). *An analysis of automobile accidents involving military personnel* (NM 005 052,33,01). Camp Lejeune, NC: Naval Medical Field Research Laboratory.

McGuire, F. L. (1981). Alcohol rehabilitation—Fact or myth? *American Journal of Drug and Alcohol Abuse, 8*(1), 131–135.

McGuire, F. L., & Tolchin, S. (1961). Group adjustment at the South Pole. *Journal of Mental Science, 107*, 954–960.

McMullin, J. J. A. (1915). Some observations on the examination of recruits. *Naval Medical Bulletin, 9*, 70–74.

Meehl, P. E. (1954). *Clinical vs. statistical prediction.* Minneapolis: University of Minnesota Press.

Miller, E. (Ed.). (1943). *The neuroses in war.* New York: Macmillan.

Mitchell, M. (1944). The clinical psychologist in a naval hospital. *Psychological Bulletin, 41*, 561–564.

Mora, G. (1967). History of psychiatry. In A. M. Freedman & H. I. Kaplan (Eds.), *Comprehensive textbook of psychiatry* (Ch. 1). Baltimore: Williams & Wilkins.

Murphy, J. (1986, March 3). A naval surgeon in the dock. *Time*, p. 68.

Napoli, D. S. (1981). Psychologists and the war. In *Architects of adjustment: History of the psychological profession in the United States* (Ch. 5). Port Washington, NY, and London: Kennikat Press.

NAVMED P-5057. (1957). *History of the Medical Department of the United States Navy, 1945–1955.* Washington, DC: Bureau of Medicine and Surgery, U.S. Navy.

Ninow, E. H. (1963). Submarine psychiatry. *Archives of Environmental Health, 6*, 579–588.

OSS Assessment Staff. (1948). *Assessment of men.* New York: Rinehart.

Palinkas, L. A. (1985). *Long-term effects of environment on health and performance of Antarctic winter-over personnel* (Report No. 85-48). San Diego, CA: Naval Health Research Center.

Palinkas, L. A., & Coben, P. (1985a). *Combat casualties among U.S. Marine Corps personnel in Vietnam: 1964–1972* (Report No. 85-11). San Diego, CA: Naval Health Research Center.

Palinkas, L. A., & Coben, P. (1985b). *Psychiatric casualties among U.S. Marines in Vietnam* (Report No. 85-47). San Diego, CA: Naval Health Research Center.

Parker, J. B. (1987). Aviation clinical psychology. *Military Medicine, 152*, 348–350.

Parsons, R. P. (1918). A search for non-physical standards for naval aviators. *Naval Medical Bulletin, 12*, 155–172.

Pillmore, G. (1919). The nervous element in aviation. *Naval Medical Bulletin, 13*, 458–478.

Plag, J. A. (1963). *The unsuitable naval recruit: His adjustment and performance during two years of service* (Report No. 63-5). San Diego, CA: Navy Medical Neuropsychiatric Research Unit.

Plag, J. A. (1964a). *The problem of enuresis in the naval service* (Report No. 64-3). San Diego, CA: Navy Medical Neuropsychiatric Research Unit.

Plag, J. A. (1964b). *The practical value of a psychiatric screening interview in predicting military ineffectiveness* (Report No. 64-7). San Diego, CA: Navy Medical Neuropsychiatric Research Unit.

Plag, J. A., & Arthur, R. J. (1965). Psychiatric re-examination of unsuitable naval recruits: A two-year follow-up. *American Journal of Psychiatry, 122*(5), 534–541.

Plag, J. A., & Goffman, J. M. (1966a). A formula for predicting effectiveness in the Navy from characteristics of high school students. *Psychology in the Schools, III*(3), 216–221.

Plag, J. A., & Goffman, J. M. (1966b). The prediction of four-year military effectiveness from characteristics of naval recruits. *Military Medicine, 131*(8), 729–735.

Plag, J. A., Goffman, J. M., & Phelan, J. D. (1967). *The adaptation of naval enlistees scoring in mental group IV on the Armed Forces Qualification Test* (Report No. 68-23). San Diego, CA: Navy Medical Neuropsychiatric Research Unit.

Plag, J. A., & Goffman J. M. (1968). *The utilization of predicted military effectiveness scores for selecting naval enlistees* (Report No. 69-6). San Diego, CA: Naval Medical Neuropsychiatric Research Unit.

Plag, J. A., Goffman, J. M., & Bowen, G. R. (1968). *Predicting the military effectiveness of naval enlistees returned to duty from the psychiatric sick-list* (Report No. 68-14). San Diego, CA: Navy Medical Neuropsychiatric Research Unit.

Plag, J. A., Wilkins, W. L., & Phelan, J. D. (1968). *Strategies for predicting adjustment of AFQT Category IV Navy and Marine Corps personnel* (Report No. 68-28). San Diego, CA: Navy Medical Neuropsychiatric Research Unit.

Plag, J. A., Goffman, J. M., & Phelan, J. D. (1970). *Predicting the effectiveness of new mental standards on enlistees in the U.S. Marine Corps* (Report No. 71-42). San Diego, CA: Navy Medical Neuropsychiatric Research Unit.

Plag, J. A., et al. (1979). Center for Prisoner of War Studies. In *Naval Health Research Center Report for 1979* (pp. 61–62). San Diego, CA: Naval Health Research Center.

Polmar, N. (1963). *Atomic submarines.* New York: Van Nostrand.

Poppen, J. R. (1923). Psychometric tests for recruiting stations. *Naval Medical Bulletin, 18,* 14–25.

Pratt, C. C. (Ed.). (1941). Military psychology. *Psychological Bulletin, 39*(6), 309–508.

Raimy, V. (1950). *Training in clinical psychology.* New York: Prentice-Hall.

Rasmussen, J. E. (1963). Psychologic discomforts in 1962 Navy protective shelter tests. *Journal of the American Dietetic Association, 42,* 109–116.

REFERENCES

Reisman, J. M. (1976). *A history of clinical psychology.* New York: Irvington.

Renner, J. A. (1963, March/April). The changing patterns of psychiatric problems in Vietnam. *Comprehensive Psychiatry, 14*(2), 169–180.

Rhoades, G. C. (1928). Examination of candidates for aviation training. *Naval Medical Bulletin, 26*, 502–514.

Richards, T. W. (1944). The psychologist in the naval hospital. *Psychological Bulletin, 41*, 565–567.

Riker, G. A. (1913). Treatment of the insane in the Navy. *Naval Medical Bulletin, 7*, 77–86.

Roe, A., Gustad, J. W., Moore, B. V., Ross, S., & Skodak, M. (Eds.). (1959). *Graduate education in psychology.* Washington, DC: American Psychological Association.

Rooks, A. H. (1935). Entrance requirements of U.S. Naval Academy. *U.S. Naval Institute Proceedings, 6*, 1468–1481.

Rosen, J. C., & Wiens, A. N. (1979). Changes in medical problems and use of medical services following psychological intervention. *American Psychologist, 34*, 400–431.

Ross, S., Rubinstein, E., Trumbull, R., & Rasmussen, J. E. (1966). Simulation, shelters, and subjects. *American Psychologist, 21*, 815–817.

Sabshin, M. (1983). The development of the American Psychiatric Association. *APA Biographical Directory 1983* (pp. ix–xi). Washington, DC: American Psychiatric Press.

Savage, D. G. (1990, February 27). High court lets military's ban on gays stand. *Los Angeles Times* (Orange County Edition), pp. A-1, A-17.

Schier, A. R. (1913). The detection of the feebleminded applicant for enlistment—The Binet-Simon scale as a diagnostic aid. *Naval Medical Bulletin, 7*, 345–360.

Schier, A. R. (1914). The feebleminded from a military standpoint. *Naval Medical Bulletin, 8*, 247–258.

Schier, A. R. (1915). Review possibilities of mental tests in the examination of applicants for enlistment. *Naval Medical Bulletin, 9*, 222–226.

Schier, A. R. (1917). A further study of mental tests in the examination of recruits. *Naval Medical Bulletin, 11*, 325–333.

Seidenfeld, M. A. (1966). Clinical psychology. In A. J. Glass & R. J. Bernucci (Eds.), *Neuropsychiatry in World War II, Department of the Army,* Vol. I (Ch. 19). Washington, DC: U.S. Government Printing Office.

Sheehan, R. (1915). Service use of intelligence tests. *Naval Medical Bulletin, 9*, 194–200.

Sheehan, R. (1916). Exclusion of the mentally unfit from the military services. *Naval Medical Bulletin, 10*, 213–249.

Sheehan, R. (1920). Neurological service in naval hospitals. *Military Surgeon, 47*, 295–302.

Shilling, C. W., & Kohl, J. W. (1947, May 25). *History of submarine medicine in World War II* (Report No. 112, Vol. VI(3)). New London, CT: Medical Research Laboratory, U.S. Naval Submarine Base.

Shneidman, E. S. (1967). Description of the NIMH Center for Studies of Suicide Prevention. *Bulletin of Suicidology, 1*, 2–7.

Smith, W. E. (1983, October 31). Carnage in Lebanon. *Time, 122*, 14–25.

Spector, R. H. (1985). *Eagle against the sun.* New York: Free Press.

Stearns, A. W. (1918). The history as a means of detecting the undesirable candidate for enlistment with especial reference to military delinquents. *Naval Medical Bulletin, 12*, 413–441.

Stearns, A. W. (1924). The detection of the psychopath and the classification of naval recruits in accordance with their intelligence. *Naval Medical Bulletin, 20*, 149–169.

Stearns, R. L., Eisenhower, D. D., et al. (1950, January). *A report and recommendation to the Secretary of Defense by the Service Academy Board.*

Stewart, R. W. (1988, February 14). Court draws fine legal line in Army—gay ruling. *Los Angeles Times* (Orange County Edition), Part I, p. 3.

Stokes, C. F. (1913). Editorial comment. *Naval Medical Bulletin, 7*, 417–419.

Strange, R. E., & Arthur, R. J. (1967). Hospital ship psychiatry in a war zone. *American Journal of Psychiatry, 124*, 281–286.

Strother, C. R. (1956). *Psychology and mental health.* Washington, DC: American Psychological Association.

Strott, G. C. (1947). *The Medical Department of the United States Navy with the Army and Marine Corps in World War I.* (NAVMED 1197). Washington, DC: Bureau of Medicine and Surgery, U.S. Navy Department.

Sutton, D. G. (1930). Psychology in Aviation. *Naval Medical Bulletin, 28*, 5–13.

Symonds, J. P. (1937). Toward unity. *Journal of Consulting Psychology, 1*, 23–24.

Taussig, J. K. (1915). The enlisted personnel of the Navy. *U.S. Naval Institute Proceedings, 41*, 1781–1831.

Thomas, G. E. (1915). The value of the mental test and its value to the service. *Naval Medical Bulletin, 9*, 200–211.

Turnbull, A., & Lord, C. (1949). *History of United States naval aviation.* New Haven, CT: Yale University Press.

U.S. Department of Commerce. (1975). *Historical statistics of U.S.: Colonial times to 1970* (p. 1141). Washington, DC: U.S. Government Printing Office.

U.S. Naval History Division. (1963). *U.S. submarine losses in World War II*, 5th printing. Washington, DC: U.S. Government Printing Office.

The value of psychometric tests in the Navy. (1924). *Naval Medical Bulletin, 20*, 213–214.

Wallin, J. E. (1961). PhDs in psychology who functioned as clinical psychologists between 1896 and 1910. *Psychological Record, 11*, 339–341.

Watson, R. I. (1953). A brief history of clinical psychology. *Psychological Bulletin, 50,* 321–346.

Webb, J. (1981). *A sense of honor.* New York: Bantam Books.

Wechsler, D. (1955). *Manual for the Wechsler adult intelligence scale.* New York: The Psychological Corporation.

Weiss, S. M. (1982). Health psychology: The time is now. *Health Psychology 1,* 81–91.

Weybrew, B. B. (1979). *History of military psychology at the U.S. Naval Submarine Medical Research Laboratory* (Report No. 917). Groton, CT: Naval Submarine Medical Research Laboratory.

White, D. F. (1987, August 16). Are they the toughest men alive? *Parade,* pp. 4–5.

Whitestone, N. E. (1973). *The submarine.* London: Davis-Poynter.

Wilentz, A. (1987, April 6). The Marine spy scandal. *Time, 129,* 21–22.

Wilkins, W. L. (1972). Psychiatric and psychological research in the Navy before World War II. *Military Medicine, 137,* 228–231.

Wilkins, W. L., Anderhalter, O. F., Rigby, M. K., & Stimson, P. (1955). *Statistical description of criterion measures for USMC junior officers* (Tech. Rep. No. 5). St. Louis, MO: St. Louis University, Department of Psychology.

Wilkinson, C. B. (1983). Aftermath of a disaster: The collapse of the Hyatt Regency Hotel skywalks. *American Journal of Psychiatry, 140,* 1134.

Witmer, L. (1907). Clinical psychology. *Psychological Clinic 1*(1), 1–9.

Witmer, L. (1908). Mental health and the Emmanuel movement. *Psychological Clinic, 2,* 295.

Wittson, C. L., & Hunt, W. A. (1951). The predictive value of the brief psychiatric interview. *American Journal of Psychiatry, 107,* 582–585.

Wittson, C. L., Hunt, W. A., & Stevenson, I. (1945). A follow-up study of neuropsychiatric screening. *Journal of Abnormal and Social Psychology, 41,* 79–82.

Wolman, B. B. (1965). Clinical psychology and the philosophy of science. In B. B. Wolman (Ed.), *Handbook of clinical psychology* (Ch. 1). New York: McGraw-Hill.

Yerkes, R. M. (1918). Psychology in relation to the war. *Psychological Review, 25,* 85–115.

Yerkes, R. M. (1919). Report of the Psychology Committee of the National Research Council. *Psychological Review, 26,* 83–149.

Yerkes, R. M., & Bridges, J. W. (1921). The point scale. *Boston Medical and Surgical Journal, 23,* 857–866.

Zilboorg, G. S., & Henry, G. W. (1941). *A history of medical psychology.* New York: Norton.

Appendixes and Indexes

Ranks in the U.S. Navy

Modern-day ranks in the Navy are identical for Line Officers and Medical Officers. The beginning enlisted rank is designated as E-1 and advances through E-9, while the officers are labeled O-1 through O-11. Warrant Officers are a group existing between the enlisted ranks and the officers. They are usually promoted from the enlisted ranks, and over the years their social and professional status has varied, ranging from "junior officers" to "super enlisted men-women."

Enlisted Personnel	Officers
E-1 Seaman Recruit	O-1 Ensign
E-2 Seaman Apprentice	O-2 Lieutenant (junior grade)
E-3 Seaman*	O-3 Lieutenant
E-4 Petty Officer 3rd Class**	O-4 Lieutenant Commander
E-5 Petty Officer 2nd Class	O-5 Commander
E-6 Petty Officer 1st Class	O-6 Captain
E-7 Chief Petty Officer	O-7 Rear Admiral (Lower Half)
E-8 Senior Chief Petty Officer	O-8 Rear Admiral
E-9 Master Chief Petty Officer	O-9 Vice Admiral
E-10 Master Chief Petty Officer of the Navy (MCPON)***	O-10 Admiral
	O-11 Fleet Admiral

Intermediate Group

W-1 Chief Warrant Officer
W-2 Chief Warrant Officer
W-3 Chief Warrant Officer
W-4 Chief Warrant Officer

---

*Depending on the needs of the service, an enlisted person may be designated as Seaman, Fireman, or Airman. A Seaman may work for Petty Officer rank in fields dealing with above-deck work (e.g., navigation); a Fireman may work in so-called below-deck ranks (e.g., engineman); the Airman would work in the Aviation Branch (e.g., aboard an aircraft carrier).

**Petty Officers are also designated in their specialty, such as Radio Operator, Signalman, and so forth.

***A position occupied by a single individual who acts as an ombudsman between the enlisted ranks and the Chief of Naval Operations. The pay grade of E-10 is honorary and carries no additional pay.

Prior to 1930 ranks for officers in the Medical Department used different terminology from that for the Line. These titles and their Line equivalents were as follows:

Former Term	**Present Term**
Acting Assistant Surgeon	Ensign
Assistant Surgeon	Ensign
Assistant Surgeon, Master	Lieutenant (junior grade)
Passed Assistant Surgeon	Lieutenant
Surgeon	Lieutenant Commander
Medical Inspector	Commander
Medical Director	Captain
Surgeon General	Rear Admiral (rank occupied by only one person)

Uniformed Navy Clinical Psychologists on Extended Active Duty, Medical Service Corps, 1948–1988

Abell, John M.
Acord, Loren D.
Adkins, David S.
Ahern, Dennis E.
Ahr, Dennis W.
Ahr, Paul R.
Aitken, John R.
Albright, Daphne
Andorfer, Joseph C.
Andrews, James G.
Anjeski, Paul G.
Ardnt, Robert G.
Arroyo, Sara G.
Bach, Gale W.
Bagby, James W., Jr.
Bailey, Larry W.
Baker, Carl D.
Bale, R. M.
Bally, Ralph E.
Baringoldz, Gregg M.
Baucom, Donald H.
Bayer, Gregory A.
Beare, Arthur N.
Beaty, William E.
Beaugrand, Marsha J.

Becker, Bruce C.
Belding, Hiram H., IV
Bellino, Thomas T.
Berry, John F.
Berry, Newell H.
Biron, Joseph E.
Blackwood, Lynn C., Jr.
Blashfield, Roger K.
Bonney, Lewis A.
Bookout, Thomas E.
Boone, Richard R.
Bory, Alexander
Bowen, Neil E.
Bowers, Clint A.
Boylan, R. J.
Bredefeld, Garry M.
Briggs, Dennie L.
Brittain, Jerry L.
Bronson, Gene
Brown, Jacob T., Jr.
Brown, John P., Jr.
Brunza, John J.
Buck, Charles W.
Bucky, Steven F.
Butler, Timothy F.

Calix, Edward C.
Calkins, Dennis L.
Callaghan-Chaffee, Martha
Calvin, James B.
Cammarata, Larry
Campbell, William W.
Carlson, Erin H.
Cathey, Robert L.
Chaffee, Roger B.
Chance, Paul B.
Chaney, Bob E., Jr.
Charlestrom, William J.
Chavoya, Gary M.
Christiansen, John C.
Churchill, Freda V.
Clarke, Norman B.
Clum, George A.
Cole, Jimmie D.
Colligan, Susan C.
Collins, Walter E.
Conger, John J.
Connery, Horace J.
Connolly, Francis J.
Crigler, Patricia W.
Cross, Michael S.

Lack of adequate records prevented listing those clinical psychologists who served in the Hospital Volunteer Corps during World War II or those who served in the Active or Inactive Reserve after the founding of the Medical Service Corps but did not serve an extended tour of duty. For the same reason, there may be some omissions among those Reservists who served a single tour of duty between 1948 and 1967. The author extends his apologies to those not included here.

Cumming, William G.
Cunningham, Mark D.
Danco, Jeffrey C. A.
Darnell, Gerald K.
DeScripkes, R. A.
Dean, T.
Demakovsky, Ronald M.
Dennis, Donald M.
Derrer, Douglas S.
Descipkes, Robert A.
Diamond, Mark D.
Dian, Duane M.
Dickenson, Robert T.
Dinuzzo, Theresa M.
Dobson, Beverly P.
Doerring, Harvey W.
Doucette, Serge R., Jr.
Eakes, John A.
Easton, Freddie L.
Edwards, Darrel
Engelstatter, Gerolf H.
Estey, Melvyn A., Jr.
Evans, A. L.
Farley, Richard L.
Ferrell, Laura J.
Figura, Clarence J.
Firestone, Richard W.
Flaherty, Edward M.
Flowers, Lynn L.
Fowler, John C.
Foxx, Stanley A.
Frederick, Richard I.
Freeman, Frank E.
Froess, James C.
Fry, George E.
Gaines, Richard N.
Garvin, Patricia C.
Gaskin, Thomas A.
Gayton, Richard R.
Gelles, Michael G.
Gellis, Ronald D.
Gerlach, Herman T.
Getka, Eric J.
Giffin, R. T.
Gilson, R. D.
Glogower, Frederick D.
Glovinski, Marvin
Goldberg, Glenn M.
Goldbert, Daniel D.
Goldstein, Henry L.

Gordon, Lisa D.
Graham-Mist, Peter C.
Greenwald, Alan F.
Gregorire, Harvey G.
Grossman, Beth L.
Grossman, Ira
Guyer, Charles G., II
Hagelis, John P.
Haller, Nancy S.
Halpern, Alan S.
Hand, Brian C.
Hardey, Thomas R.
Hargraves, David T.
Harmon, Robert W.
Harper, Warren E.
Harrelson, Patricia C.
Harris, Jesse G., Jr.
Harte, James P.
Hashimoto, Don M.
Haskell, Carolyn A.
Hawkinson, John R.
Hayes, Larry C.
Hazen, Douglas L.
Hazlehurst, Charles D.
Held, Patricia G.
Herrmann, Robert S.
Hester, Samuel B.
Hiland, David N.
Hilmo, John A.
Hilton, Clifford H.
Hitchko, Michael J.
Holland, Terrill R.
Holmes-Johnson, Elizabeth
Hopkins, John B.
Hoppe, Edward W.
Horn, Charles H.
Horvath, Arthur C.
House, John F.
Howell, William L.
Hughes, Anne S.
Hughes, Herschel, Jr.
Hughes, William G.
Hunt, James A.
Hysham, Charles J.
Inman, Elmer E.
Jacobson, Dorothy
James, Larry C.
Jenkins, Z.
Johnson, J. H.
Jones, John G.

Jones, Randel R.
Jones, T. N.
Kado, Randolph
Kalkines, Christopher T.
Kay, Gary G.
Keen, Raymond P.
Kelly, Dennis A.
Kelly, Kenneth S.
Kelly, Stephen J.
Kilpatrick, Ted D.
Kleiger, James H.
Kleitsch, Edward C., Jr.
Knapp, Robert R.
Kosof, Peter L.
Kramer, Douglas W.
Kretchmer, Robert S.
Krug, Ronald S.
Laudenslager, John M.
Lazor, Paul S.
Lefever, Bryce E.
Levine, Bernard
Lindstrom, Lorel L.
Long, Gerald M.
Long, Mark A. D.
Lore, James I.
Louy, J. William
Luedtke, Kurt A.
Lyon, Waldo B.
Lyons, Lawrence G.
Machir, Dan F.
Mahoney, David J.
Marcy, Michael R.
Marrs, Aimee W.
Martin, Cynthia F.
Mather, David B.
May, Jerry R.
Maynard, William S., Jr.
McCullah, Robert D.
McGrael, Lawrence, J.
McGuire, Frederick L.
McMichael, Allen E.
McRay, John F.
McWilliams, Richard T.
Mea, William J.
Meegan, William J.
Meier, Lonny R.
Meyer, William J.
Miller, Harriet I.
Miller, Lloyd A.
Minagawa, Rahn Y.

Molish, Herman B.	Randazzo, Catherine E.	Spingarn, James A.
Montgomery, Craig S.	Rasmussen, John E.	Stanek, Richard J.
Moore, Jeffrey L.	Rathjen, Eric D.	Stein, Mark L.
Moran, Michael R.	Reed, Robin A.	Steingarten, Karen A.
Morgan, Carl E.	Regts, John M.	Stephenson, Norman L.
Mountz, Thomas C., Jr.	Reinhart, David F.	Sterner, Gary A.
Moyer, Ronald C.	Rickus, G. J., Jr.	Stockton, Phillip
Mullins, Frank A., Jr.	Ridge, Bradley B.	Stoltz, Richard F.
Murphree, Henry B., Jr.	Riffe, Dudley	Svendsen, Mary L.
Murphy, Harry B.	Ritchie, Louise R.	Tal, Carolyn S.
Murphy, Wayne A.	Rivero, Carol A.	Theo, Peter
Murray, Thomas	Roberts, David C.	Timm, Stephen A.
Narut, Thomas E.	Rock, Samuel M.	Toole, James
Nathan, Howard W.	Rogers, Paulette A.	Tucher, John J.
Navradszky, Laszlo I.	Rosen, Howard S.	Turian, Judith E.
Newfield, Norbert L.	Rumann, Donald J.	Vanden Bossche, Ronald L.
Nobers, Donald R.	Russ, Carol A.	Venn, Jonathan
Noble, Howard F.	Sammons, Morgan T.	Viglione, Donald J., Jr.
Nolen, Leslie C., Jr.	Sampson, Raymond N.	Von Stuck, Murlow L.
O'Briant, Dennis A.	Sanders, George M.	Wagner, Carl M.
O'Brien, Clayton S.	Sands, Ronald G.	Walls, Lynda E.
O'Brien, Harriet I.	Scaramozzino, James A.	Wasileski, Maryann E.
O'Hern, Karen S.	Schaeffer, Richard F.	Webster, Bruce D.
Olson, Gary M.	Schlegel, Robert M.	Weiner, William J.
Orcutt, Ted L.	Schoenrock, Raymond P.	Westphal, Carl R.
Parker, James B.	Schratz, Paul R.	Wheeler, John T.
Parks, Ronald S., II	Schwartz, Michael L.	Whitley, Michael Q.
Patten, Thomas G.	Sexton, John L.	Wilcox, Robert H.
Paul, Frank E.	Shaffer, Scott C.	Wilkes, R. L.
Pecorelli, Joseph P.	Shelnutt, Jack B.	Willis, Don C.
Penkunas, John J.	Sheperd, Walter P.	Wilson, Justin M.
Pereira, Robert P.	Sherman, Forrest A.	Winkle, Bernard
Petrillo, Martin A.	Shimberg, Edmund	Wong, Dennis E.
Phelps, Harrison	Simone, Stephen S.	Wood, Arlis G.
Philhour, P. R.	Singer, Fredric L.	Wood, Dennis P.
Pine, Harry	Slater, Charles B.	Wright, Duff R.
Piper, William E.	Smiley, Colleen S.	Wright, Michael R.
Pishel, R. G., Jr.	Smith, Randall J.	Young, James C.
Platner, Donald J.	Smith, Vann A.	Younger, Robert D.
Poirier, John M.	Spaulding, David L., Jr.	Youniss, Richard P.
Rachlin, Daniel (n)	Speir, Herbert A., III	Zimmerman, Thomas A.

Suggestions for the Management of Psychological Services in the U.S. Navy

Compiled by Frederick L. McGuire

In the process of research for this book, a number of ideas emerged for the enhancement of clinical psychology in the Navy. Many of these ideas are not new and have been considered by current and past administrations. However, it is not always possible to implement a good idea on demand. In order not only to emphasize them but to preserve them until their time may come, they are listed separately in this appendix.

1. The Navy should provide its personnel with access to psychological services at least equal to that of the Army and Air Force personnel. In 1988 terms, to implement this would require raising the number in the entering class of clinical psychology interns to 30 per year, plus an appropriate increase in fellowships and scholarships.

2. Clinical psychologists should be given bonus pay for being board-certified.

3. A formal program should be instituted for assisting newly commissioned interns to complete the work toward their PhDs—especially the dissertation requirement.

4. Subspecialties should be created in aviation and submarine clinical psychology.

5. There should be an increase in billets that can enhance the operational readiness of the Navy, such as now exist in SEAL and SERE programs.

6. At the U.S. Naval Academy, a separate academic Department of Psychology should be created, including majors in fields of psychology relevant to the naval establishment.

7. There should be a formal program for the recruitment of high-quality clinical psychologists, with members of the Active Reserve being given primary roles in this activity and awarded retirement credits for their work.

8. The maximum entry-level age for newly commissioned clinical psychologists should be raised to 42 and the age for mandatory retirement raised to 65.

9. A comprehensive system of psychological and social services should be created for active-duty personnel and their dependents—perhaps modeled after Employee Assistance Programs in the civilian sector.

10. The clinical psychology internship should be increased to 2 years, with a corresponding length of committed service. One of these years should be in an operational environment.

11. In all major naval hospitals, a separate Department of Psychology should be created with status equal to that of other professional departments.

12. Increased communication among individual clinical psychologists on active duty should be formally supported. Among other techniques, Navy meeting(s) at the annual meetings of the American Psychological Association should be reinstituted.

13. A naval liaison committee should be formed within the American Psychological Association. This committee should be charged with advising and assisting the naval establishment in matters concerning psychology, and it may also act as an advocate with Congress and other sectors of the American public.

NAME AND AUTHOR INDEX

Acord, Loren D., 71
Adde, N., 145
Aldous, Mary, xv
Allport, Gordon, 46
Angell, James R., 25
Angelo, L. E., 55, 67
Arthur, R. J., 107, 108–111, 163

Bachman, R., 172
Bagby, James W., 50, 71
Bailey, P., 156, 157–158, 159
Baird, John B., 25
Baldwin, B. T., 23
Balley, Ralph E., 138
Bancroft, George, 147–148
Banning, K., 148
Beach, Edward L., 169–170
Beck, Samuel, 170
Becker, Bruce, xv, 63, 207
Bentley, Madison, 25
Benton, Arthur L., 37, 38
Bernreuter, R., 4
Bingham, Walter V., 18
Bisch, L. E., 15, 88–91
Bobbitt, Joseph M., 44
Boomer, Walter, 186
Boring, E. G., xii
Bosio, Sue, xv
Bourne, P. G., 163
Bowen, G. R., 117
Braceland, Frances J., 40, 44
Bradley, Omar (General), 125
Bremner, M. K., 37, 67
Bridges, J. W., 83
Briggs, Dennis, 168
Broomhead, Elizabeth, 63, 67
Brotemarkle, R. A., 46
Burton, H. W., 100
Burtt, Harold E., 20, 173
Butts, H., 13, 14, 78–79, 80, 84, 125

Calvert, James, 150
Carlson, E., 68–69
Carmichael, Leonard J., 46

Carter, Billy, 138
Catell, R. B., 201
Cattell, James McKean, 3–4, 7, 18
Caulkins, William C., 50
Chermol, B. H., 160
Coben, P., 164
Coe, George A., 25
Colbach, E. M., 62, 116
Conger, John J., 152–153
Connery, Michael, 154
Crigler, Patricia W., xv, 67, 123, 136, 207
Crowe, R. R., 116
Cumming, William G., Jr., xv, 59, 63, 71, 207

Dallenback, Karl M., 46, 47
DeCamp, Graydon, 147, 149, 150
DeFoney, C. G., 33, 176
Deutsch, Albert, 125–126
Dix, Dorothea, 11
Dodge, Raymond, 25, 26, 28, 29, 31, 47, 118
Drury, M., 161
Duff, I. F., 167
Dunlap, Knight, 25, 172

Eisenhower, Dwight D., 66, 151–152, 153, 169–170
English, Horace B., 38
Erie, J. R., 49

Faucett, R. E., 168
Fechner, Gustave, xii
Felix, Robert, 44
Fernald, Grace, 14, 65
Fernberger, S. W., 3, 4
Finley, Peter, 186
Firestone, Richard W., 118
Fisher, J., 103
Ford, A., 69, 187
Ford, Betty, 138
Franz, Shepard I., 13, 14, 24, 25, 84
Freud, Sigmund, 132

Friedman, P., 141

Galton, Sir Francis, xii, 173
Gannon, John H., 50, 51
Garfield, S. L., xii
Gerstle, M., 102
Glass, Albert J., 12, 13, 81, 159, 160, 161
Goddard, Henry M., 14, 15
Goffman, J. M., 112, 116, 117
Gough, H. G., 174
Gravitz, Melvin A., xi, 63
Gray, E., 169
Grinstean, Allen D., 177
Guilford, Joan S., xv
Gunderson, Eric K., 137, 140, 193, 195
Guthe, Carl E., 46

Hall, G. Stanley, 3, 18
Halpern, Alan S., xv
Harris, Daniel H., 118
Harris, Jesse, 177–178
Hart, Thomas C., 149
Hazelhurst, Charles D., 138
Healy, M., 69
Helgesson, O., 130
Helmholtz, Hermann von, xii
Henmon, V. A., 175
Henry, G. W., xii
Herrmann, Robert S., xv, 50, 52, 67, 71, 123
Hiland, David N., 185–186
Hildreth, G. H., 7
Hinckley, John W., Jr., 11
Hobby, Oveta Culp, 66
Hoch, E. L., 5
Hoiberg, A., 141
Holden, Constance, 140
Holtzman, W. H., 103
Hopper, Grace, 58
House, John F., xv, 72, 192, 207
Howard, A., 67, 217
Hunt, Edna B., 100
Hunt, William A., x, xi, xii, 36–37, 40, 45, 59, 71, 73, 96, 97, 98, 99, 100, 101, 102, 103, 114, 115, 116, 117, 118, 124, 130
Hunter, Edna J., 196
Hunter, Walter S., 46, 99

Jacoby, A. L., 32, 80, 81

Jenkins, H. E., 14
Jenkins, John G., 37, 38, 47, 177
Jenkins, L., 183
Johnson, Laverne, 193
Johnson, Lyndon B., 116
Jones, M., 186
Jones, Randall R., xv, 33

Kauffmann, Draper, 154–155
Kennedy, John F., 183
Kelley, G. A., 44
Kilburg, R. R., 124
Kilpatrick, Ted D., xv
Knapp, Robert R., 190–191
Knox, Howard A., 15, 88
Kohl, J. W., 166
Kolb, D., 137, 140
Korchin, I. J., xii
Korman, M., 5
Kuhlman, Frederick, 14

Landers, S., 12, 141
Landis, Carney, 98
Langfield, Herbert S., 25
Lanzetta, John T., 74
Lashley, K. S., 24
Laudenslager, John M., 71, 154
Lewin, Kurt, 193
Lewinsky, R. J., 37
Lincoln, P. S., 96
Lord, C., 171
Louttit, C. M., 5, 6, 32, 35, 36, 37, 38, 67, 96, 97
Lovell, J. P., 147, 148, 155
Lowndes, D. H. T., 13, 77, 78
Lynn, L., 141

Malzberg, B., 12
Mann, W. L., Jr., 14
Manning, R. A., 183
Marcy, William L., 147
Marrs, Aimee, 67
Masson, J., 132
Matarazzo, Joseph D., ix–x, 74, 135, 216
MacCorquodale, Kenneth, 74
McAfee, Mildred, 66
McCarthy, Joseph, 185
McCaughey, B. G., 141, 142–144
McCubbin, H. I., 179
McCullah, Harry F., 49, 53

McCullah, Robert D., xv, 53, 71, 72, 123, 207
McDaniel, F. L., 29
McGuire, Frederick L. (the author), ix–x, 58, 67, 140, 190, 193, 195
McMichael, Allen E., xv, 59, 153–154, 162–163, 193
McMullin, J. J. A., 14, 84, 86
Meehl, Paul E., 105–106
Menninger, William, 40
Mensh, Ivan N., xv, 74
Meyer, Adolph, 80
Miles, Walter R., 46
Miller, E., 87, 156, 158, 159
Miller, James Grier, 44
Mitchell, Mildred, 37
Mogridge, George, 14
Molish, H. Barry, xv, 50, 168, 169
Mora, G., xii
Mountz, Thomas C., 183–184
Mullins, Frank A., Jr., xi, xv, 59, 72, 207
Mullins, Sam, 161
Murphy, J., 52
Murray, Henry, 175

Napoli, D. S., 36, 39
Nardini, John E., 193
Navradszky, Laszlo, 178
Nelson, Paul D., 52, 193, 207
Newman, P. P., 168
Nimitz, Admiral, 66
Ninow, E. H., 167
Nixon, Richard M., 74

O'Brian, Daniel J., 49
O'Connor, Johnson, 96
O'Hern, Karen, 67

Packard, David, 74
Palinkas, L. A., 164, 195
Parker, J. B., 179, 217
Parsons, R. P., 21, 172, 173
Pennington, L. A., 37
Pershing, John J. (General), 87, 114
Phelan, James D., 116
Pillmore, G., 172
Plag, John A., xv, 105, 106–114, 116, 117, 176, 193, 195, 196
Polk, James K., 147
Polmar, N., 166

Poppen, J. R., 32
Pratt, Carroll, 46

Raimy, V., 5
Raines, George N., 50, 161, 193
Rasmussen, John E., xv, 71, 192–193
Reagan, Ronald, 11, 183
Reisman, John M., xii
Renner, J. A., 163, 164
Rhoades, G. C., 173–174
Richards, Thomas, 37–38
Riker, G. A., 14, 127–129
Roe, A., 5
Rogers, Edith Nourse, 66
Rohr, John H., 74
Rooks, A. H., 151
Roosevelt, Eleanor, 66
Rorschach, Hermann, 175
Rosen, J. C., 217
Rubenstein, Eli A., 74

Salmon, T. W., 157
Savage, D. G., 134
Scaramozzino, James A., 72
Scherer, Isidor, 63
Schier, A. R., 14, 84–86
Scott, Walter Dill, 21
Seashore, Carl E., 18, 25
Seidenfeld, M. A., 36, 39, 40, 43, 59
Sells, Saul B., 74, 103
Sexton, John L., 182, 208–209
Sheehan, R., 14, 120
Sherman, Forrest A., 178, 186–187
Shilling, C. W., 166, 167
Shipley, Walter, 98
Shneidman, Edwin S., xv, 164
Sidwell, L. T., 14
Smith, Denzel D., 74
Smith, W. E., 141
Spector, R. H., 65, 148–149
Spencer, Philip, 148
Spingarn, James A., 190–191
Stearns, A. W., 80, 81, 92–95, 150
Stearns, Robert, 151–152, 153
Stevenson, I., 44, 98, 99, 100
Stewart, R. W., 134
Stokes, C. F., 13
Stone, Irving R., 177
Strange, R. E., 163
Stripling, Terry J., xv

Strother, C. R., 5
Strott, George C., 158
Sutton, Dallas G., 33, 35, 38, 40, 175–176

Taussig, J. K., 12
Terman, Lewis M., 25
Thomas, G. E., 14, 83
Thorndike, Edward, 18, 20, 21, 25
Thorne, Frederick, 43, 44
Thurstone, L. L., 25
Titchener, Edward, ix, 17
Tolchin, Sidney, 194–195
Towne, Clara H., 65
Troland, L. E., 173
Trumbull, Richard, 74
Turnbull, A., 171

Watson, J. B., 18, 24, 25
Watson, R. I., xi, 13
Webb, J., 154
Wechsler, D., 92
Weiss, S. M., 136

Weybrew, Benjamin B., 168, 170
White, D. F., 182
White, William Alanson, 12, 80
Wiens, A. N., 217
Wilentz, Amy, 186
Wilkins, W. L., xv, 31, 73, 95, 103, 116, 193
Wilkinson, C. B., 141
Witmer, Lightner, 3, 4, 5, 6, 7, 14, 45, 214
Wittson, C. L., 41, 96, 98, 99, 100, 102, 104, 114
Wolfle, Dael, 46
Wolman, B. B., xii
Woodworth, Robert S., 24, 25, 35, 161
Wright, George D., 152
Wright brothers (Orville & Wilbur), 171
Wundt, Wilhelm, xii

Yerkes, Robert M., 14, 17–20, 22, 25, 26, 27, 28, 31, 38, 46, 83, 87, 102, 103
Zilboorg, G. S., xii

SUBJECT INDEX

Accident research
  at NMRFL, Camp Lejeune, NC, 190
Air Force Academy, Colorado Springs, 147,
  155
Alcohol and·drug abuse
  automobile accidents, 137
  evaluation of, 139–140
  role of psychologists, 140
  treatment units
    location and type, 137–139
    USNH Long Beach program, 138–139
American Association of Clinical Psychology (AACP), 4
American Board of Professional Psychology (ABPP), 5, 212
American Psychiatric Association (ApA),
  11, 126, 132, 133
American Psychological Association (APA),
  3, 4, 5, 11, 17, 18, 27, 61, 63,
    123, 135, 203, 212, 216
  Committee on Physical and Mental Tests
    (1896), 4
  content of clinical training programs, 6
  Division of Clinical Psychology, 5
  Society of Psychologists in Manage-
    ment, 124
Annapolis, Naval Academy at, 147–155
  between Athens and Sparta, 150
  criticisms of, 148–149, 151–152, 153
  earliest exposure to clinical psychology,
    150–151
  founding of, 147–148
Armed Forces Qualification Test (AFQT),
  112, 113, 116
Army, U.S.
  Alpha Test, 20, 138
  crash at Gander, Newfoundland, 145
  earliest model for military psychology,
    xiii
  "early" use of clinical psychologists,
    WWII, 38–40
  Psychology School, Oglethorpe, GA,
    WWI, 20

Army, U.S. (*continued*)
  screening program
    during WWI, 159–160
    during WWII, 99
  Assignments for Navy psychologists, 121–
    122
American Association for Applied Psychology (AAAP), 5, 38
Aviation, naval
  early role in WWII, 38
  existing aviation billets, 178
  first psychologists in, 177–179
  Flight Surgeon, role of, 173–174
  Naval Aerospace Medical Institute (Pen-
    sacola), 178
  pilot selection after WWI, 47, 171–172
  psychologists as aviation specialists, 179

Basic Test Battery, GCT, 47
Binet-Simon Test, 3, 14
  use of Binet-type items, 13–14, 32, 83–
    86, 88–92, 98

Clinical psychology
  definition of, 6–7
  lack of parity with Army and Air Force,
    212–213
Coast Guard Academy, New London, CT,
  147
Crisis intervention (see also Chapters 21
    and 22)
  examples of, 141
  SPRINT, 142–146
  USS *Belknap*, 141–142
  USS *Iowa*, 145–146
  USS *Kennedy*, 141
  USS *Stark*, 145

Deep Freeze, Operation, 170, 194–195

Ellis Island
  screening of immigrants, 15

247

Emergency Committee in Psychology (1940), 45–47
Enuretics
    suitability for service, 117–118
"Experimentalists, The," 17

General Classification Test (GCT), 32, 47, 96, 106, 107
German military psychology (1941), 46

Health psychology
    definition of, 135
    forerunner of in WWI, 22–24
Health Promotion Division, 123, 135–137
Hospital care for Navy mental patients
    model for, 127–130
Hospital Corps, 49–50

Journal of Clinical Psychology, 44, 45

Korean War
    billets served overseas, 59
    recall of psychologists, 55–57
    treatment of battle fatigue, 161–163
    use of hospital ships, 59

"Lone Ranger" type of billet, 45, 58, 174, 178, 184, 208

Marine Corps, U.S., 59, 61–62, 161–162
    Marine Security Battalion (Embassy guards), 186–187
    Second Division (WWI), 158
Medical Service Corps, 72
    creation and development of, 49–53
    social workers in, 55

National Research Council Psychology Committee (WWII), 45–47
Naval Health Research Center, San Diego, CA, 192–194
    Operation Deep Freeze, 194–195
    prisoner of war studies, 195–197
        family service centers as outgrowth of, 196–197
Naval hospitals
    Bethesda, 12, 61, 63–64, 67
    first assignment of psychologists to, 130
    overseas, 59, 131

Naval hospitals (*continued*)
    Portsmouth, 64
    San Diego, 64
Naval Medical Field Research Laboratory, Camp Lejeune, NC, 58, 190–191
Naval Medical Research Institute, Bethesda, MD, 190, 191–192
Naval Security and Investigative Command (NSIC), 185–186
    role of psychologist in, 185–186
"New Science," the, 3, 7

Odds-for-effectiveness tables, 112–113
Office of Scientific Research and Development (OSRD), 47
O'Rourke Intelligence Test, 33

Personal Data Questionnaire
    forerunner of pencil-paper personality tests, 24, 101–102
Psychological Clinic, The, 4

Recruit screening program(s)
    NOB, Hampton Roads, VA, 88–92
    NTC, Newport, RI, 97–104
    NTC, San Francisco, CA, 92–95
    NTS, Farragut, ID, 114
    NTS, Great Lakes, IL, 100–101, 103, 113–114
    NTS, Sampson, NY, 100–101
    NTS, San Diego, CA, 101–102, 114
Red Cross social workers, 55

SEALs, 180, 182–184
    Team 6, 183–184
    psychologist's role, 183–184
Sexuality
    as a cause of insanity, 79, 132–133
        listing in DSM, 132–133
    homosexuality in Navy, 133–134, 185
    masturbation, 79, 132
    need for Navy psychologist to be informed, 135
    rape and sexual abuse, 135
    the issue of, 132–135
St. Elizabeths Hospital (USGHI), 11–12, 78–80, 125
Submarine service
    MRL (Groton, CT), 123, 168, 170–171, 327

Submarine service (*continued*)
  screening after WWI, 31–33
  screening during and after WWII, 167–168
  the *Nautilus*, 168
  the *Thresher*, 169
  the *Triton*, 169–170
Surgeon General of the Navy
  attitude toward specialties, 31
  call for use of Binet-Simon, 13
  description of psychologist's duties in WWII, 97
  WWII announcement for psychologists, 35–36

Uniformed Services University of the Health Sciences (USUHS), 74, 145–146

Vietnam War
  prisoner of war studies, 195–197
  SERE program, 179–182, 196
    psychologist's role in, 181
  treatment of battle fatigue, 163–165

Walter Reed Hospital, 23, 145
West Point
  Military Academy at, 147
Women
  in Armed Forces, 65–67
  in Navy clinical psychology, 67–69
  need for more in future, 217–218
  on Embassy duty, 187
World War I
  committees to support war effort, 18–25
  French methods of treatment, 157–158
  Naval Training Station, Hampton Roads, VA, 29
  Navy's use of psychologists, 27–29
  participation of psychologists in, 17–18
    response of APA, 17–18
  Second Marine Division, 158
  types of "shell shock" or "war neurosis," 156–157
World War II
  categories of psychologists commissioned in Navy, 37